Masterpieces

of American Furniture
from the
Munson-Williams-Proctor Institute

Contributors

Kenneth L. Ames KLA

Donald Scott Bell DSB

Michael K. Brown MKB

Anna Tobin D'Ambrosio ATD

Ed Polk Douglas EPD

Donald L. Fennimore DLF

Jerry V. Grant JVG

Katherine C. Grier KCG

Barry R. Harwood BRH

Judith S. Hull JSH

Jack L. Lindsey JL

Robert D. Mussey Jr. RM

Donald C. Peirce DCP

Jodi A. Pollack JP

Timothy D. Rieman TDR

Page Talbott PT

Charles L. Venable CV

Catherine Hoover Voorsanger CHV

Gerald W. R. Ward GWRW

Janet Zapata JZ

Philip Zea PZ

Anna Tobin D'Ambrosio
Editor

John Bigelow Taylor
Principal Photographer

Distributed by Syracuse University Press

Published with the exhibition *Masterpieces of American Furniture from the Munson-Williams-Proctor Institute*, on view May 2 through October 31, 1999, at the Munson-Williams-Proctor Institute Museum of Art, Utica, New York, and February 18 through May 28, 2000, at the Cincinnati Art Museum, Cincinnati, Ohio.

The exhibition and catalogue were funded in part by a grant from **The Henry Luce Foundation, Inc**. Additional funding was provided by **Furthermore**, the publication program of **The J. M. Kaplan Fund**.

Generous support provided by **Syracuse Colour Graphics, Ltd**.

Photographers: Principal photography by John Bigelow Taylor, New York, New York, except cat. no. 18 and 22 and figs. 3-6, 8-11, 13-15, 27, 28, and 32 by Gale Farley, Utica, New York; figs. 1, 2, 7, 12, and 16-19 by David Revette, Syracuse, New York; cat. no. 43 by Richard Goodbody, New York, New York; detail, p. 130 by the Williamstown Art Conservation Center; or as otherwise cited in the credit lines.

Manuscript editor: Barbara McLean Ward
Designer: Nadeau Design Associates, Utica, New York
Printer: Syracuse Color Graphics, Syracuse, New York

Distributed by Syracuse University Press, Syracuse, New York, and the Munson-Williams-Proctor Institute.

Library of Congress Cataloging-in-Publication Data

Munson-Williams-Proctor Institute.
Masterpieces of American Furniture
from the Munson-Williams-Proctor Institute / Anna Tobin D'Ambrosio, editor ;
John Bigelow Taylor, principal object photographer.
p. cm.

Catalogue of an exhibition held
at the Munson-Williams-Proctor Institute, Utica, New York, May 2-Oct. 31, 1999.
Includes bibliographical references and index.
ISBN 0-8156-8127-5 (hardcover : alk. paper)
1. Furniture—United States—History—19th century—Exhibitions. 2. Furniture—New York (State)—Utica—Exhibitions. 3. Munson-Williams-Proctor Institute—Exhibitions. 4. Cabinetmakers—United States—Biography. I. D'Ambrosio, Anna Tobin. II. Title.
NK2407.M86 1999
749.213'09'03407474762—dc21 98-45261
CIP

Contents page: *Cabinet* (detail), ca. 1865-75. Maker unknown, probably New York, New York. See catalogue number 35.

Contents

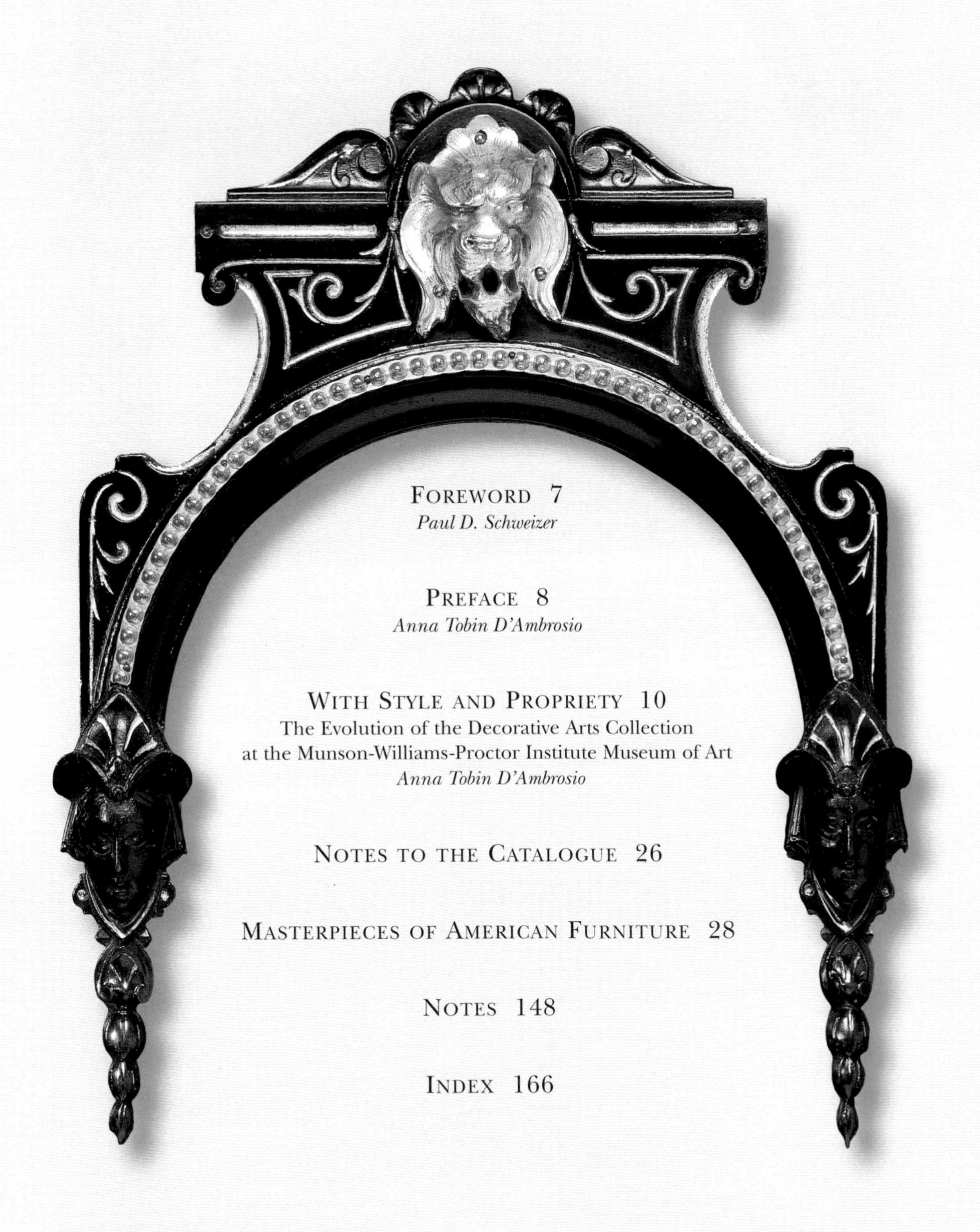

Foreword

In the 1980s the Munson-Williams-Proctor Institute Museum of Art initiated an ambitious plan to publish scholarly catalogues of the most noteworthy parts of its wide-ranging collections. The first in this series, a catalogue of the museum's American painting collection, was published in 1989. This was followed in 1994 with a catalogue of fifty-eight of the Institute's finest American drawings. The present catalogue is the first systematic study the museum has published of its distinguished collection of nineteenth-century American furniture.

This landmark study, the fruit of several years of scholarly endeavor, documents the pioneering role the Munson-Williams-Proctor Institute Museum of Art has played in collecting, researching, and interpreting nineteenth-century American furniture. The collection is distinguished by its breadth and quality. It includes examples of every major nineteenth-century style and virtually all of the period's decorative and construction techniques. Additionally, it contains works that are the most significant examples of particular craftsmen's contributions to the history of American furniture design. The origins of the collection can be traced to the Institute's founders' patronage of several preeminent nineteenth-century American cabinetmakers.

Projects as ambitious in scope as this are the result of a happy set of circumstances. Chief among these are the taste, enthusiasm, and dedication of Anna T. D'Ambrosio, who since 1989 has been the museum's Curator of Decorative Arts. Her efforts to broaden the scope, range, and quality of the collection are supremely evident throughout the pages of this publication. The Henry Luce Foundation also played a key role by funding both the research for and publication of this volume, one of a few collection catalogues of American furniture ever supported by the Foundation.

One of the principal goals of this catalogue, to advance the study of nineteenth-century American art and culture, has been furthered by the organization of the catalogue, which should appeal to an interested general audience and to specialists in the field. Discussions about nineteenth-century American culture, taste, and the history of collecting are interspersed with numerous illustrations and with technical, bibliographical, and biographical information that form the basis of sound scholarship.

Aesthetic quality, historical importance, and available documentation on the maker or owner of a piece are three criteria that figured prominently in Anna D'Ambrosio's decision to include a particular work in the catalogue. Readers should be aware that, in certain instances, works featured in the catalogue do not necessarily represent the full extent of the museum's holdings by a specific cabinetmaker. This is especially the case with Charles Baudouine and John Henry Belter.

Some of the works discussed in the catalogue are already known to collectors and scholars, whereas others are published for the first time. Fourteen works were originally owned by the Williams and Proctor families. Fifteen pieces were acquired by the museum since 1989. Space considerations required the exclusion of several other examples of fine nineteenth-century American furniture whose makers are unknown at present.

This project is a professional collaboration in the best sense. The essays were written by twenty-one authors who have specialized knowledge of one or more of the pieces featured in the catalogue. The tremendous amount of information they have brought forth offers a tantalizing glimpse of the burgeoning field of nineteenth-century American furniture studies. Gerald W. R. Ward, the Carolyn and Peter Lynch Associate Curator of American Decorative Arts and Sculpture, Museum of Fine Arts, Boston, graciously agreed to collaborate with Anna D'Ambrosio in reviewing the content of all the essays. At The Henry Luce Foundation, Henry Luce III, Chairman; John Wesley Cook, President; and Ellen Holtzman, Program Director for the Arts, supported this project by awarding the museum one of the foundation's first American collections enhancement initiative grants. This program was established to provide support for museums with significant holdings to advance the study of American art. It is intended to highlight important collections that are not widely known but should be. To that end it is hoped that this catalogue will stimulate further research and enthusiasm for the field of nineteenth-century American furniture, that it will prove useful to collectors and scholars, and that it will provide greater access to and knowledge of the Munson-Williams-Proctor Institute's rich holdings in this area.

Paul D. Schweizer, Ph.D.

Director and Chief Curator
Museum of Art
Munson-Williams-Proctor Institute

Preface

While furniture most often serves a utilitarian purpose and can have the power to enhance the character of a home, it always manifests the interactions of artisans with form and material. Each piece of furniture described and illustrated in *Masterpieces of American Furniture from the Munson-Williams-Proctor Institute*, in addition to its aesthetic attributes, informs us of multiple influences on design, reveals the creativity of its maker, communicates the taste and social status of its owners, and illustrates a chapter in the history of American cabinetmaking and interior decoration. Above all, these objects exhibit artistry that transcends function.

The objects, selected for their artistic and historical importance, are from the furniture holdings of the Institute's Museum of Art. They are only a fraction of the more than ten thousand decorative arts objects in the museum's collection. The essays, commissioned from furniture scholars around the country, include research data on many cabinetmakers who have not been well documented, as well as new information on familiar names. It was an honor and a pleasure to work with these colleagues on this undertaking, a truly collaborative effort. Each author has contributed his or her expertise to the project, resulting in a text that offers the most current evaluation of the collection and of the many cabinetmakers represented in it. Research for this catalogue has also deepened our understanding of the complex and fascinating web of relationships that existed within the nineteenth-century furniture trade, especially in New York City, where many of the museum's furniture pieces were made.

The museum's decorative arts collection originated in the 1850s with James and Helen Williams's purchases for their Italianate mansion, Fountain Elms. Their eye for quality passed to their daughters, Rachel Williams Proctor and Maria Williams Proctor, who preserved their parents' legacy and greatly increased the family's decorative arts possessions. Fountain Elms, part of the original family bequest that created the Munson-Williams-Proctor Institute (MWPI), was refurbished and opened to the public in October of 1960 as a showcase for the Museum of Art's decorative arts holdings. This effort firmly established the importance of the decorative arts within MWPI. Over almost forty years the collection has been carefully honed by its curators—Barbara Franco, Carol Gordon Wood, Christopher Bensch, and myself—to the point where it now comprises one of the strongest assemblages of nineteenth-century American furniture in any public institution the size of MWPI.

This project would not have been possible without generous funding from The Henry Luce Foundation. The Luce Foundation funds enabled us to undertake scholarly research and to present our findings in an exhibition and a publication. Additional support for the catalogue was provided by Furthermore, the publication program of The J. M. Kaplan Fund. Munson-Williams-Proctor Institute funding for the accompanying exhibition was provided by an endowment established at MWPI by David E. and Jane B. Sayre Bryant.

In 1996 I was awarded a research fellowship at the Henry Francis du Pont Winterthur Museum, Garden and Library that enabled me to begin gathering information to enhance the Institute's furniture scholarship files and to prepare for this book. I wish to thank Winterthur Library staff members Eleanor McD. Thompson, Richard McKinstry, Bert Denker, and former assistant librarian Gail Stanislow for helping me to nearly double the thickness of my object files. Winterthur curators Wendy Cooper and Donald Fennimore offered perceptive comments on my notes, and Brock Jobe kindly made recommendations about the course of my research. Patricia Elliott's assistance also ensured a pleasant sabbatical.

Many individuals made informal contributions to this catalogue during the early stages of my research. A battalion of curators, librarians, and scholars—Wesley G. Balla, David Barquist, David Conradsen, Ulysses Grant Dietz, Stacy Pomeroy Draper, Russell Grills, Kristin Herron, Peter M. Kenny, Mary Alice Mackay, William D. Moore, John Scherer, Gilbert T. Vincent, Deborah Dependahl Waters, and the staffs of the Avery Library at Columbia University and the library of the Cooper-Hewitt National Design Museum, Smithsonian Institution—generously shared their expertise with me. I am especially indebted to Barry R. Harwood of the Brooklyn Museum of Art and Catherine Hoover Voorsanger of the Metropolitan Museum of Art who have encouraged my endeavors since the beginning of the project and have provided information and guidance throughout its development.

Many art historians, historians, collectors, and dealers—Alex Brammer, W. Scott Braznell, Margaret Caldwell, Katherine Grier, Mary de Julio, Peter Hill, Margot Johnson, Jon King, Hyman Meyers, Peggy Tuck Sinko, and Priscilla St. Germain—were forthcoming with their expertise. Several graduate students were generous with their time and information. The efforts of D. Scott Bell, an MWPI decorative arts department intern during the summer of 1996, contributed biographical data on many of the cabinetmakers represented. Jeni Sandberg's research in New York City helped us document several objects further. Medill Higgins Harvey and Cynthia Schaffner, who worked in the Department of American Decorative Arts at the Metropolitan Museum of Art, provided solid scholarly information. Sarah Pinchin, a volunteer intern at MWPI, assisted with general office duties related to the publication.

The meticulous work of conservators Hugh Glover, Alex Carlisle, and Monica Berry at the Williamstown Art Conservation Center in Williamstown, Massachusetts, restored the splendor of a number of the objects. Conservation work was also enhanced by the efforts of John Buscemi, Rabbit Goody, Kathleen Kiefer, Mimi Sherman, and Gwen Spicer. Bruce Hoadley's painstaking wood analysis of all the furniture in the book offers new insight into the origins of several pieces.

I would like to extend my appreciation to Gerald W. R. Ward, who read the manuscript for historical accuracy and clarity, and to Barbara McLean Ward, who served as manuscript and copy editor. Their expertise, perceptive comments, and guidance strengthened the presentation. Complementing the prose in this book are the striking photographs taken by John Bigelow Taylor with the assistance of Dianne Dubler. Gale Farley and David Revette also contributed distinctive photographs. Nadeau Design Associates brought the text and images together in an exceptional presentation; it has been a pleasure to work with all of them.

Many people at MWPI contributed to the book and exhibition. The endorsements of the MWPI Board of Trustees and MWPI President Milton J. Bloch, as well as the support of the Institute's staff, have been firm assurances that this multifaceted project would run smoothly. Museum of Art Director Paul D. Schweizer and I initially discussed this effort in 1989, and his guidance has been tireless. I am grateful for Paul's encouragement over the last ten years.

Librarian Cynthia Barth provided immeasurable assistance obtaining books, microfilm, periodicals, and archival materials. Marianne Corrou offered steadfast aid with manuscript preparation and administrative work. Fellow curator Mary E. Murray offered her support and sound counsel. The organizational skills of Debora Ryan, museum registrar, were an asset during every step of the undertaking. Michele Murphy's direction ensured that the publication remained on schedule.

Each member of the decorative arts department staff—Suzanne Costanza, Serafina Gape, Louise O'Connell, N. Beth Christian, Sally Williams, Dawn Rougeux, and Lena Thomas—assisted with research queries, departmental coordination, and office management. I would especially like to acknowledge the persistent efforts of Helen G. Gant whose research in the Williams and Proctor family papers in the collection of the Oneida County Historical Society turned up fascinating, and at times humorous, facts and anecdotes. In addition, her writing skills and attention to detail have enhanced the manuscript.

The exhibition at MWPI that accompanies this book was accomplished through the dedication of Elena Lochmatow, exhibition coordinator; Bonnie Conway, preparator; and Eric Ramirez-Weaver, technician, as well as of numerous members of the physical plant division. These individuals helped with many phases of the project by moving large and fragile objects for photography, wood analysis, and exhibition installation. Education programming for the exhibition was the work of Elaine dePalma-Sadzkoski and her staff.

My most heartfelt acknowledgment is to my husband Paul and daughter Julia. Julia spent far too much time during the first two years of her life listening to me discourse about this project. Paul offered perceptive comments on the manuscript, but, most importantly, he kept me relatively calm and kept our lives balanced. I find my work endlessly engaging and fulfilling, but without Paul and Julia, it would be inconsequential.

Anna Tobin D'Ambrosio

Curator of Decorative Arts
December 1998

With Style and Propriety

The Evolution of the Decorative Arts Collection at the Munson-Williams-Proctor Institute Museum of Art

The architect thinks we have a pretty difficult house to manage for architectural effect, and with a view to economy of expense. He likes the plan of the interior, and thinks you are a woman of sense.[1]

Fig. 1

THESE WORDS, written by James Williams (fig. 1) in March 1850 to his wife Helen Munson Williams, seem to foreshadow the careful, reasoned approach used to guide the couple's home through numerous permutations over the following 150 years. That home—Fountain Elms—has housed the decorative arts division of the Munson-Williams-Proctor Institute Museum of Art since 1960. Among the country's earliest Victorian house museums, Fountain Elms incited interest in the relatively new field of Victorian studies. Today it continues to reveal the complex world of Victorian taste to visitors and scholars.

The growth of the museum's decorative arts collection is intimately linked to a similar development that works of art at Fountain Elms and the Williams family records and anecdotes reveal—the evolution of attitudes toward Victorian-era decorative arts and interiors in the twentieth century. The home offers an effective background for the analysis of the museum's furniture collection and enhances our understanding of the impact of collecting on provincial communities.

Alfred Munson (1793-1854), who moved to Utica from Connecticut in 1823 shortly after marrying his cousin Elizabeth Munson (1798-1870), amassed the family fortune in industrial interests such as burrstone manufacturing in Utica, coal mining in Pennsylvania, and canal development in upstate New York. He and Elizabeth had two children, Helen (1824-94) and Samuel (1826-81).[2] Helen (fig. 2) entered school at age three and later attended the Utica Female Academy, where the curriculum included algebra, geometry, French, physics, logic, and Latin. She also accompanied her father on his business travels to major East Coast cities. At a time when many young women were encouraged to concentrate on domestic skills, Helen was uncommonly well educated.

The family's regard for fine and decorative arts began after Helen's marriage to Utica lawyer James Watson Williams (1810-73) in 1846. Williams soon became involved in his father-in-law's business affairs and also served as a lobbyist on his behalf in Albany. Shortly after his daughter's marriage, Alfred Munson offered to pay for the construction of a new home for her and his son-in-law. In 1850 the couple engaged Albany architect William Woollett Jr. (1815-74) to design a home in the Italianate style on property at the outskirts of Utica.[3] Its location permitted the family to enjoy, in effect, a suburban life—the conveniences of city dwelling and a substantial area for gardens and other rural amenities. The Williams home (fig. 3), named Fountain Elms in the 1870s,[4] included state-of-the-art conveniences such as water closets, coal gas lighting, and hot air heat. The Williamses were a wealthy family living at a considerable remove from large urban centers, but they emulated the lifestyles and tastes of their more urban, and often wealthier, counterparts.

Letters between the architect and the couple outline James and Helen's thinking as the design for Fountain Elms evolved. Complementing the correspondence, meticulous account books detail all construction material expenses (wood, brick, pipe, paint, nails) and wages paid to laborers and tradesmen, and nearly every bill of sale for interior and exterior expenses survives.[5] Little pictorial or physical

Fig. 2

Fig. 1. *James Watson Williams*, ca. 1855, Henry F. Darby, American (1829-97). Oil on canvas, 12 x 10 in. Proctor Collection.

Fig. 2. *Helen Elizabeth Munson Williams*, ca. 1855, Henry F. Darby, American (1829-97). Oil on canvas, 12 x 10 in. Proctor Collection.

Fig. 3

evidence of the 1850 interior decor endures because the home was often renovated and updated during the eighty-three years of family occupancy. Excerpts from correspondence and bills of sale recount the types of interior decorating materials the Williamses considered, such as wallpapers and the variety of floor coverings, but their ultimate choices in pattern and color have yet to be discovered.

James and Helen were keenly aware that Alfred Munson was paying for their new home, and, no doubt, they felt some obligation to limit costs.[6] Compared with Italianate homes in larger urban settings, the modified center hall plan of Fountain Elms was a conservative adaptation of a style that was usually asymmetrical and more flamboyant. In one of his regular letters to Helen, James, who frequently traveled from Utica to Albany and New York City, justified his preference for the more conventional—but, to his way of thinking, still fashionable—plan: "The estimate is founded on quite plain work, inside and outside, but such as cannot be objected to for want of taste."[7] In another letter he noted, "The finish of the interior, I would wish to be as plain as possible; all wood work perfectly so. A simple cornice for the best rooms would please me."[8]

James's desire for an interior that was moderate in cost challenged his aspiration for a fashionable home. An April 1850 letter to Helen recounts his deliberations on the purchase of stylish wallpaper for the best rooms:

> One word as to painting walls. If they crack, the paint does not hide the defect. Papering does. Very fine and appropriate paper is made now, and more ornamental than any painting that is not quite expensive. I rather admire some of the papers particularly for dining room and library. The cost of painting and papering is on the whole rather in favor of the latter.[9]

Although the Williamses clearly considered using wallpaper, evidence indicates that, for some reason, the walls were simply painted while they lived at Fountain Elms. This choice may have resulted from James's conventional taste. Or perhaps the Williamses decided not to proceed with any extra flourishes. The actual construction costs of the house were more than double the initial estimates of six to eight thousand dollars.[10] The couple did, however, carpet the dining room, drawing room, and library with costly Brussels carpeting and purchased cheaper "Tapestry Venetian" floor covering for the less formal rooms in the home.[11]

Fig. 3. Fountain Elms, ca. 1885-90, attributed to Rachel Munson Williams. Albumen print on paper. Proctor Collection.

Whereas James and Helen relied on Utica, Troy, and Albany businesses for utilitarian items for Fountain Elms, they turned to the finest New York City cabinetmakers to appoint the public spaces in their home.[12] In the early 1850s James Williams made numerous visits to the eminently popular craftsmen in the Bowery area to compare styles and prices. Afterwards, almost daily, he wrote to Helen for her opinion on the expense and character of the furniture he was to acquire. These letters make evident that James found the selection of costly, stylish furniture a taxing undertaking. The procurement of a parlor étagère nearly proved to be his nemesis.[13] "Étagères, and all sorts of furniture, are higher now than when we purchased before," he wrote Helen in November 1853. "I saw one at Hutchin's [*sic*] (where I got the side board for $65.00) that suits me pretty well. All the rest were $125 to $500."[14] James was still trying to find an appropriate étagère in April 1854, five months later. "I do not see any étagères for the parlor which in all respects satisfy me, price included," he confided to Helen. "There is one without back, and with twisted supports, which I should take if I thought it would please you. Its price is $300. But I will look further."[15] His letter the following day contains an inkling of desperation:

> I am at a loss about a rosewood étagère. I saw a neat one yesterday at $38 with open back. They all have twisted uprights. Another with a drawer at the bottom and a mirror as a back to the bottom shelf, but otherwise of the same style, costs I think about $65. . . . You might telegraph me as early as possible tomorrow "Get the mirror etagere" or "Get the plain etagere." [16]

Still, the Williames did not settle on an étagère for another eight months. On December 30, 1854, James ordered one from the New York shop of Julius Dessoir, from whom the couple also purchased a library table, two mahogany étagères, and four hanging étagères.[17]

The Williamses also bought furniture from the New York cabinet shops of Edward Hutchings, James Miller, Charles Baudouine, and others. John Henry Belter, perhaps the city's preeminent manufacturer of elaborate rococo revival furniture, was not among their suppliers, however. The Williamses preferred the conservative interpretation of this style, as is evident in the parlor

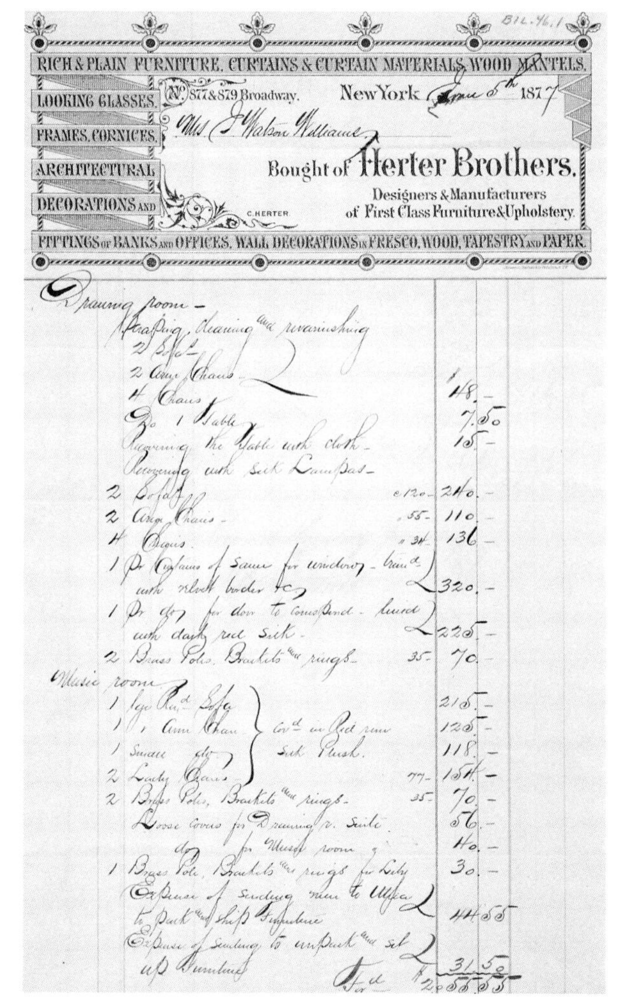

BIL.46.1

RICH & PLAIN FURNITURE, CURTAINS & CURTAIN MATERIALS, WOOD MANTELS,
LOOKING GLASSES, FRAMES, CORNICES, ARCHITECTURAL DECORATIONS AND
FITTINGS OF BANKS AND OFFICES, WALL DECORATIONS IN FRESCO, WOOD, TAPESTRY AND PAPER.

No. 877 & 879 Broadway. New York June 5th 1877

Mrs J. Watson Williams

Bought of Herter Brothers.
Designers & Manufacturers of First Class Furniture & Upholstery.
C. HERTER

Drawing room –
Scraping, cleaning and revarnishing
2 Sofas
2 Arm Chairs
4 Chairs — 148. –
Do 1 Table — 7.50
Recovering the Table with cloth — 15. –
Recovering with Silk Lampas –
2 Sofas — 120 — 240. –
2 Arm Chairs — 55 — 110. –
4 Chairs — 34 — 136. –
1 Pr Curtains of Same for windows – trimd with velvet border &c — 320. –
1 Pr do for door to correspond – lined with dark red silk — 225. –
2 Brass Poles, Brackets and rings — 35 — 70. –
Music room
1 lge Reclining Sofa — 215. –
1 " Arm Chair — Covd in Red ... Silk Plush — 125. –
1 Small do — 118. –
2 Lady Chairs — 77 — 154. –
2 Brass Poles, Brackets and rings — 35 — 70. –
Loose covers for Drawing r. Suite — 56. –
do for Music room — 40. –
1 Brass Pole, Brackets and rings for Lib'y — 30. –
Expense of sending men to Utica to pack and ship furniture — 44.55
Expense of sending to unpack and set up furniture — 31.50
Fwd — 2055.55

Fig. 4

suite they purchased from Charles Baudouine (see cat. no. 27).[18] After the initial furnishing of the home, the Williamses apparently did little to Fountain Elms for nearly twenty years, except to alter the service areas of the house. They did, however, actively acquire decorative and fine arts such as Parian ware (porcelain sculpture) and works by the painter Henry Darby and the sculptor Erastus Dow Palmer.

In 1873 James Williams died, and Helen and her two daughters, Rachel (1850-1915) and Maria (1852-1935), adopted a more affluent lifestyle. Helen had traveled with her husband, but after his death the Williams women traveled more extensively to fashionable locales, spending weeks at a time in New York City, Newport, and Europe. With the expanded vacationing came increased expenditures, thousands of dollars spent on jewelry, clothing, and household items. Their heightened

Fig. 4. Bill of sale, ink on printed paper. Herter Brothers to Mrs. James Watson Williams, 1877. Collection of the Oneida County Historical Society, Utica, N.Y.

awareness of the fashions that trendsetting families in larger urban centers chose no doubt influenced the choices the women made. Moreover, as a keen and astute investor who increased her inheritance severalfold, Helen was able to spend more grandly on furnishings and to gather the core of what was to become the family's art collection.[19]

In 1876 the Williams women began refurbishing the interior of Fountain Elms, a project that included buying new furniture and textiles and restructuring the use of first-floor rooms. The space designated as a master bedroom on the architectural drawings of 1850 was used as a family sitting room at least as early as 1864, as Maria documented in her diary:

> I am going to describe the room I am in so I may remember it when I grow old. There are four doors . . . [and] only one window though it is a large room and that is on the side with the fire-place. . . . The window looks out on the garden. . . . We have no grate in the fire-place only andirons. There are six tables in the room two under the window long oak ones those are ours [Rachel and Maria's] and have desks then there is a marble topped table near the window in the middle of the room a sofa table with leaves and in one corner, a little round table. There are two arm-chairs and two rockingchairs besides four others variously dispersed and a great sofa at one end.[20]

After the 1870s renovations and refurbishment, the Williams women used this room for dining. The original dining room was converted to a music room, which was also referred to as the "back parlor."

For the interior embellishments of their redesigned rooms, mother and daughters turned to the celebrated cabinetmakers and interior decorators of the time—Léon Marcotte and Company, Herts Brothers, Pottier and Stymus Manufacturing Company, Daniel Cottier, Alexander T. Stewart, and Herter Brothers. They called on many of these shops numerous times as they continued to upgrade the furnishings and interior decor of Fountain Elms through the 1880s.

To initiate the changes, the first-floor rooms were recarpeted in 1876. The women chose Axminster carpeting with borders for the drawing and music rooms and a Persian rug for the dining room.[21] They also contracted with Herter Brothers (fig. 4) for cleaning, revarnishing, and reupholstering in a silk Lampas a suite of furniture that appears to be the set James and Helen had purchased from Baudouine in 1852.[22] Herter Brothers also supplied matching draperies with velvet trim and a table covering to complete the ensemble. For the music room the same firm provided a suite of furniture covered in "red raw silk plush," coordinating covers for a table and the piano "of red cloth trimmed with black velvet," and curtains.[23]

The second-floor rooms received analogous treatment. Helen bought Brussels carpeting in a pink daisy pattern and Wilton rugs, presumably for bedchambers.[24] In 1877 Leon Marcotte and Company supplied a suite of butternut bedroom furniture (dressing bureau and washstand with marble tops; bedstead, dressing case, and assorted chairs with painted ornamentation) and upholstered furniture covered with "pink ground and Satin figured chintz ornamented with Gimp, ruffles

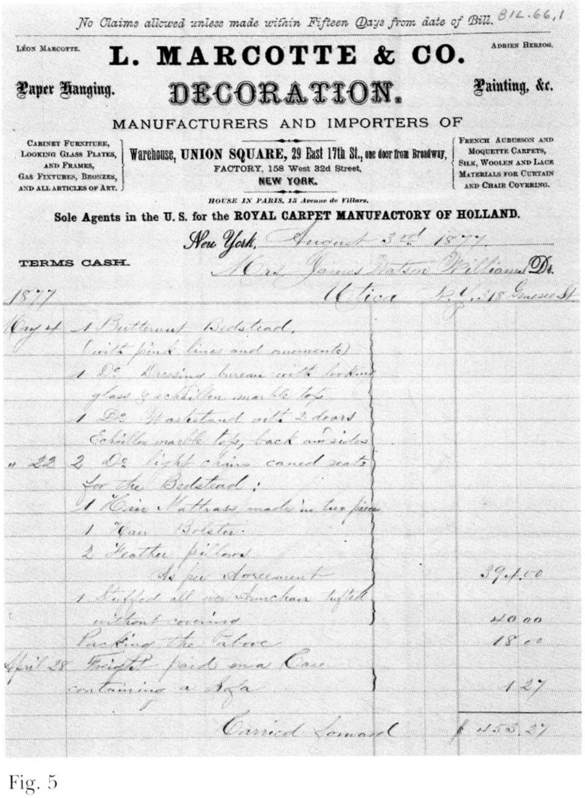

Fig. 5

Fig. 5. Bill of sale, ink on printed paper. Leon Marcotte & Co. to Mrs. James Watson Williams, 1877. Collection of the Oneida County Historical Society, Utica, N.Y.

Fig. 6

and flounces."[25] Summer covers of "striped dimity" (a cotton fabric) were also provided (fig. 5). Rounding out her patronage of fashionable cabinetmakers, Helen asked Pottier and Stymus to provide library furniture, gilt reception chairs, and other miscellaneous items.

To complement her updated interior, Helen chose to collect Asian ceramics varying from small items to large vases.[26] Her preference for Chinese and Japanese ceramics was no doubt influenced by the developing design reform initiative known as the aesthetic movement.[27] At the same time, Helen began to build a painting collection. In one five-year period, between 1876 and 1881, she purchased thirty-one major paintings and numerous works on paper.[28]

Nineteenth-century bills of sale and correspondence chronicle the spending habits of Helen and her daughters, but they do not reveal the development of their tastes. Helen's initiation into the arena of fine art collecting, however, illustrates the diverse influences on her choices and how her aesthetic sensibilities grew. Extensive actual and armchair travel exposed the Williams women to fine and decorative artworks from throughout the world, but it appears that Helen and her daughters were strongly influenced by factors other than travel. One of the earliest influences on Helen's taste were the art exhibitions organized by the Utica Art Association.[29] Many of the works of art shown were by painters whose canvases Helen later acquired for her collection—John W. Casilear, Frederic E. Church (fig. 6), Mauritz F. H. De Haas, Sanford R. Gifford (fig. 7), and William Hart. Helen's personal relationship with artists was an additional factor in the development of her aesthetic sense. She was familiar with John J. Audubon through her husband's association with the artist, Albert Bierstadt through personal ties, and Samuel F. B. Morse through her acquaintance with his second wife, Sarah.[30] The Williams family also had close ties with the portrait painter Henry Darby, who captured every member of the Williams family (even Maria's pet bird, "Birdie") on canvas.[31] As Helen began to acquire a variety of works of art, she appears to have initially relied on Darby's advice.[32]

Helen, Rachel, and Maria expanded their knowledge by arranging to view the collections of prominent New Yorkers. In 1886, for example, they went to see the collection of Mrs. Alexander T. Stewart, wife of the prominent New York City dry-goods merchant.[33] That same year, attending the New York sale of Mary Jane Morgan's fine and decorative arts collection, they purchased several items for Fountain Elms. They may also have viewed the 1883 Pedestal Fund Art Loan Exhibition, which included works by many of the artists Helen chose to represent in her private collection.[34]

Perhaps what is most enlightening about Helen's artistic eye is what is revealed in her correspondence with New York City fine arts dealers. Consistent with her choices of first-rate interior designers, she worked with some of the best-known dealers, men who also

Fig. 6. *Sunset*, 1856, Frederic Edwin Church, American (1826-1900). Oil on canvas, 24 x 36 in. Proctor Collection.

guided the collections of wealthy New Yorkers. All of the correspondence between Helen and three of these dealers survives, leaving a comprehensive record of her deliberations. From these letters it is evident that Helen was not solely interested in the aesthetic properties of an artwork. Again paralleling her quest for works from principal cabinetmakers and interior decorators, Helen sought works by artists represented in noteworthy collections. She trusted dealers and interior decorators to be the best guides in shaping her collection.

Helen's venture into the decorative and fine arts market in the 1870s is exemplified in her transactions with New York City art dealer Daniel Cottier. Their correspondence reflects her ambitions as well as her insecurities. Cottier was a seasoned dealer whose letters exert persuasive and aggressive salesmanship. As Cottier tried to educate Helen to see a work in a larger context, he assumed the role of coach and art historian. In 1878, for example, he urged Helen to acquire a painting by the French artist Jean-Baptiste-Camille Corot. "Even the holders of poor collections have a Corot," Cottier told Helen; "I am certain that this great master of modern landscape will grow upon you and when you do begin to feel the art in his work, you will find it a liberal education in art."[35] The acquisition of a Corot was adventuresome, as his tonal compositions were considered progressive in some circles, including the provincial setting in which Helen was situated. Consequently, she initially responded to Cottier with uncertainty:

> I am well aware that if I should purchase it, it will be for the gratification chiefly of myself, and that there will be a great difference of opinion concerning it among my friends. Indeed, I was told by a gentleman in New York whose judgment was recommended to me that if I wished to buy a picture that artists would dispute about I would buy a Corot.[36]

Even after Cottier persuaded her to secure the Corot at the discounted price of thirty-five hundred, she petitioned him not to let anyone know of her purchase:

> The publicity that is given in these days to the most inconspicuous persons and the most ordinary transactions will be my excuse for making this request. While I purchase the picture not merely for the pleasure it gives myself and my family, but hoping that if it should ever become necessary for us to part with it, it may prove not a bad pecuniary investment . . . I dislike unnecessary notoriety. Besides, the price even with the reduction is one that for this meridian would subject me to criticism in some quarters and importunities in others.[37]

Helen's aesthetic choices clearly reflect her concern for how her acquisitions would be viewed in upstate New York. The family was not enamored of avant-garde

Fig. 7

Fig. 7. *Galleries of the Stelvio—Lake Como*, 1878, Sanford R. Gifford, American (1823-80). Oil on canvas, 30½ x 24½ in. Proctor Collection.

Fig. 8

artists or styles. Although Helen considered her purchase of a Corot daring, his work was more conventional than the spontaneous brushstrokes and high-colored palettes of the Impressionist painters, who were not yet widely accepted in the United States. Instead, the family turned its attention to works of the French Barbizon School painters, whose sentimentalized depictions of peasants and country settings appealed to conventional tastes. Similarly, they chose the best interior design firms but decorated their homes conservatively, disregarding the European furniture and the reform interiors many other affluent and stylish people favored.

In the late 1870s and early 1880s, Helen turned primarily to the New York City galleries of William Schaus, Gustav Reichard, and M. Knoedler and Company to purchase works by artists such as Léon J. F. Bonnat, Narcisse-Virgile Diaz de la Peña, Jules Dupré, Johann G. Meyer von Bremen, and Jean François Millet. From a variety of sources she procured American works by Hudson River School artists John W. Casilear, William Hart, and David Johnson.[38]

Without a comprehensive collecting plan to guide her, Helen made fine and decorative art purchases in both pragmatic and personal ways. She appears to have acquired works for three main reasons. First among them was to garner prestige by buying from the galleries and shops that distinguished New Yorkers patronized. Helen Williams would never be a part of the social circles she emulated, but she may have reasoned that buying similar works from the same dealers might enhance the status of her two unmarried daughters, then in their thirties. Second, the accessories Helen bought for her home were in keeping with the family's stature in the community; third, she hoped that the intrinsic value of these items would increase.

Helen's collecting habits were adopted by her daughters, Rachel and Maria, although they seem to have collected for the pure pleasure of the hunt and for the joy of owning objects that were personally meaningful. Helen desired to collect on a grander scale and to display her prestigious paintings in a tasteful, private setting; her daughters purchased works of art at more modest levels.

Rachel and Maria married men whose collecting habits were similar to their own. In 1891 Maria married regional hotel owner Thomas R. Proctor (1844-1920) (fig. 8). Shortly after their marriage, Helen purchased the house next to Fountain Elms for her daughter and son-in-law. The couple redecorated the home in the 1890s to create an elegant interior (figs. 9 and 10). Helen Williams died in 1894. A few months after her mother's death, Rachel married Thomas's half-brother Frederick T. Proctor (1856-1929), and the couple (fig. 11) took up residence at Fountain Elms. The unions of the Williams sisters and

Fig. 9

Fig. 8. Thomas and Maria Proctor, ca. 1910.
Albumen print on paper. Proctor Collection.

Fig. 10

the Proctor brothers brought together two of upstate New York's most illustrious surnames.

The couples, neither of whom had surviving heirs, continued to collect and travel extensively. In addition to enlarging the fine and decorative arts collection inherited from their mother, Rachel and Maria, enthralled by popular Victorian-era habits of collecting spoons, thimbles, and fans, pursued a "bric-a-brac" aesthetic. In their travel diaries they noted visits to European museums and sites and commented at length on architectural details or on a particular artist's style. But afterward, they would scour the area for a thimble to add to their collection. The women's thimble collection is one of the earliest American examples of its kind and contains numerous superb and rare specimens among more typical souvenir thimbles.[39]

The sisters' husbands had a corresponding flair for amassing suitable "male" objects such as European watches and timepieces dating from the sixteenth through the twentieth centuries. The Proctor men published catalogues of their collections. Noteworthy for its many elegant and rare examples and its comprehensive scope, the museum's collection of their timepieces also includes finely crafted fakes that, in spite of the men's connoisseurship, duped Frederick and Thomas. The Proctor men also vigorously collected rare books, historical prints, walking sticks, coins and medals, bookplates, and holographs. The autograph collection, for instance, includes thousands of signatures ranging from Darwin to Dickens to Doubleday.

The Proctor couples also bought Louis C. Tiffany art glass, Asian ceramics, lacquerware, and cloisonné objects and augmented these smaller collections with paintings. Maria and her husband Thomas bought works by the French masters Rosa Bonheur and Léon Lhermitte and the Austrians Adolf Echtler and Franz Unterberger, along with a selection of European pastoral scenes.

After their marriage, Rachel and Frederick purchased works of art and furniture to modernize the interior of Fountain Elms. One of their major painting acquisitions was a large canvas by Jules Bréton, *Young Women Going to a Procession* (1888), which they placed at the head of the main staircase (fig. 12).[40] Between 1896 and 1915 Rachel and Frederick made numerous physical

Figs. 9 and 10. Thomas and Maria Proctor's home, Utica, N.Y., ca. 1905-10; demolished in 1959. Modern silver prints on paper from ca. 1905-10 glass plate negatives. Proctor Collection.

Fig. 11

changes to the house as well, including the installation of a pipe organ in the music room and the updating of light fixtures, fireplaces, mantels, and the heating system. In 1908 the house was enlarged on the north side with a two-story addition—a first-floor morning room with a mosaic fireplace surround, an organ chamber (for the pipes), and two second-floor bathrooms separated by a pergola with a mosaic tile floor.

Photographs of the foyer, dining room, drawing room, and one second-floor bedroom are the only known visual evidence of what the house looked like in the early twentieth century (figs. 13, 14, and 15). These images reveal that more stylish colonial revival and heavily carved Edwardian furniture had been purchased and used with some of the furnishings of the 1850s. The origins of the newer furniture are unknown, but an 1896 letter to Maria in Utica from Rachel, staying at the Plaza Hotel in New York City, mentions new pieces: "The furniture is now all decided on and is to be pushed to completion."[41]

The photographs also disclose walls arrayed with family portraits and paintings; all visible horizontal surfaces bedecked by silver, porcelain, and other objects Rachel and Frederick collected on their extensive travels to Europe and Egypt; and floors covered with Oriental rugs. At unspecified times during the couple's occupancy, some of the first-floor rooms were papered. The hall was papered with "bronze colored Lincrusta Walton which had a raised design. . . . On the drawing room walls was flock-paper with conventionalized floral design, pale pink in the front room and pale yellow in the [music room]."[42]

The family's collecting habits and steady rejuvenation of its domestic settings were outdone by its philanthropy. James and Helen Williams contributed to a number of causes and many civic needs, and Rachel, Maria, and their husbands continued the family tradition. They donated much of the land for the expansive city park system and supported local hospitals, the county historical society, disadvantaged children, the city library, and the Episcopal church. During the Great Depression, Maria helped assure the financial security of local banks and had decrepit buildings she owned torn down to give work to unemployed men. She contributed to lesser-known causes such as local and national war memorials and the campaign to place Braille books in libraries across the country.

This magnanimity, combined with the family's collecting penchant, created the Munson-Williams-Proctor Institute. Helen Williams instilled in her daughters an appreciation of art as an educational tool, although she had collected for personal enjoyment, status, propriety, and investment. Rachel and Maria were more oriented to future edification of their community. Shortly after Rachel's death in 1915, the three remaining

Fig. 12

Fig. 11. Rachel and Frederick Proctor in the foyer of Fountain Elms, ca. 1910. Gelatin silver print on paper. Proctor Collection.

Fig. 12. *Young Women Going to a Procession*, 1888, Jules A. Bréton, French (1827-1906). Oil on canvas, 49½ x 69 in. Proctor Collection.

Fig. 13

members of her family—sister, husband, and brother-in-law—formulated a broad concept for a cultural organization. In 1919 the Munson-Williams-Proctor Institute was chartered as a multifaceted organization—"an artistic, musical and social center"—that would officially and publicly commence operation upon the death of the last family member.[43]

Thomas Proctor died in 1920, Frederick in 1929. After Frederick's death, Maria envisioned that her residence and Fountain Elms would house the organization, and she was determined that the family's homes would retain the "human element" even when they began to be used as public spaces. She anticipated that one or both of the houses would be left in situ, "as examples of the residence of people of culture," and she hoped to restore Fountain Elms to approximate her recollection of her childhood.[44] To this end, Maria explored the operations of other house museums, such as Pendleton House, part of the Rhode Island School of Design.[45] Failing health, however, inhibited her progress.

The Institute officially opened in May 1936, eleven months after Maria's death. At first both houses were open for tours, but by 1937 Fountain Elms was used as the Community Arts Building. Soon thereafter the Institute modified the layout of the house to create more practical exhibition and programming space. Maria and Thomas's home continued to operate as a house museum with space for offices and public rooms for the presentation of music programs.

Within twenty years, the Munson-Williams-Proctor Institute outgrew the limiting dimensions of the two family homes. In the late 1950s the Institute commissioned architect Philip Johnson to design a new museum

Fig. 14

Fig. 13. Fountain Elms parlor, ca. 1910-20.
Cyanotype. Proctor Collection.

Fig. 14. Fountain Elms bedroom, ca. 1910-20.
Albumen print on paper. Proctor Collection.

Fig. 15

of art. Under the administration of Dr. Richard B. K. McLanathan, director of the Community Arts (later called Museum of Art) program from 1957 until 1961, the decision was made to restore Fountain Elms to the era of the Williamses' initial occupancy (1852). Decorative arts scholarship in the late 1950s was primarily focused on the colonial and federal periods; the Victorian era had received little scholarly attention. The Institute staff thus had limited primary and secondary sources on which to base historical and aesthetic decisions about the alterations. Beyond identifying types of furnishings, the extant bills of sale for Fountain Elms did not shed light on the 1850s interior decor. Museum staff believed, however, that the Williamses' aesthetic deliberations may have been influenced by published works such as the six-volume *Journal of Design and Manufactures* (London, 1849-52), published in conjunction with the Great Exhibition of 1851, and two titles by American architect and arbiter of taste Andrew Jackson Downing; these books remain in the museum's collection from the Williams family library. The restoration was based on these guides and on surviving period interiors in analogous upstate New York homes. The Institute acquired nineteenth-century architectural elements from some of these houses, many of which were being dismantled, sold, or destroyed in the name of urban renewal, to replace twentieth-century modifications in Fountain Elms.

The five, main, first-floor rooms were returned to the *functions* indicated on William Woollett's 1850 architectural drawings, and they were furnished in an extravagant fashion that later research determined did not accurately reflect the Williamses' taste.[16] Scalamandré Wallpapers, Inc., for example, created sumptuous wallpapers, adapted or extrapolated from period design sources, for each room—a rich, yellow-gold, moiré wallcovering to heighten the formality of the drawing room (fig. 16); a paper of classical extraction for the bedroom (fig. 17); a rococo-patterned, red-flocked wallpaper for the dining room to coordinate with circa 1850s draperies purchased for installation in that room (fig. 18); flocked paper of a simple stripe executed in deep purple for the library (fig. 19); and a Gothic-inspired motif for the foyer.[17] Scalamandré Silks, Inc., provided coordinating textiles for upholstery and window treatments. Some of the draperies and lambrequins were based on period objects or design sources.[18] For floor coverings, museum staff chose Wilton carpeting

Fig. 15. Fountain Elms dining room, ca. 1910-20.
Cyanotype. Proctor Collection.

Fig. 16. Fountain Elms drawing room period setting, 1998.

Fig. 17

executed in derivations of nineteenth-century patterns and colorways and woven on period looms by Hugh Mackay and Company, Ltd., of Durham, England.[49]

The four rooms and foyer were generously filled with high-style furniture, many pieces of which had a New York State provenance—an overmantel mirror and chandelier from the Taggart home in Watertown, a pier mirror and table from the Randall mansion in Cortland, and a John Henry Belter suite from Syracuse.[50] Williams family furnishings, porcelains, glass, and silver were incorporated in the settings.

The restoration provided inspiration for the preservation of nineteenth-century decorative arts and interior architectural elements that would otherwise have been lost as similar homes were renovated or demolished. Moreover, this widely publicized project, among the earliest Victorian house restorations, helped to elevate contemporary regard for mid-nineteenth-century decor and to spur research into a field that was just emerging.

The renovation of Fountain Elms, which included the creation of gallery space on the second floor, solidified MWPI's commitment to the decorative arts. Building on the collections of the Williamses and Proctors, the museum acquired many objects that are more difficult to secure in today's market—a parlor suite by John Henry Belter; labeled furniture by Edward W. Hutchings and Anthony Quervelle; a painted chair by John and Hugh Finlay; outstanding examples of New York and Philadelphia furniture from the first half of the nineteenth century; gasoliers, mantels, and window valances in original condition; and even unusual works such as a labeled, patented, fancy-painted sofa bed by Chester

Fig. 17. Fountain Elms bedroom period setting, 1998.

Johnson and furniture designed by Richard Upjohn for a house in New York City. The decorative arts holdings have been amplified through the generosity of numerous patrons including Emily Lowery Beardsley, John Devereux Kernan, H. Randolph Lever, Mrs. James L. Lowery, Mrs. Edmund Munson and Watson Lowery, Otto A. Meyer and Helen and Jane Meyer, Mr. and Mrs. William C. Murray, Sarah T. Norris, Mrs. Erving C. Pruyn, and Verne S. Swan, all of whom had ties to the Williamses or Proctors or to the city of Utica. The largest single donation to the decorative arts collection—more than 180 objects—came in 1986 from Jane B. Sayre Bryant and David E. Bryant in memory of the Sayre family.

In 1960 the then-uncommon practice of housing part of an art museum in a historic home, as opposed to restoring the house to represent a specific period of occupancy, led early MWPI staff members to approach the decorative arts from a dual perspective, as history and as art. Accordingly, the collection encompassed a spectrum of domestic objects with historic value as well as artistic merit from the seventeenth through the nineteenth centuries. Subcollections varied from silver and glass to wrought-iron cooking implements and spinning wheels.

The family's initial gift and the selected focus of the period rooms provided the collection with a strong representation of high-style goods made between 1830

Fig. 18

Fig. 18. Fountain Elms dining room period setting, 1998.

and 1870. During the last ten years the collection has been refined to reflect this strength, and in 1990 the Institute's Board of Trustees endorsed a revised collection policy that limited the scope of the collection to nineteenth-century America.[51] Significant items predating this focus, such as a William and Mary-style chair with its original upholstery and a *kast* from Bergen County, New Jersey, were placed with museums specializing in these areas.[52]

Through an active acquisition campaign, the museum staff seeks works representative of the finest craftsmanship produced in America during the nineteenth century. Including examples of nearly every principal nineteenth-century style and virtually all of the period's major decorative and construction techniques, the collection is a notable cross section of American art history. It contains objects that document European influences on American furniture, trade and shop practices, the employment of innovative materials or techniques, changing concepts of style and taste, specialization of forms, the impact of changing American lifestyles on the country's furniture, the overt use of historical references, and regional craftsmanship.

Recent efforts have centered on filling chronological gaps and on adding greater interpretive depth to the collection. Acquisitions have therefore included the styles and works of cabinetmakers that would have graced a home such as Fountain Elms from the 1870s through the 1890s—furnishings in the Elizabethan, renaissance revival, *néo-grec*, aesthetic, and arts and crafts styles representing the works of J. and J. W. Meeks, Alexander Roux, Kilian Brothers, A. Kimbel and J. Cabus, Joseph P. McHugh, and other artisans well known in their day. Two noteworthy acquisitions of works by Herter Brothers illustrate portions of the stylistic range and decorative techniques the firm employed. The Institute also acquired a silver-plated table by Tiffany & Company, featured in the firm's display at the World's Columbian Exposition, and an elaborate cabinet-on-stand by an unknown maker that exhibits a sweep of finely crafted *néo-grec* motifs.

The entire decorative arts collection of more than ten thousand objects is a mosaic of materials—silver, glass, and porcelain, with subcollections ranging from jewel-encrusted European watches to locally made stoneware—with infinite interpretive possibilities. This interpretive potential was strengthened in 1995 when the museum's education wing was built between Fountain Elms and the Philip Johnson-designed building, physically joining the fine and decorative arts galleries.

The success of Fountain Elms lies in its combination of a historic structure, period room settings, and exhibition and study storage galleries, a configuration that permits the art museum to exhibit the decorative arts as art and as documents of social history. Because Maria Williams Proctor and Thomas and Frederick Proctor had the foresight not to restrict the use of their homes, the Institute has been able to retain "the human element" Maria envisioned through the creation of four period-room settings, while modifying the structure to meet evolving needs of the museum with public study storage galleries on the second floor.

In 1850 when Helen and James Williams were establishing their home, they could not have foreseen that the house they lovingly designed and the items they painstakingly gathered would form the foundation of an internationally known art museum. Nor could they have imagined that their home would become a window to a better understanding of nineteenth-century material culture and a reflection of twentieth-century cultural values.

Anna Tobin D'Ambrosio
Curator of Decorative Arts

Fig. 19. Fountain Elms library period setting, 1998.

Notes to the Catalogue

This catalogue is the third volume in a continuing series of books devoted to aspects of the Museum of Art's permanent collection. The goal of these publications is to present new scholarship on the collection and to make it available to a broad audience.

Masterpieces of American Furniture presents 68 pieces from the museum's furniture collection. Objects were chosen for their importance in an art historical context. In some instances, only one or two works from a larger suite are illustrated.

Each entry contains a descriptive title of the piece, date made, maker and active dates of maker, and place of manufacture. Measurements, inscriptions, materials, condition notes, provenance, and the museum's credit line and accession number are recorded at the end of each essay.

Dimensions: Three dimensions are given for each object to the nearest eighth of an inch. The maximum measurements of height, width, and depth take into account all carving, upholstery, and any other protrusions.

Inscriptions: In most cases, an inscription is limited to the maker's marks. Exact wording of labels, stamps, and handwritten inscriptions are noted.

Materials: Wood analysis for nearly all the objects was undertaken for this catalogue. In a few instances where it was not possible to collect a wood sample without potential damage to the object, woods were identified visually rather than microscopically. Woods are listed from primary (show) to secondary (structural and/or minor decorative); other materials used in the construction of the object are listed last. Upholstery is also described. "Original upholstery" assumes the covering is the only one the piece has had. "Reproduction upholstery" means that object's original fabric has been replicated or that a new fabric, the design of which is documented to the nineteenth century, was used. "Replacement upholstery" means that a nineteenth-century fabric was used to recover the object. "Modern upholstery" indicates that a fabric is new and is not a reproduction of a nineteenth-century textile.

Condition: Major conservation work, when known, is noted. Minor repairs and surface damage are not noted. Many of the pieces have undergone some type of work on the finish during their history. When MWPI has undertaken such work, the entry notes that fact.

Provenance: The entry also cites the history of ownership as it is documented in the museum's collection records. When the object has a significant, well-documented provenance, this history is recounted in the catalogue essay. Objects that are part of the museum's Proctor Collection are signified by "PC" at the beginning of the accession number. Except for a desk by R. J. Horner (cat. no. 53), the "PC" items were part of the original furnishings for Fountain Elms. All of the Proctor Collection furnishings descended directly to the Museum of Art from James and Helen Williams, through their daughters Rachel Williams Proctor and Maria Williams Proctor.

ATD

Masterpieces
of American Furniture from the Munson-Williams-Proctor Institute

1

Side Chair, ca. 1790–1820

Maker unknown
New York, New York

By the 1770s a completely new interpretation of classicism was being introduced to colonial America. Inspired by archaeological excavations at the ancient cities of Pompeii and Herculaneum, the English designer Robert Adam and his contemporaries reinterpreted and reconfigured classicism in their designs for architecture and the decorative arts. The vigorous motifs central to the rococo idiom gave way to classically derived elements such as bellflowers, swags, acanthus leaves, and urns. Although introduced in the colonies just prior to the Revolution, neoclassicism was not popularized and integrated into the arts until after the war.

By the 1780s Americans were becoming more acquainted with the style through published sources such as George Hepplewhite's *Cabinet-Maker and Upholsterer's Guide* (1788), which continued the tradition of earlier furniture design books by making the latest patterns available to craftsmen and their patrons. By contrast, Thomas Sheraton's more technical publications, *The Cabinet-Maker and Upholsterer's Drawing-Book* (1791-93) and *The Cabinet Dictionary* (1803), were specifically compiled for artisans in the trade.

The *Drawing-Book* had a profound impact on American neoclassical furniture; the MWPI side chair, for instance, is patterned after plate 36, number 1.[1] Described at the time as "a Square Back Chair," this design was particularly favored in New York where its popularity is confirmed by numerous surviving examples and by descriptions in *The New-York Book of Prices for Cabinet and Chair Work* of 1802, a volume compiled to establish prices for specific forms and designs within the trade. The basic square-back side chair consisted of "a drapery bannister, with a feather top; a splatt on each side, to form an arch with the top rail; bannister and splatts pierc'd; sweep stay and top rail, with a brake in ditto; sweep seat rails, for stuffing over ditto; plain taper'd legs."[2] In addition, the client and master craftsman could review a series of optional treatments for the finished chair. The final purchase price varied according to the overall configuration and surface treatment.[3]

A series of these subtle options, albeit not enumerated in the 1802 price book, is handsomely manifested in the MWPI chair. This distinctive chair diverges from the conventional form in that its principal elements—capitals, drapery, and plumes—are brilliantly interpreted in contrasting inlays rather than carving. In American furniture, individual chairbacks that incorporate the skills of a carver and an inlayer are highly unusual and indicate the substantial contribution specialist craftsmen made in the design and production of the finest furniture.[4] This particular chair may represent the collaboration of a chairmaker and a specialist inlayer, or it may display the skills of a single craftsman such as Benjamin Atkinson, who described himself in the city directory as an "inlayer and cabinet-maker."[5] Here, the use of inlays—accentuated by darkened incising—produces an arresting effect, of greater contrast and definition than is realized in the carved version of this same design.[6]

MKB

36 x 21½ x 18⅞ in.
Mahogany, white ash, soft maple, eastern white pine, reproduction upholstery
Provenance: Believed to be from the Cogswell family of Albany or New York, New York; Mrs. Edward W. (Grace Cogswell) Root, Clinton, New York; MWPI.
Museum Purchase, 67.112

2

Side Chair, ca. 1785–93

Possibly John Seymour III (active 1785–93)
Falmouth (renamed Portland, 1786), Maine

This chair is linked to examples from at least three closely related sets that vary from one another only in the details of their painted decoration.[1] All of these chairs have long been considered to be the work of either John Seymour II (1738-1818) or his son John Seymour III (1765?-93). This attribution is based on an inscription by a Seymour descendant on a single chair.[2]

The Seymours originally came to America from the southwest English county of Devonshire and arrived in Falmouth in the "Casco Settlements" of what is now Maine in the fall of 1784.[3] By early December of that year, John II was supplying cabinetwork to Thomas Robison, an enterprising Falmouth merchant.[4]

Although John Seymour II's primary artisanal training was as a leatherworker, he probably had worked with his father John I (d. 1784?), a "Master Joiner," in Axminster.[5] John Seymour II in many ways was the ideal immigrant. He came to America accompanied by his wife Jane Brice (1748-1816), who had been formally apprenticed in England in one of the needle trades, and at least three sons.[6] John III, Thomas (1771-1849), and Joseph (dates unknown) practiced furniture making and, along with their father, performed an amazing variety of services in several trades including furniture construction and repair, finish shipjoinery, carpentry, and coffinmaking.[7] John III joined his father's cabinetmaking business but worked primarily as a painter. Records show that his tasks included "painting at the store," priming and painting "the vessels," and "painting the Cabbin of the Brigg Ranger."[8]

This chair may well be an example of John Seymour III's painterly efforts. Although the attribution cannot be documented by other means, the combination of relatively crude workmanship and painted neoclassical decoration is consistent with a provincial Falmouth-Portland provenance and the young Seymour's trade skills. The chair's structure and joinery show that the maker was clearly a novice. All of the elements are rough, uneven, asymmetrical, and halting. The joints are not accurately cut or fitted, and the overall stance is skewed. The caned seat is laid on top of the leg and seat-rail frame and attached to it with five tapered and squared wooden pins, all of which are imprecisely fitted.

In contrast, the painted "Etruscan" decoration on the chair is sophisticated in conception and intent. The neoclassical inspiration for the splat painting derives from a design by English architect Robert Adam for the country house Osterly Park in Middlesex County, England. Adam's work was popularized and disseminated by designers such as Thomas Sheraton, and it is likely the painter of the MWPI chair worked from plate 36, number 1, in Sheraton's *Cabinet-Maker and Upholsterer's Drawing-Book* of 1793.[9] The ornamentation on the chair includes many of Adam's favorite classical motifs. The central splat is in the form of a vase with blue and white "Wedgwood" ground, adorned with a drapery swag and acanthus leaves. Flanking columns, suggesting a classical order, are marbleized in the contrasting "Etruscan" colors of gray, white, ochre, and red earth. The paired, stylized roses on the back crest and stay rails and on the front seat rail derive from a neoclassical English tradition of painted decoration. The stylish overall design of the chair was at the height of fashion in post-Revolutionary Portland.[10] If John Seymour III did paint this chair, it probably dates to just before his death in Portland in 1793. At that time Seymour had the artistic experience to execute the sophisticated painting.

RM

36 x 20 x 15⅞ in.
"IIII" in chisel marks on inner edge of left caned rail
Birch, oil paint, modern caned seat
Provenance: Sotheby Parke Bernet & Co., *Property from the Collection of Boscobel Restoration Inc.*, sale cat. (New York, Jan. 22, 1977), lot 171; MWPI.
Museum Purchase, 77.65

3

Card Table, ca. 1790–1820

Maker unknown
Coastal Massachusetts, probably Boston area

While this is one of the most dazzling and elaborate federal-period card tables made in New England, its precise place of origin remains unclear. Numerous construction and design features point to its manufacture in northern coastal New England, as indicated by the method established by furniture scholar Benjamin A. Hewitt for analyzing the anatomy of these tables. The shape of the MWPI table (square with elliptic front and serpentine ends), its three-part facade with light panels of flame birch or satinwood outlined in dark she-oak, and its pointed double-taper legs strongly indicate that it was made in Boston, Salem, or New Hampshire. Similarly, the patterned inlays—used to strong visual effect on this table—are also seen on card tables and other objects from the same regions.[1]

The construction features of the MWPI table are also consistent with a Boston, Salem, or New Hampshire place of manufacture. Hewitt found the single-board construction of its rails predominately in New Hampshire, western Massachusetts, and the cities of Newburyport, Salem, and Boston. Its hinged-rail design was common in New England (as well as in Philadelphia and Annapolis), and although its flush back-rail construction was atypical, it was not unknown in New England. The flyleg construction is a type common to Massachusetts and New Hampshire. A single rear leaf-edge tenon, used to help support the top when it is in the open position, was common in all areas of New England; the use of multiple tenons was more typical of other cabinetmaking centers.[2]

This table is closely related to tables labeled by Elisha Tucker (d. 1827) of Boston, especially to examples in the Winterthur Museum and the Honolulu Academy of Arts. Some construction features of the Winterthur and Honolulu tables are similar to the MWPI table: all three have the same type of hinged rail, flush back-rail construction, plane flyleg construction, and one rear leaf-edge tenon.[3] However, the MWPI table has single-board rails, while the Winterthur and Honolulu tables have laminated rails with a cross-brace behind the front curved rail. Hewitt was not able to find a consistently significant statistical difference between single lamination and solid rail construction, however, leaving open at least the theoretical possibility that this table was made in Tucker's shop.[4]

Card tables were often made in pairs, and an apparent mate to this table has survived in a private collection.[5] Although visually the two seem identical, they differ in some of their construction details. Such variations may merely reflect the practices of a large urban shop containing a number of workbenches staffed by journeymen and apprentices. But Elisha Tucker is a little-known figure; his modest estate inventory gives no strong indication that he was a major furniture producer, and only a few surviving objects bear his label.[6]

The secondary woods of the MWPI table—white pine and birch—are common to Massachusetts and New Hampshire furniture. One unusual feature of the MWPI table is the apparent use of Australian she-oak (*Casuarina* spp.) veneer for the crossbanding that outlines the panels of figured birch or satinwood on the facade. This distinctive wood, similar to mahogany, rosewood, beefwood, and other imported exotic hardwoods, has distinct dark streaks or stripes. It was also known as Botany Bay wood in the period; the Boston cabinetmaker Stephen Badlam had quantities of "Botany Bay oak" in his 1815 estate inventory, and London price books of the period list "Botany-bay" veneers. Its use is recorded on Portsmouth furniture (as on a federal secretary in the collection of the Strawbery Banke Museum), and it appears on Salem and Boston pieces as well.[7] A later English cabinetmaker's guide notes that this wood "is imported from New South Wales, in round logs about nine feet long, and from 9 to 14 inches in diameter. In general colour, it is more intensely red than mahogany, with occasionally dark veins, small, slightly curled, and minutely dispersed throughout the entire surface. Some specimens are pretty."[8]

On balance, it seems most reasonable to attribute the MWPI table to a maker working in the Boston area. It is a sophisticated and beautiful example that is closely related visually to labeled Boston work. Whatever its exact place of manufacture, it reflects the widespread craze for card playing that swept America during the federal period.[9]

GWRW

29¾ x 35⅞ x 17⅛ in.
29¾ x 35⅞ x 34 in. (open position)
Mahogany, birch, eastern white pine, veneers of birch
or satinwood and probably she-oak, inlay of various woods
Provenance: Seymour house, Utica, New York; Robert Palmiter, Bouckville, New York; MWPI.
Museum Purchase, 56.306

4

Pembroke Table, ca. 1800–1810

Attributed to Holmes Weaver (active ca. 1799–1815)
Newport, Rhode Island

The Pembroke table was a new form of furniture in federal-period America. Small in size and fitted with folding leaves and a drawer, Pembroke tables were often used for breakfast but also served a wide range of other functions. The maker of this table apparently turned to a source such as plate 62 in George Hepplewhite's *Cabinet-Maker and Upholsterer's Guide* (1794) for inspiration. Dated September 1, 1787, this plate depicts two Pembroke tables, one of which has rectangular leaves and inlaid urns flanking the drawer; the less elegant inlay on the MWPI table is suggestive of the Hepplewhite example. The text notes that "Pembroke Tables are the most useful of this species of furniture: they may be of various shapes. The long square [as with the MWPI table] and oval are the most fashionable."[1]

It is possible to attribute this table to Holmes Weaver (1769-1848) of Newport, Rhode Island, largely on the basis of its four, distinctive, inlaid urns (inset). Although patterned inlays and some pictorial inlays were made by specialists and used by many cabinetmaking shops, pictorial inlays of the type seen here (termed "single unit" inlays by the scholar Benjamin A. Hewitt) were made within individual shops and therefore can be used as a diagnostic feature. Inlays similar to those on the MWPI table—consisting of urns with a rounded cap resting on a plinth, decorated with engraved decoration, and intertwined stringing terminating in tassels on the legs—are found on a Pembroke table bearing Weaver's label in the collection of the Museum of Fine Arts, Boston.[2] Scholars have used the MFA table as the basis for attributing a group of stylish Pembroke tables and card tables to Weaver; all have inlaid urns and tassels, and some have inlaid tulips as well.[3]

In the case of the MWPI table, the attribution is strengthened by the existence of a labeled table, without inlay, of virtually the same form and with the same short rectangular leaves.[4] In addition, Weaver's newspaper advertisement in the *Newport Mercury*, which first appeared on November 16, 1802, and ran through March 1, 1803, depicts a small table not unlike the MWPI example and a second Pembroke-type table as well.[5] However, because the engraver probably used stock images rather than attempting to depict actual products of Weaver's shop, the resemblance of the print to this table may be only coincidental. Variations among labeled Weaver tables in features such as cross braces complicate making an attribution to Weaver based on construction details.[6]

Weaver was born in Middleton, Rhode Island, on July 24, 1769, the son of Alice and Thomas Weaver of Portsmouth, Rhode Island. Although it is not known with whom he apprenticed, he was running his own shop in Newport before the end of the eighteenth century. His shop, opened at least by the time of his first newspaper advertisement in 1799, was initially located on Meeting Street; between 1806 and 1815 Weaver was situated on the north side of Broadway. In addition to tables, his labeled work includes chests of drawers and clock cases.[7] Although his printed label, engraved by Henry Barber Jr. (ca. 1780-1856), refers to Weaver as a "Cabinet & Chair Maker," no chairs bearing his label are currently known.[8] The *Newport Mercury* published Weaver's obituary on February 19, 1848, noting that he had served as clerk of the Supreme Court for the county and was "a man respected by all who knew him."

The MWPI table and others like it indicate that Newport cabinetmakers, who had not embraced the rococo style with any degree of enthusiasm, quickly adopted neoclassicism. Many federal-period Pembroke tables made in Newport have rounded or D-shaped leaves, although some, like this table, retain the rectangular leaves more typical of examples made before 1790. Newport Pembroke tables labeled by Robert Lawton and by Stephen and Thomas Goddard also sometimes have inlaid urns, although they are of a different character than Weaver's.[9]

GWRW

28⅞ x 19⅜ x 29⅞ in.
28⅞ x 31⅞ x 29⅞ in. (open position)
Mahogany, probably maple, brass
Repair to proper left front and proper right rear leg
Provenance: Mrs. Francis M. Metcalf, Utica, New York; MWPI.
Gift of Mrs. Francis M. Metcalf; 66.98

97 x 21⅛ x 10¾ in.
Clock face: "SHUBAEL STORRS."
Pencil inscription inside case door: "C. [France ?] (Clock C[?] 5) S[?]. Iw./Washington Mills/Oneida Co., N.Y." "H. G. Sanford Watchmaker" "Mr. W. S. Taylor 62 Genesee Street-May 26, 1897"
Works: brass, silvered brass, iron, steel
Case: mahogany, cherry, eastern white pine, satinwood, inlay of various woods, glass, brass
Provenance: Sherman family, Utica, New York; Mrs. Sanford Sherman; Robert Palmiter, Bouckville, New York; MWPI.
Museum Purchase, 50.37

 5

Tall-Case Clock, ca. 1805

Works: Shubael Storrs (active 1803–28)
Utica, New York
Case: Maker unknown
Probably New York State

During the 1790s, market towns including Utica quickly grew along the turnpikes and rivers of upstate New York. As citizens accrued wealth to build fine homes, they encouraged specialists to create elegant furnishings for their new residences. Silversmiths, clockmakers, and instrument makers occupied the top of the hierarchy of craftsmen. Their social standing was defined by the intrinsic worth of the raw materials they used, relative to the value of their own labor. In smaller towns during the early nineteenth century, individuals often combined the crafts of silver-smithing—working with gold, silver, copper, and copper alloys such as brass—and clockmaking. Because of the small number of patrons who could afford these emblems of status, craft specialization was limited.

Shubael Storrs (1778-1847) of Utica is an example of the kind of craftsmen who worked in the main-street shops of early federal America. Born in Mansfield, Connecticut, on December 13, 1778, he was the son of Ebenezer and Lois Southworth Storrs.[1] He served his apprenticeship in Springfield, Massachusetts, probably with Jacob Sergeant (1761-1843), a one-time neighbor who in 1784 advertised a "shop in Mansfield [where he] makes clocks and watches, gold and silversmith work."[2] Sergeant moved to Springfield about 1789 and probably took Shubael as an apprentice in 1792, when the boy was about fourteen. Shubael may have replaced his older first cousin, Nathan Storrs (1768-1839), who left Sergeant to settle in Northampton, Massachusetts, about 1790.[3] In any case, Shubael moved to Utica in 1803 and opened his own shop in 1808.[4]

Storrs made his living by offering an evolving range of products based on demand. Some items he made; others he purchased for retail sale. In Utica's first *City Directory* (1817), Storrs presented himself as a gold- and silversmith at 30 Genesee Street. Four years later, he advertised that he had "commenced the manufacture" of mathematical and surveying instruments.[5] In 1828 Storrs called himself a watchmaker and silversmith. After 1837 he changed the entire scope of his livelihood when he began making trusses, probably for bridge construction. Storrs died on July 10, 1847.

The MWPI tall clock is testimony to the quality of life in Utica during the first years of the nineteenth century and to Storrs's skills as a businessman and clockmaker. The clock is imposing in several ways. Physically it is large—eight feet tall—and has an oversized, thirteen-inch, English "Osborne" dial. Storrs assembled the clock,

a sophisticated mechanical almanac, from primarily imported English parts. The case was most likely made by a specialist who was able to combine dramatic veneers and inlays to visually unite classicism with nationalism and opulence.[6] Despite its showy exterior, the structure of the case is relatively simple. The maker rabbeted the sides of the base to receive the veneered facade and constructed the stubby feet as extensions of the base.[7]

Although the cabinetmaker is unidentified, the earliest inscription on the back of the door places the clock's owner in nearby "Washington Mills/Oneida Co., N.Y."[8] The clock was probably made during Storrs's first years in Utica, before Jefferson's Embargo Act and the War of 1812 temporarily halted the importation of English goods. Furthermore, the sixteen stars flanking the prominent eagle inlay (above) suggest that the inlay was manufactured between 1796, when Tennessee became the sixteenth state, and 1803, when Ohio joined the Union as the seventeenth state.[9] The maker of the case may be one of the cabinetmakers recorded in Utica's 1817 street directory—Joseph B. Prescott, Rudolph Snyder, William Tillman, or John Todd.

Storrs and his cabinetmaker placed an expensive mechanism in a complex case that features costly imported veneers and pictorial inlays in combination with native lumber and homemade inlays at the base of the columns. The clock, which reflects a provincial enthusiasm for New York City and Albany prototypes, is punctuated with the confidence that Utica craftsmen could perform just as well.[10]

PZ

 6

Side Chairs, ca. 1805–30

Maker unknown
New York, New York

The Empire style, appropriately referred to as "Grecian" at the time it was introduced, came to America through the English-trained architect Benjamin H. Latrobe (1764-1820).[1] Compared with neoclassicism, it was a more historically correct interpretation of the ancient past and one deemed appropriate for the emerging republic. Even after Americans declared their political independence from England, they continued to emulate English culture and to purchase English manufactured goods for their homes. Throughout the Grecian period London publications influenced American decorative arts. *The London Chair-Makers' and Carvers' Book of Prices* (1802), Thomas Sheraton's *Cabinet Dictionary* (1803), Thomas Hope's influential *Household Furniture and Interior Decoration* (1807), and Rudolph Ackermann's monthly series *The Repository of Arts, Literature, Commerce, Manufactures, Fashions and Politics* (begun 1809) coincide with the earliest American manifestations of this new fashion.[2]

In New York the first hint of the style is perceptible as early as 1807 in a set of chairs supplied to the merchant William Bayard by Duncan Phyfe (1768-1854), the city's preeminent cabinetmaker. These mahogany chairs retain neoclassical elements; their "sprung" legs and scrolled backs, however, signify the introduction of a more archaeologically correct taste.[3] Shortly thereafter, a more fully developed interpretation, one patterned after the ancient *klismos* chair, became the requisite form of seating furniture in the most fashionable households. Characterized by gracefully inward curving front and rear legs, the chair had its genesis in classical sources, probably vase paintings or sculpted stelae.[4]

The MWPI side chairs are classic New York interpretations of the *klismos* form. At the time they were made they were described as "scroll-back" side chairs. Incorporated into the finest examples, such as these, are realistic carvings of animal paws, acanthus leaves, and ornamental reliefs; paired cornucopias embellish the crest rail. A less commonly found feature on these chairs is the reeded front seat rail, which corresponds to the continuous seat rails and stiles. These chairs also have graceful, scrolled strapwork splats in place of the more usual lyre, harp, or curule shapes. This alternative may be best understood as a combination of the Grecian curule with a tripartite element that is reminiscent of the trio of plumes often seen on the backs of neoclassical-style New York chairs (see cat. no. 1). This same distinctive splat embellishes a set of eight matching side chairs now in a private collection; perhaps the MWPI side chairs were originally part of that suite.[5]

The number of New York City chairs known from this period and the range of discrete variations that exist among them are indicative of the phenomenal growth in the city's cabinet trade during this dynamic era. Between 1800 and 1810 New York's population increased by more than 50 percent, making it the most populous city in the young nation. Scholars have habitually assigned scroll-back chairs of this type to Duncan Phyfe's prominent Fulton Street shop, purportedly the largest and finest establishment in early nineteenth-century New York. Phyfe's shop certainly produced similar examples, but the design was widely admired, and scores of cabinetmakers throughout the city fashioned chairs of this type. Attribution of scroll-back chairs to a specific artisan or shop is therefore complicated, if not impossible.[6]

Exactly what role Duncan Phyfe played in the development of the Grecian style in early nineteenth-century New York is not clear. In the past, decorative arts scholars have credited him with its introduction. Some enthusiasts have suggested that Phyfe originated the style and have named it after him, despite the fact that there is no documentation to support their lofty claims. What can be safely inferred from contemporary records is that Duncan Phyfe's cabinet shop was synonymous with a standard of excellence admired in his day by clientele and competitors alike.[7]

MKB

32⅛ x 18½ x 18⅝ in.
Mahogany, soft maple, reproduction upholstery
Repair to splat on one chair
Provenance: Mrs. C. Barton Wyncoop, Utica, New York; MWPI.
Museum Purchase, 60.315.1-2

7

Grecian Couch, ca. 1815–25

Maker unknown

Probably New York, New York

This couch is an elegant variant of the popular Empire sofa form made fashionable by English and French designers of the early nineteenth century. The couch form is distinguished from the sofa form in that one end of the couch is higher than the other.[1] Based on Roman models, English examples of the couch form may date from as early as 1795; French examples may date from as early as 1788.[2] Popularized by the French and made famous by Jacques-Louis David's (1748-1826) *Portrait of Mme. Récamier* (1800), the form was included in widely circulated English design books such as Thomas Sheraton's *Cabinet Dictionary* (1803) and George Smith's *Collection of Designs for Household Furniture and Interior Decoration* (1808).

The historian John Morley noted that the "Grecian" couch form was more Roman than Greek with its "rolled back arm and lion paw feet" and that the imprecisely named "Grecian" squab (couch) soon became "indispensable in most Regency drawing rooms."[3] In America the form was equally ubiquitous, but it developed with distinctive local characteristics as its production spread to nearly every region of the United States. American couches feature a range of ornament from highly figured veneers to richly grained surfaces, from elaborate ormolu mounts to detailed stenciled designs, and from cut-brass inlays to a variety of carved elements that include floridly carved legs and paw feet.

New York couches can be distinguished from those made in other East Coast centers by their lavishly carved and gilded surfaces and by the use of contrasting colors—red, brown, or black ground color; gold stenciled ornamentation; gilded carving; and *vert antique* accents. The MWPI example, made of maple but painted to simulate rosewood, has refined gilding and *vert antique* paw feet capped by carved and gilded botanical clusters. Caning gives the couch delicacy and stylishness, and the repeated curves of the arms and back add to the overall feeling of lightness.

New York couches often employ cornucopias as part of their decorative vocabulary. While the MWPI example does not include this element, a bracket of fruit and leaves crowns each front paw foot. Related couches are in the collections of the Metropolitan Museum of Art; the Museum of Fine Arts, Boston; and the Cleveland Museum of Art.[4] The gilded decoration on the couch in the Metropolitan Museum includes small cornucopias, eagles, masks, swans, and scrolls, many of which are also found on the MWPI couch.[5] The quality of this decoration is of the highest level, suggesting the hand of an accomplished artisan, perhaps someone skilled in the art of engraving.[6] Another common feature among this group of couches is the use of gilded metal or wooden rosettes (as on the MWPI example) at the termination of the couch ends and on the back crest rail.

PT

$32\frac{1}{2}$ x $83\frac{1}{2}$ x $24\frac{1}{2}$ in.
Soft maple, birch, cherry, paint, gilding, caned seat and back, modern cushion
Provenance: Yonderhill Dwellers; MWPI.
Museum Purchase, 60.67

8

Pier Table, ca. 1828

Maker unknown
New York, New York

This table and its mate, a pair of matching center tables, and two pier mirrors were part of the original furnishings of the 1828 Cortland, New York, mansion of William Randall and his wife Betsey (Bassett) Randall.[1] These items were featured in a private sale in November 1935 following the death of Marian B. Wilson, the last member of the Randall family to live in the magnificent house.[2] According to the sale notice, "The pieces offered . . . are all from the furnishings of the Randall home and were reserved by the Randall heirs when the less sophisticated things were sold at auction a few weeks ago."[3]

William Randall and his brother Roswell, both of whom came to Cortland in 1812 from Stonington, Connecticut, built a general store that flourished at an auspicious location near the banks of the Tioughnioga River. William later founded the Randall Bank, and Roswell built the Eagle Store and served as the town's postmaster. The brothers also had extensive landholdings in the southern and eastern parts of Cortland.[4]

William and Betsey Randall built two houses on Main Street, one in 1821 (sold to Roswell Randall in 1828) and another, next door to the first, in 1828. In a 1928 history of the William Randall mansion, local historian and former newspaper editor Edward D. Blodgett stated that Betsey and William Randall had gone by stage, packet boat, and steamship to New York "to buy suitable furniture for their pretentious dwelling." They purchased the most "beautiful things which the city afforded," Blodgett wrote, and added that it took months to haul these goods "by river, canal and land" back to the "country, which, less than 25 years before had been a forest wilderness." The furnishings were "for the long drawing room of the Randall mansion, occupying the south side of the house," which in 1928 was "still furnished as William Randall designed it, 100 years ago." He commented on the Randalls' excellent taste and noted that the drawing room contained "flowered carpets . . . long peer [*sic*] mirrors with onyx console tables at their bases . . . Empire chairs and . . . long red damask draperies at the windows," all "perfect examples of the best styles of Empire interior decorations of that early period."[5] The MWPI pier table is one of the "onyx console tables" Blodgett mentioned.

While pier tables of this overall form must have been ubiquitous in fine New York houses of the period, the Randall table is a superior example, distinguished by its rosewood veneer, black-veined marble top, front columns with elaborate gilt bronze capitals and bases, carved and gilded conical feet, and the formalized gilt rinceaux decorations on the apron and platform.[6] Considering the options available to a prospective buyer of fine furniture in New York City in the 1820s, the Randalls clearly chose the finest that money could buy. Although the name of the maker is unknown, the Randalls' suite is remarkable for the story of its journey from New York to Cortland and for its pristine provenance.

The freehand gilding on this pier table is skillfully executed and employs classical motifs derived from European pattern books of the time. Imitating French and English ormolu mounts, freehand gilding, according to furniture conservator Cynthia Moyer, was achieved by "applying gold leaf to an oil size painted in a pattern on a smooth two-dimensional surface. Over the leaf, thin, dark lines were then either etched with a stylus or painted in with a fine brush, making the oil-gilded decoration look three dimensional."[7] It is possible that the decorator used pin pricks and lithopone to transfer patterns of symmetrical classical motifs onto the surface of the table. This provided an outline for the craftsman who completed the final design by hand.[8]

PT

38⅞ x 46¼ x 19⅛ in.
Mahogany, black ash, eastern white pine, yellow-poplar, marble, glass, gilded gesso, gilded bronze, gilding
Front feet regilded
Provenance: William Randall, Cortland, New York; Wilhelmina Randall (1820-1913), Cortland, New York; Marian B. Wilson (d. 1935), Cortland, New York; Robert Palmiter, Bouckville, New York; MWPI.
Museum Purchase, 59.125

9

Pier Mirror, ca. 1830–35

Isaac Platt (active 1815–ca. 1860)
New York, New York

Fig. 20

This pier mirror bears the label (fig. 20) of Isaac L. Platt (1793-1875), a frame and looking-glass maker and retailer and a print seller who conducted business at 178 Broadway in New York City from 1825 to 1837.[1] Born in Freehold, New Jersey, to Stephen (1762-1800) and Dorcas (Hopkins) Platt, Isaac Platt first appears in New York City directories in 1815 with a looking-glass store at 196 Broadway. In addition to his frame and looking-glass business, Platt was a founder of the Chemical Bank and the Pennsylvania Coal Company and served as vice president of the Delaware and Hudson Canal Company.[2]

With its four split turnings, carved corner elements, symmetrical decoration, and overall sculptural quality, this mirror is of a type that became popular in the 1830s.[3] It was probably made between 1830 and 1835 and has elements of both federal and rococo revival styles: The simple split-turned sides suggest the federal style, but the carved bosses, floral motifs, and C-scrolls evoke the rococo revival style. At one time, looking glasses of this type were thought to have been made later than those with cornices and side turnings, but more recent scholarship suggests that the designs were made contemporaneously and that clients could chose between the two.[4] Of the known mirrors with a Platt label, the MWPI example is one of the most richly ornamented.[5]

This pier mirror is one of a pair that originally hung in the drawing room of the Randall family mansion on Main Street in Cortland, New York. One of the pair can be seen in situ above a marble-top pier table (see cat. no. 8) in a photograph in a brochure for the November 1935 sale of the Randall house contents.[6] A mirror is also described in the text of the brochure as a "magnificent mirror with gold leaf frame, thirty-nine by sixty-nine inches in size." Further documentation of the Randall provenance can be found in the inventory of the estate of Marian B. Wilson, last member of the Randall family to live in the mansion, which lists "2 Gold frame Peer [*sic*] glasses" valued at seventy dollars among the contents of the drawing room.[7]

Platt's correspondence with another family provides interesting documentation of the pitfalls of transporting fragile merchandise to customers living at a great distance from New York City. Hyde Hall, on the north end of Otsego Lake in central New York State, was built to the specifications of its owner, George Clarke (1768-1835), between 1817 and 1833. The house was primarily furnished with goods brought from Albany and New York City, and records now at Cornell University document many of these purchases.[8] In an 1833 letter to Clarke, James A. Smith, auctioneer at 92 Broadway, mentioned looking glasses for the drawing room "packed by Mr. Platt, and forwarded, as per order."[9] Platt's bill to Clarke lists one "Looking Glass Plate 72" x 36" framed 4½ Inch fluted molding Gilt back at the sides" and two other glasses measuring sixty-six inches by sixty inches among merchandise totaling $597.[10] These suffered somewhat in transit to the storage warehouse of Messrs. Warner & Company in Fort Plain, New York, about twenty miles from Hyde Hall, as Platt indicated:

> one of the frames was injured—this I had before been apprised of by the young man from Mr. Gardner's. Such damage if in the City would be of trifling consideration, and could be repaired with little trouble or expense. I am aware that the case is widely different situate as you are, and trusted that the care taken in packing and storing them safe on board the vessel would have prevented any damage.[11]

Living so far from the city, Clarke was left to make the necessary repairs on his own. The Randalls were lucky that their pier glasses apparently made the trip from New York to Cortland without incident.

PT

78⅝ x 39 x 3¼ in.
Paper label (fig. 20): "ISAAC L. PLATT,/LOOKING GLASS MANUFACTURER/AND/IMPORTER./WAREHOUSE/Nº 178 Broadway,/NEW YORK."
Eastern white pine, glass, gilded gesso, gilding
Provenance: William Randall, Cortland, New York; Wilhelmina Randall (1820-1913), Cortland, New York; Marian B. Wilson (d. 1935), Cortland, New York; Robert Palmiter, Bouckville, New York; MWPI.
Museum Purchase, 59.127

10

Dressing Bureau, ca. 1825–29

Attributed to Edward Holmes and Simeon Haines (active 1825–29)
New York, New York

The presumed makers of this dressing bureau, Edward Holmes and Simeon Haines, worked in partnership in New York City from 1825 to 1829.[1] A partial paper label (fig. 21) in the frieze drawer does not specify the partners' shop location, but a similar dressing bureau at the Museum of Fine Arts, Boston, bears a Holmes and Haines stenciled label that gives the firm's working address as 48 Broad and 20 Beaver Streets.

A sizable body of furniture is now recognized as the work of this partnership, and seven labeled examples are known—a sideboard, a drop-leaf table, two pier tables, a two-drawer stand, and two dressing bureaus.[2] The bureaus are in the collections of MWPI and the Museum of Fine Arts, Boston. A small group of unlabeled dressing bureaus is also associated with Holmes and Haines.[3] The labeled and unlabeled bureaus have many formal and decorative features in common. Each consists of a central case with side columns, two large drawers, and one smaller (usually convex) frieze drawer. Small drawers are set back on the cases, and acanthus-carved S-scrolls support the mirrors. Each case has painted and stenciled gold decoration and stamped-brass, rosette-shaped drawer hardware with circular pulls. Variations among the bureaus are found in the shape of the feet, the configurations of the set-back drawers, the amount of hand-painted and stenciled decoration, and the orientation of the mirrors. Two types of feet are found on the bureaus—crisply turned feet or distinctly carved paw feet with splayed toes topped by carved acanthus leaves. In all cases the rear feet are rather crudely executed stumps.

The painted decoration on the MWPI bureau and on related bureaus is primarily limited to linear, geometric borders on the drawers and mirror. This ornamentation was probably stenciled or executed with a roller or stamp to create an outline, which was later filled in with gold leaf.[4] This type of decoration simulates cut-brass inlay featured on French and English furniture of the early nineteenth century.[5]

A labeled dressing bureau by Alexander P. W. Kinnan and States M. Mead of New York City (active 1823-30) bears many similarities to Holmes and Haines bureaus and suggests the preference for this form in New York City.[6] It also calls into question the tendency to attribute unlabeled furniture to a specific firm. The maker of a case piece may not have produced each component in his own shop. Ebonized and stenciled columns, turned feet, scroll supports, and looking-glass frames were available from many specialists. Further study may provide clues that will allow scholars to attribute unlabeled examples of this popular form to particular makers.

PT

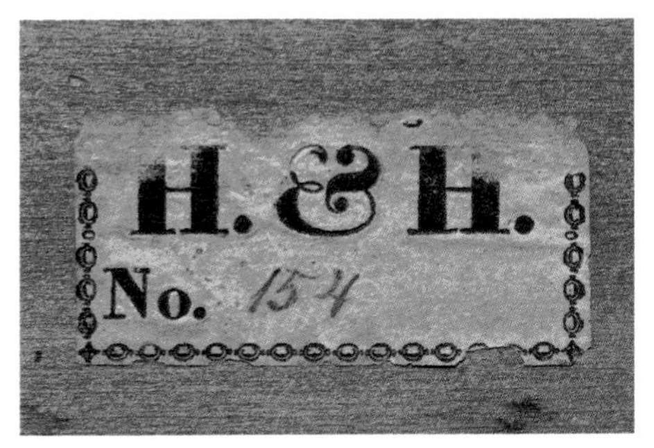

Fig. 21

69 x 37 x 23¾ in.
Paper label (fig. 21): "H. & H./No. 154"
Mahogany, yellow-poplar, Spanish cedar, eastern white pine, glass, brass, gilding
Provenance: Mrs. Edward Hyland, Utica, New York; MWPI.
Museum Purchase, 60.271

11

Dining Table, ca. 1825–35

Maker unknown
New York State

By the time of the American Revolution, separate dining rooms equipped with specialized furniture became customary in the homes of the very wealthy. Many of these rooms, however, continued to be used for multiple purposes and included furnishings such as desks and reading chairs.[1] Even in the early nineteenth century, when rooms designated as dining rooms became more common, dining room and parlor functions were interchangeable. When a family was not entertaining guests, it was apt to eat informal meals in more intimate spaces such as the back parlor or the sitting room.[2]

The basic form of the MWPI dining table is typical of those made in the United States during the second quarter of the nineteenth century. What distinguishes this particular dining table from other examples is the quality of the veneer, the caliber of the carving, and the abundant painted decoration. The table is an early and handsome example of the extension table form that became ubiquitous in dining rooms later in the nineteenth century. Consisting of two matching parts—each with rounded apron corners and a drop leaf—that can be combined to form an impressive eight-foot-long pedestal table, it would have been suitable for large-scale entertaining in a fashionable residence.[3] The two halves of the table are joined together by lifting the drop leaves and rotating them ninety degrees over the aprons to distribute the weight more evenly. Brass clips, which fit into brackets on the underside, lock the two sections together. In formal dining rooms, the dining table was placed in the center of the room. Each part could be detached and, with the leaf down, placed against a wall to function as a side table. Casters allowed the separated table parts to be moved with ease to the sides of the room.

The most common form of support for extension tables in the first half of the nineteenth century is the so-called "pillar-and-claw" pedestal.[4] The carved hairy legs and the acanthus leaves topping the pedestal on this table are representative of fancy late-neoclassical furniture made in New York City. Thomas Hope, George Smith, and other English designers incorporated this combination of motifs, originally found on Greek and Roman furniture, into their designs of the Regency period. The highly figured veneer, highlighted by hand-painted and stenciled decoration, is another typical feature of high-style New York furniture.[5] The gold decoration on the apron, rendered realistically and with superior detail, imitates more expensive ormolu mounts.[6] Painted gold lines inscribe the rectangular panels on the base of the pedestal and encircle the plinth in emulation of inlaid brass stringing.

PT

28⅞ x 48⅛ x 24⅛ in.
28⅞ x 48⅛ x 96⅛ in. (two tables joined)
Mahogany, eastern white pine, cherry, white ash, gilding, brass
Provenance: Green family, Syracuse, New York; Maude Moyer Ward; MWPI.
Museum Purchase, 60.199

35 x 80⅛ x 24 in.
Stenciled label (fig. 22): "C. JOHNSONS. PATENT."
Soft maple, beechwood, yellow-poplar, cherry, rush, paint
Provenance: Emily Lowery Beardsley, Utica, New York; MWPI.
Emily Lowery Beardsley Bequest, 61.65

Fig. 22

12

Convertible Settee, ca. 1827

Chester Johnson (active 1819–20, 1826, and 1827–54)
Albany and New York, New York

This convertible settee bears the stenciled name of its maker (fig. 22), Chester Johnson (1796-1863), a fancy chair manufacturer who worked in Albany, New York, and New York City. Few extant pieces are attributed to him, and it appears that the only products bearing Johnson's label were the patented settees he produced in the 1820s and 1830s.[1]

Albany directories list Johnson as a city resident in 1819, 1820, and 1826. His Albany business, located on State Street, is listed only in 1819, at which time Johnson was in partnership with an individual named Bates.[2] According to Bates and Johnson's 1819 trade card, the firm offered "Fancy, Windsor & Common chairs, viz. Rose Wood, Curled Maple & Painted Chairs & Settees" as well as painted signs and did general furniture repairing.[3] An 1819 advertisement in the *Albany Argus and Daily City Gazette* declared that the partners "have taken pains to obtain some of the best workmen in the city of New-York—Also, the modern patterns of Chairs in Europe and New-York."[4]

Johnson relocated to New York City between 1820 and 1826. From 1827 through 1854 Johnson appears in New York City directories variously as a "cabinetmaker," a maker of "sofa bedsteads," or a "sofa-bed maker." He continued to promote his products in the upstate area, however, evidently making them available through a local distributor. The last line of text in his *Albany Argus and Daily City Gazette* advertisement of April 1827 reads, "All orders will be punctually attended at the settee factory of CORNWELL WILLIS, no. 291 North Market street, Albany."[5] Johnson's reasons for leaving Albany after being in business for only one year and his whereabouts between 1820 and 1826 are unknown.

Although Johnson's 1819 trade card lists "Johnson's Patent Portable Settees, convenient for sitting or lodging for two persons," the recorded patent date for Johnson's "improvement in the manufacture of sofas" is 1827, suggesting that in that year he had revised an earlier patent for a convertible settee or that he advertised the patent before it was actually granted.[6] An examination of MWPI's Johnson-made settee and descriptions of the form in the maker's advertisements explain how the object, with two sets of front legs, converted into a bed. Although the MWPI example has been altered and no longer opens, it is clear that originally the front seat rail and the first set of legs were meant to be pulled forward, thereby drawing out an extra section that doubled the depth of the settee so it could be used as a bed. Johnson explained that a settee "made with a bottom of 19-inches in width, by the gearing attached to it, will admit of a bed four feet in width."[7] Johnson also noted that the extended settee was "calculated to contain bed and bedding."[8]

In 1829 Johnson advertised the "sofa and settee bedstead" as "economy and luxury combined." He explained that his product "is constructed on principles peculiar to itself: with the size, strength, and convenience of the ordinary four poster Bedstead, it possesses the symmetry, beauty and finish of the ornamental parlor Settee or Sofa."[9] Johnson stated in an 1832 advertisement that there was extraordinary demand for his patented sofa bedstead and that "upwards of seven Hundred of them have been manufactured by the Patentee within a short period, their [combined] value at a fair estimate, being sixty Thousand Dollars."[10]

Johnson made his settees to conform to the standard form and decoration of fancy chairs and other simple seating furniture (see cat. no. 14). His settees were designed essentially as elongated fancy chairs with turned legs and stiles, turned or flat crest rails, and horizontal slats. The MWPI rosewood-grained settee has turnings highlighted by painted rings and flat surfaces ornamented with well-executed, bronze-powder, naturalistic stenciling that is enhanced by black pen work.

ATD

13

Side Chair, ca. 1820–30

Attributed to John and Hugh Finlay (active 1800–1837)
Baltimore, Maryland

Few groups of nineteenth-century furniture have been so closely scrutinized as the painted chairs, settees, and tables made by John (1777-1851) and Hugh (1781-1831) Finlay of Baltimore. Scholars recognized this furniture as exceptional even before its makers were identified. The antiquarian and writer Edgar Miller, for example, included an elaborately painted table owned by the Brown family of Baltimore in *American Antique Furniture* (1937).[1] With the landmark scholarship by Gregory R. Weidman, the painted furniture of John and Hugh Finlay now takes its place among the best-documented American furniture in the late neoclassical taste.[2]

John Finlay first worked in Baltimore as a coach painter in 1799 and was joined by his brother Hugh by 1803. For the next three decades the brothers appear in city directories and newspapers as workers in the furniture trade at various shop locations within the area of Frederick, Baltimore, and Gay Streets in Baltimore. Their advertisements refer to a wide range of furniture "in all colors, gilt ornamented, and varnished in a style not equalled on the continent."[3] Weidman has established that the Finlays' shop was "almost the sole supplier of stylish and diverse suites of furniture to prosperous Baltimoreans and others throughout the region."[4]

This chair is one of a set owned by the Abell family at Woodbourne, its Baltimore estate. The chairs descended in the family of Arunah Shepherdson Abell (1808-88), founder of the *Baltimore Sun*. The set, attributed to the Finlays, reflects the high style of craftsmanship and decoration that is emblematic of Baltimore work between 1815 and 1825.[5] Chairs of this type are based on the Roman *klismos* form and consist of a crest rail with broad curved tablet, turned tapered front legs, and sharply raked rear legs and back. Finlay *klismos* chairs have painted decoration and, in overall form, relate to French and English precedents.[6] A model for this archaeologically correct classical chair was published in 1790 in a French album entitled *Mobilier de Madame Elisabeth.* A more widely circulated version was published by English designer Thomas Hope in *Household Furniture and Interior Decoration* (1807).[7]

The Abell chairs are especially notable because each of the nine known chairs (from an original set that probably numbered twelve) features a different design on the curved tablet. A motif of either swans, deer, griffins, unicorns, or other mythological creatures, painted on the black-green background of each chair, is flanked by Grecian scrolls. The Finlays derived these designs from plate 56 of the 1803 edition of Thomas Sheraton's *Cabinet-Maker and Upholsterer's Drawing-Book.* Each chair is painted gold with green, red, white, and black decoration.[8] Designs of a dart with crossed torches on the center rail, diamonds and anthemia on the side rails, a fasces flanked by wreaths on the front rail, and swags and stylized palmettes on the legs were inspired by motifs found in the published drawings of Frenchmen Charles Percier (1764-1838) and Pierre-François-Léonard Fontaine (1762-1853), designers to the court of Napoleon Bonaparte.

The attribution of the Abell chairs is based on their similarity to documented furniture made by the Finlays for wealthy Hagerstown, Maryland, merchant Richard Ragan (1776-1850) and for Baltimore merchant James Wilson (1775-1851). The Finlay attribution is strengthened by comparisons of the Abell chairs with two other suites of furniture—the suite the brothers made for William Waln (1775-1826) of Philadelphia in 1808 and the suite they made for the drawing room of the White House in 1809 after the designs of architect Benjamin H. Latrobe (1764-1829). The Abell chairs are caned, a cool alternative to an upholstered slip seat. During the winter, they undoubtedly would have held cushions to protect sitters from drafts.

PT

34 x 20⅜ x 22½ in.
Soft maple, yellow-poplar, paint, gesso, modern caned seat
Minor inpainting
Provenance: Arunah S. Abell (1806-88), Baltimore, Maryland; by descent to Margaret Abell Fenwick; Norton Asner Antiques, Baltimore, Maryland; the Metropolitan Museum of Art, New York, New York; MWPI.
Museum Purchase, by exchange with the Metropolitan Museum of Art, 77.66

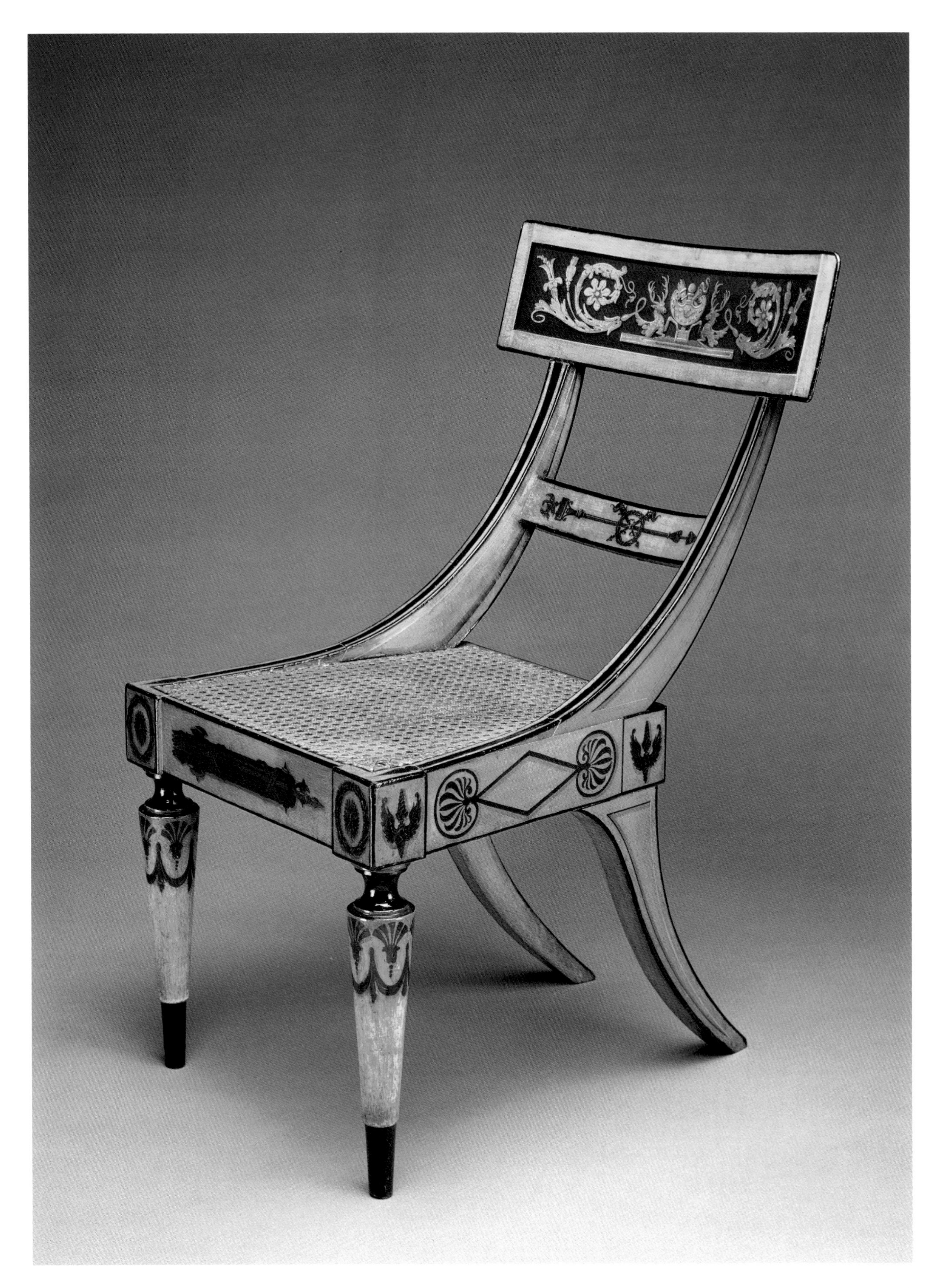

32⅞ x 18 x 19¼ in.
Soft maple, yellow-poplar, hickory, rush, paint
Provenance: Robert Palmiter, Bouckville, New York; MWPI.
Museum Purchase, 59.126.1-2

14

SIDE CHAIRS, ca. 1820–40

Maker unknown

Probably Philadelphia, Pennsylvania; possibly Baltimore, Maryland

DURING THE EIGHTEENTH and early nineteenth centuries, urban artisans involved in furniture making generally specialized in specific areas of the craft. In 1803 Thomas Sheraton observed that "chair-making is a branch generally confined to itself; as those who professedly work at it, seldom engage to make cabinet furniture. . . . The two branches seem evidently to require different talents in workmen, in order to become proficients [*sic*]. In the chair branch it requires a particular turn in the handling of shapes, to make them agreeable and easy."[1]

Among the most active urban chairmakers were those who made Windsor and fancy chairs, both of which were inexpensive and relatively easy to fabricate. While Windsor chairs consist primarily of turned elements painted a single color, fancy chairs have turned and sawn components decoratively painted in polychrome patterns to imitate formal furniture.[2]

A fancy chairmaker was responsible for the design and fabrication of the MWPI chairs. He may or may not have relied on other artisans for the painted and gilded decoration. The different parts of fancy chairs were made of various types of local woods, each chosen for its particular physical properties. The diverse woods were visually integrated through the use of paint. These chairs have been grained to imitate rosewood, an expensive imported tropical wood that was used in more formal furniture. The chairs were then ornamented with a decorative scheme of gilded patterns that corresponded to expensive, imported, French and English gilded-brass furniture mounts.

The motifs used here, including the Greek key design on the crest rails, *paterae* on the front stretchers, and acanthus leaves on the legs, allude to ancient classical prototypes. The most highly charged of these motifs are the paired griffins—mythological beasts, part eagle and part lion—who, according to legend, guarded the gold of the ancient kingdom of Scythia. These stenciled decorations were executed in gold leaf that was applied to a tacky surface, usually shellac. Furniture decorators owned dozens, even hundreds, of precut stencils made of heavy paper or metal. They could use these stencils, each of which depicted a specific motif, individually or in combination to create an infinite variety of designs tailored to the size of the space being ornamented. Requisite detail was painted over the gold leaf in black or red.

At the time these chairs were made, numerous individuals in the Philadelphia community advertised their expertise in creating this type of decoration. Among them were William Delaveau, ornamental painter; William Haydon, ornamental painter; William Stewart, ornamental painter, gilder, and japanner; and Samuel Bavies, chair painter and ornamenter. Others, including John Meyers, fancy chairmaker and painter, and James Montgomery, chairmaker and painter, advertised that they both made and decorated fancy chairs.[3] Peter Martin, Stephen H. Simmons, and partners Melchoir Burkhard and Thomas W.(?) Smith identified themselves as "fancy and Windsor chairmakers."[4] The 1833 billhead of Abraham McDonough, another specialist in this area, lists him as a fancy and Windsor chair manufacturer and pictures a side chair almost identical with the MWPI examples.[5] The chair on the billhead has a curved crest rail with a rolled top edge that extends beyond the stiles. The rush seat has a vertically reeded front edge; and the front legs, turned in the form of inverted balusters surmounted by scrolled vases, flank a flat, shaped stretcher.[6] The MWPI chairs were probably part of a larger set and almost certainly emanated from the shop of one of Philadelphia's many fancy-furniture establishments.

DLF

15

PEDESTAL, ca. 1825–35

Maker unknown
Philadelphia, Pennsylvania

PEDESTALS WERE USED in ancient Greece and Rome to support vases and figures and became increasingly visible in stylish European rooms during and after the Renaissance, when they typically held clocks, busts, vases of flowers, and cases for eating implements.[1] By the nineteenth century, pedestals had evolved to serve an additional purpose. In 1818 prolific English social commentator Rudolph Ackermann noted that "the pedestal is designed to correspond in style and material [with other furniture in a room], and is suited to bear a group of figures in bronze or ormolu, terminated by branches for lights. These are properly placed in the angles of large rooms, that will otherwise be gloomy."[2]

The seven-armed candelabrum atop this pedestal appears to be unmarked, but most likely it is of French origin. Made of brass, its finish is primarily gilded with the balance patinated to simulate antique bronze. It was probably manufactured between 1800 and 1830 and, like many French and English lighting devices, was undoubtedly imported into the United States when newly made. The pedestal gives every appearance of having been made specifically to support the candelabrum.

Pedestals for lighting devices were fairly commonplace in fashionable continental European and English houses by the early nineteenth century, but they remained rare in American interiors until after midcentury. This example, probably originally one of a pair, is in the classical revival style, as are the few other documented pedestals of the same date.[3] Features that spring from ancient designs include the triangular base with stenciled decoration, carved borders of acanthus leaves, a reeded column, and carved palmettes with painted highlights.

Greek and Roman motifs found their way into American cabinetmakers' and chairmakers' shops via European design books, increasing numbers of which were published during the late eighteenth and early nineteenth centuries. Among the more popular volumes that included designs for pedestals were Thomas Hope's *Household Furniture and Interior Decoration* (1807) and George Smith's *Collection of Designs for Household Furniture and Interior Decoration* (1808). Books like these were intended for furniture makers and were readily available in subscription libraries such as the Library Company of Philadelphia.[4]

The form, materials, and ornamental treatments of this pedestal correlate with a small group of furniture assignable to Philadelphia cabinetmakers. Lewis Redner, who worked between 1829 and 1838, placed his name on an upright piano case that is strikingly similar to the MWPI pedestal.[5] Entirely veneered in rosewood, the piano case is embellished with gold stenciled motifs that correspond to the stenciled composite image repeated on the three sides of the base of the MWPI pedestal. The two front supports, carved in the form of monopod eagles, are antiqued with verd and gold in the same manner as the reeded columnar section of this pedestal.

Another Philadelphia cabinetmaker, Isaac Jones (active 1818-40), made a large bedroom suite that also closely relates to the MWPI pedestal.[6] Made for wealthy wine and liquor merchant Elijah Vansyckel (d. 1855) and his wife Sarah (d. 1872) about 1833, the suite was designed for their house at 187 Mulberry Street in Philadelphia and passed through four generations of Vansyckel descendants until it was sold in the 1980s.[7] Like the Redner piano case, the Jones bedroom suite is veneered in rosewood. Its carved components and moldings are detailed in gold that shades to verd, and its flat surfaces are embellished with a large number of gold-stenciled designs. Many parts of the repeated stenciled motifs—pineapples, scrolls, acanthus-decorated volutes, and palmettes—appear to be identical with those on the MWPI pedestal. The 1855 inventory of the Vansyckel's house itemizes the bedroom suite and lists both candelabra and "2 Lamp Stands."[8] Those stands may well have been similar to, if not identical with, the MWPI pedestal.

DLF

41¼ x 16½ x 14⅜ in.
Mahogany, rosewood, yellow-poplar, gilding, paint
(Candelabrum, 35¼ in. h.; gilt and patinated brass)
Provenance: Carriage House Antiques; MWPI.
Museum Purchase, 60.58

25⅝ x 36⅝ x 18¾ in.
25⅝ x 36⅝ x 78½ in. (two tables joined)
Mahogany, yellow-poplar, eastern white pine, basswood, cherry
Corner blocks replaced
Provenance: Israel Sack, New York, New York; MWPI.
Museum Purchase, 60.20.a-b

16

Dining Table, ca. 1820–40

Maker unknown
Philadelphia, Pennsylvania

During the eighteenth century the standard American dining table had two hinged leaves that hung vertically when not required for eating. When necessary, the leaves were raised to a horizontal position and, supported by hinged legs, formed an oval, circular, or rectangular tabletop.[1] During the last quarter of the century, drop-leaf tables with rectangular leaves were sometimes lengthened by attaching two separate ends to a center section. Dining tables of this type were always supported by legs affixed at the perimeter. When not in use for dining, these separate ends were placed against a wall to serve as side tables.[2]

During the nineteenth century the dining table form evolved to accommodate changing lifestyles. In 1845 Thomas Webster noted that dining tables are "necessarily of various sizes and forms, to suit the apartments, numbers of guests, and other circumstances. Various methods have been contrived for increasing the size of tables on occasion, and of causing them to occupy less space when out of use."[3]

By the third decade of the nineteenth century, dining tables like the MWPI example were usually supported by central pedestals. The central support was a distinct improvement over legs at the perimeter because it allowed diners to sit comfortably with their knees under the table. Tables of this kind typically consisted of two identical ends, each with a hinged leaf. The leaves were swung to a horizontal position and rotated to form a large dining surface supported by the pedestal. The two ends could be used individually, or if more space was needed, one architect pointed out that they could "be placed together so as to form one square [actually rectangular] table, made fast by thumbscrews."[4]

Most pedestal tables had only a single, plain, cylinder-on-cube support and four-toed claw feet (see cat. no. 11). The MWPI table, however, described as "a round cornered end table on pillar and claws" in *The Philadelphia Cabinet and Chair Makers' Union Book of Prices for Manufacturing Cabinet Ware* (1828), is an unusual and attractive variant.[5] The price book lists, and gives prices for, optional extra features including a distinctive detail present on this table—the canting of the front edge of the skirt decorated with applied leafy panels. This feature is described in the 1828 Philadelphia price book as "eased away not to exceed five inches from the square of the corner." Two more options listed in the price book appear on this table—the two-part pedestal base carved in the form of a vase holding fruit and leaves, and the eagle-headed claw feet.[6]

The pedestal carving is deep, realistically executed, dramatic, and of excellent quality. The vase overflows with fruit and is flanked by eagle-headed monopods. Carving of this type represents the Philadelphia school at its best and is comparable to related designs on contemporary furniture bearing the paper labels or stencils of renowned early nineteenth-century Philadelphia furniture makers such as Anthony G. Quervelle, Michel Bouvier, Charles H. White, and Lawrence Sink.[7] Although these men were undoubtedly capable of executing this type of carving, they frequently assigned the work to specialist carvers who were either in their employ or were self-employed jobbers.

The configuration of dining table ends like these, with extensive carved sections on only one side, makes it clear that they were intended to be placed against walls when not in use for eating; they would be moved into a room and set up for dining when the need arose. When the tables were brought together and topped with a tablecloth, for all practical purposes the carved features were completely obscured. The consistent presence of casters on the feet of such tables underscores their portability.

DLF

 17

Secretary Bookcase, ca. 1825–35

Anthony Gabriel Quervelle (active 1820–56)
Philadelphia, Pennsylvania

Fig. 23

The imposing proportions, rich surface ornament, and fine craftsmanship of this secretary bookcase reflect the influence of French taste and style on Philadelphia cabinetmakers and their patrons during the late classical period of the 1830s. Anthony Gabriel Quervelle (1789-1856), maker of this secretary bookcase, arrived in Philadelphia from France about 1817 and enjoyed a long and prosperous career as one of the city's leading cabinetmakers. His business was regularly listed in Philadelphia city directories from 1820 until his death, and he prominently advertised that customers could find an array of elegant furniture forms in the latest style at his United States Fashionable Cabinet Ware Rooms at 126 South Second Street.[1]

The MWPI secretary bookcase demonstrates the consequence of Quervelle's French training and his exceptional skill as a cabinetmaker and designer.[2] Its brilliantly figured crotch-grain mahogany-veneered surfaces—with shaped, convex, applied ornaments and rich applied carving—illustrate the art of the *ébéniste* or veneer worker, as well as Quervelle's eclectic yet informed familiarity with traditional French and English cabinetry designs and techniques.[3] The radiating fan that decorates the lower doors of the case is composed of applied rounded wedges veneered with figured mahogany and burl ash. This ornamentation relates to decorations prescribed by French designer Pierre de la Mésangère.[4] The diamond-and-arch mullion patterns on the case doors are closely associated with "Chinese" and "Gothic" designs published in George Smith's *Collection of Designs for Household Furniture* (1808). Smith's design book, widely distributed in Philadelphia, seems to have been a major source of inspiration for Quervelle.[5]

Five similar secretary bookcases of this form are either firmly documented to Quervelle by labels or provenance or are attributed to him on the basis of similar decoration and construction.[6] Quervelle submitted a larger and more ornate version of this form to one of a series of early exhibitions of mechanical arts organized by the Franklin Institute of Philadelphia in 1827. He received a silver medal for a desk and bookcase that the committee referred to as "a splendid piece of furniture from the establishment of this excellent workman" and "the best piece of furniture of that description exhibited for premium." The judges further remarked that "the parlor secretary and lady's dressing table by the same [shop] are fair specimens of the present style of work."[7]

Quervelle, obviously proud to be recognized for his skill and the resultant quality of his work, applied five labels to the winning piece that are identical in format to the label found in the MWPI example. The Franklin Institute award gained an even wider circle of wealthy and influential patrons for Quervelle. He received numerous important orders from members of Philadelphia's elite merchant class and in 1829 was commissioned by President Jackson's administration to produce a series of marble-topped center and pier tables for the East Room of the White House.[8]

A recently discovered manuscript pattern book with script notations in Quervelle's handwriting includes a pen-and-ink drawing of a secretary bookcase (fig. 23).[9] The overall form, case divisions, and placement of ornaments in the drawing correspond to the MWPI example and to a secretary bookcase in the collection of the Philadelphia Museum of Art.[10] Furthermore, the sketch shows raised veneered panels similar to those on the lower doors of the MWPI and PMA examples and includes the same center drawers and stepped-back plinths (above the lower columns) that appear on the MWPI secretary bookcase. Two other features of the sketch parallel the MWPI piece—the rendering of the carved capitals on the lower case and the carved paw feet. Moreover, the Quervelle sketchbook has several drawings of sideboard, pier table, and center table columns that are analogous in design to the carved, urn-form bases and capitals on the columns of the upper case of the MWPI secretary bookcase.

JL

102¼ x 50¾ x 23⅝ in.
Paper label inside drawer: "126/ANTHONY G. QUERVELLE'S/CABINET AND SOFA MANUFACTORY,/ SOUTH SECOND STREET A FEW DOORS BELOW DOCK,/PHILADELPHIA."
Mahogany, eastern white pine, basswood, yellow-poplar, bird's-eye maple, glass, brass, gilded gesso
New gilding on column bases and capitals, replacement drawer pulls
Provenance: R. Pietsch & Sons, Inc., Utica, New York; MWPI.
Museum Purchase, 60.257

Fig. 23. Sketch, attributed to the workshop of Anthony Quervelle, ca. 1820-35. Pen, pencil, and ink on laid paper. Collection of Philadelphia Museum of Art. Photo: Lynn Rosenthal

18

Worktable, ca. 1825–35

Anthony Gabriel Quervelle (active 1820–56)
Philadelphia, Pennsylvania

During the federal period small, finely crafted worktables with fitted interior compartments and drawers became elegant and popular additions to the decorative furnishings of stylish American domestic interiors. The earliest forms—light in proportion, embellished with exotic wood veneers, and fitted with ornately pleated and trimmed textile work bags—were promoted in English and French pattern books and fashion periodicals during the late eighteenth century.[1] By the 1820s the French Empire and Restoration styles with their curved profiles and larger dimensions had transformed these specialized tables. In Philadelphia, tables became larger and more architectural in their configurations, textile work bags disappeared, and delicate turned legs and bases gave way to a variety of ornately carved central supports with platforms or feet.

A number of Philadelphia's leading cabinetmakers produced elegant versions of the "work" or "toilet" table.[2] MWPI's richly veneered example bears the engraved label (fig. 24) of Anthony Gabriel Quervelle (1789-1856) (see cat. no. 17), who is known to have made several variations of this form.[3] In 1831 he submitted a "Ladies Work Table" to an exhibition of mechanical arts at the Franklin Institute, where it was acknowledged to be a well-crafted, successful, and tasteful design.

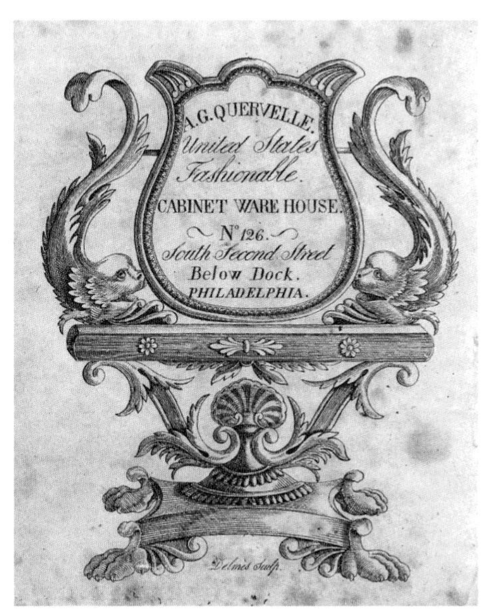

Fig. 24

The form, which grew in popularity during the 1820s and 1830s among several Philadelphia cabinetmakers, is described in *The Philadelphia Cabinet and Chair Makers' Union Book of Prices for Manufacturing Cabinet Ware* (1828) as a "work table with pillar and 4 claws." Quervelle probably utilized this same base configuration, with slight decorative variations, on gaming, dining, and center tables as well.

The support column of the MWPI example is carved with scrolled leafage that is flanked above and below by crisply turned concentric rings of varying diameters. The concave sides of the veneered platform on which the column rests and the carved scroll-and-paw feet are closely related to elements found on the engraving of a dressing stand depicted on Quervelle's label and in the drawings of his manuscript sketchbook.[4]

The rounded corners, convex upper drawer front, and architectonically arched and recessed facade of the deep lower drawer are elements that can be found on other worktables attributed to Quervelle's shop. They are combined in the MWPI example to produce a simple, yet graceful, balance to the form of the table. Quervelle produced striking, symmetrically centered patterns on the facade of the case using richly figured, crotch-grained mahogany veneers. His talent for combining decorative elements to create a successfully unified design is evident in the way he used inlaid banding of contrasting rosewood to outline the top of the table, employed crossbanded veneer to emphasize the arch of lower drawer, and applied gadrooning to the lower edges of the case and the platform to soften the geometric forms.

JL

30⅝ x 23 x 16⅞ in.
Paper label (fig. 24): "A. G. QUERVELLE./United States/Fashionable./CABINET WARE HOUSE./N° 126./South Second Street/Below Dock./PHILADELPHIA."
Mahogany, yellow-poplar, pine, rosewood, glass, brass, fabric
Repairs to lid
Provenance: Mark Shoemaker, Utica, New York; MWPI.
Museum Purchase with funds from the Sarah T. Norris Fund, in honor of Carol E. Gordon, Curator of Decorative Arts from 1974 to 1983, 83.15

19

BOOKCASE, TABLE, PEDIMENT, AND MIRROR, ca. 1844–46

Design attributed to Richard Upjohn (active 1834–78)
Maker unknown
Probably New York, New York

THE DESIGN OF THE LIBRARY FURNITURE from the home of Mr. and Mrs. Robert Kelly has long been attributed to the architect Richard Upjohn (1802-78).[1] The design of the row house in which it stood at 9 West 16th Street, New York City, was also credited to Upjohn.[2] The home and its furnishings are important as one of a small group of projects Upjohn completed between 1839 and 1846 when his contract as the architect of Boston's Trinity Church limited additional work. As part of one of Upjohn's most complete residential interiors, the library suite illuminates his practice in furniture design, and it represents part of an exceptional New York City 1840s interior.[3]

The context for the Kelly home was an elegant residential area near Union Square. Beginning in 1839 this neighborhood became increasingly fashionable.[4] In 1842 a developer initiated a building project consisting of nine similar, elegant row houses situated on wider-than-usual lots.[5] The exteriors of these homes featured Boston bow fronts rather than the typical New York flat fronts, which supports the hypothesis that Upjohn, well acquainted with Boston and with speculative housing schemes, either designed or provided drawings for the project. Stylistic evidence and Kelly family papers indicate that Upjohn also completed much of the interior of the residence between 1844, when Kelly and his bride Arietta Hutton returned to New York City after their honeymoon, and 1845, when they are said to have moved into their home.[6]

Photographs, taken about 1927 when the family sold the house, show a high-style interior.[7] Visitors were greeted in the front hall with a sweeping stairway curve that invited attention to the rich profiles of the balusters and to the Gothic details on the newel post and stair brackets. Gothic motifs were sustained in the parlor woodwork, reminiscent of interiors at "Oaklands," the splendid house designed by Upjohn and built between 1835 and 1842 for the Gardiner family in Gardiner, Maine. The elaborate treatment and weight of the cornice and overmantel in the Kelly parlor recall another important Upjohn house of the 1830s, the Rotch-Jones-Duff house in New Bedford, Massachusetts. In contrast, the rococo revival furniture suite from the shop of Alexander Roux and the encrusted parlor fireplace are incompatible with Upjohn's style, which suggests that other designers contributed some interior elements to the Kelly house.[8]

In a letter dated February 14, 1846, Robert Kelly stated that he had contracted with Mr. H. Parsons for a suite of library furniture and asked Upjohn to furnish plans for a table, two high-backed chairs, and six low-backed chairs.[9] Unfortunately, no other documentation confirms that Upjohn provided the designs. Because Kelly mentioned neither bookcases nor mirror and pediment, they must have been made separately, possibly somewhat earlier.

Upjohn's furniture is intriguing from several perspectives. It is congruent with then-current theories of affective psychology, which asserted that the environment shaped human response and, therefore, character. Thus, Gothic revival architects designed the *Gesamtkunstwerk*, or total work of art. Accordingly, Upjohn sought to coordinate interior and exterior; his church designs, for example, included plan, section, and elevation, as

Table: 29¾ x 59¾ x 40½ in.
Walnut, unidentified secondary woods
Provenance: Robert Kelly, New York, New York; Mrs. Erving Pruyn, New York, New York; MWPI.
Gift of Mrs. Erving Pruyn, 60.169

Bookcase: 108⅞ x 75¼ x 23½ in. (one of a pair in MWPI collection; see n. 3)
Black walnut, eastern white pine, glass
Provenance: Robert Kelly, New York, New York; Mrs. Erving Pruyn, New York, New York; MWPI.
Gift of Mrs. Erving Pruyn, 60.164

Fig. 25

well as interior fittings, decoration, and furniture in a compatible style. In both large architectural objects and in small, movable pieces of furniture, Upjohn presented simple masses with careful detailing. He sustained the guiding precept of the Gothic revival—honest expression of purpose, construction, and materials.

The library furniture departs from the Gothic motifs visible elsewhere in the house. By the mid-1840s Upjohn had designed churches in the *Rundbogenstil* or Romanesque revival style and houses in the closely related Italianate mode. His choice to combine these styles in the Kelly library suite represents an evolution of classicism befitting Robert Kelly's large library and considerable fluency in ancient and modern languages.[10] The pediment, breaking high above the line of the flat cornice in two of the bookcases, is a motif from Upjohn's Italianate houses; the arcades appear in churches and residences. At the top of each tall door, in a gesture of ebullience suitable to the Kellys' circumstances, Upjohn took a Romanesque arcade, deformed it, and created the cusped arch of Islam.

The aesthetic qualities that most reveal Upjohn's hand in the design of this suite are the restrained use of detail and the emphasis on the overall mass of the object. Like the woodwork in the Kelly and Gardiner houses, the furniture relies on architectural features rather than applied decoration or elaborate carving for ornamentation. Two exceptions are the capitals of the colonnettes and the stipple work of the extrados on the doors of the bookcases. Even this carved detail is offset by broad areas created by the moldings. Using eastern white pine with black walnut as "show wood," Upjohn characteristically avoided veneers, and the bookcases appear to be solid walnut.[11] The pediment and mirror, similar in style and material to the bookcases, were installed over the fireplace in the Kelly library (fig. 25). Like the pediments of the two bookcases, that of the mirror has "dripping" arches that terminate with carefully detailed drops, a motif found in several contemporary Upjohn houses.[12]

Photographs of the Kelly house show the library adjacent to the parlor.[13] Thus, far from simply equipping a sequestered study with utilitarian furniture, Upjohn's library suite fittingly defined a public space in the house. Robert Kelly—first in his class at Columbia College—was reputed to have entered commerce rather than the learned professions to be able to retire early and to devote the remainder of his life to study. The library served as both a scholar's haven and a symbol of Kelly's aspirations.

JSH

Fig. 25. Early 20th-century photograph of the library in the Robert Kelly residence, West 16th Street, New York City. Collection of the Museum of the City of New York.

Pediment: 37½ x 55 x 9⅜ in.
Black walnut, unidentified secondary woods

Mirror: 64 x 43½ x 3½ in.
Black walnut, yellow-poplar, eastern white pine, glass, gilding
Provenance: Robert Kelly, New York, New York; Mrs. Erving Pruyn, New York, New York; MWPI.
Gifts of Mrs. Erving Pruyn, 60.170.1-2

20

Dining Table, ca. 1844–46

Charles F. Hobe (active 1839–64 or –65)
New York, New York

This massive table is a subtle example of the Gothic revival style. The round top, with an applied band of ripple molding on its skirt, is supported by a four-sided, columnar pedestal. Each side of the central support features a double-arch pattern—a trefoil-topped arch surrounded by an ogee arch—flanked by engaged columns. Four legs extend from the bottom of the base and terminate in hexagonal feet with quatrefoil ornamentation.

The extension mechanism on this table consists of metal slides incorporated within wooden supports and is stamped "Hobe's Patent N.Y" in several places. Charles F. Hobe, cabinetmaker, appears in New York City directories beginning in 1839. After leaving his Grand Street shop address, he established a business on Broadway, where it remained in operation until 1868.[1] Hobe placed an advertisement for his "Patent Metalic [*sic*] Slide Extension Dining Tables" in the *New-York Mercantile Register* in 1848 (fig. 26).[2] The pedestal of the MWPI table differs from the table Hobe illustrated in his advertisement in that the MWPI pedestal divides as the table is separated. An octagonal leg, housed in the hollow space of the pedestal when the table is closed, supports the middle of the table when it is extended.

Hobe advertised that his patented mechanism allowed the table to function with ease, even when used "in the hottest parlor . . . or in a damp place," and, therefore, he recommended his tables "for the use of steamboats." Hobe added that he manufactured "all desirable forms and patterns."[3]

The design of the MWPI table was previously attributed to Richard Upjohn. Because the table shares a provenance with the library furniture designed by Upjohn for Mr. and Mrs. Robert Kelly (see cat. no. 19),[4] and has elements that recall the Gothic characteristics Upjohn incorporated into the stairwell of the Kelly residence, this attribution has seemed plausible. However, Upjohn's characteristically rigorous application of an architecturally accurate Gothic vocabulary is absent, and the employment of the motifs seems more in keeping with the types of devices a decorator would use. In addition, the use of veneers on some sections of the table does not correspond to Upjohn's belief in honest construction. Hobe may have relied on a cabinetmaker's handbook for the design, or perhaps he built the table according to a client's request.

ATD and JSH

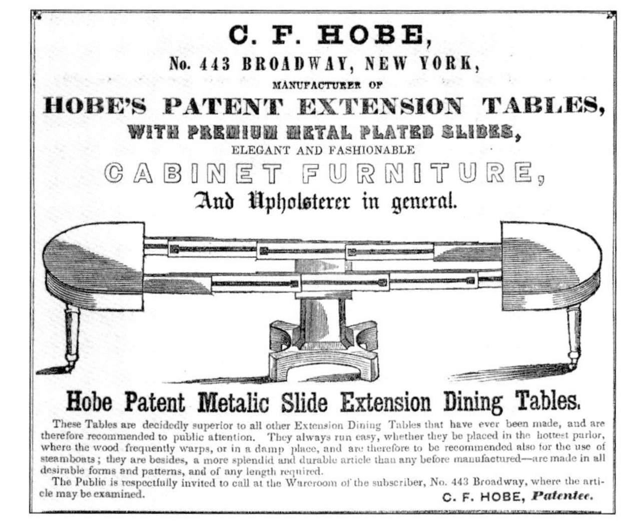

Fig. 26

Fig. 26. Advertisement for C. F. Hobe's "Patent Metalic [*sic*] Slide Extension Dining Tables" from T. Morehead, *The New-York Mercantile Register for 1848-49.* Courtesy, The Winterthur Library: Printed Book and Periodical Collection.

32 x 54 in. diam.
Stamped on extension mechanism: "HOBE'S PATENT N.Y"
Mahogany, black walnut, ash, eastern white pine, metal
Provenance: Robert Kelly, New York, New York; Mrs. Erving Pruyn, New York, New York; MWPI.
Gift of Mrs. Erving Pruyn, 60.171

 21

Étagère, ca. 1840–60

Maker unknown
Probably New York, New York

Popularized by architect-designers Alexander Jackson Davis (1803-92) and Andrew Jackson Downing (1815-52), American-made Gothic furniture reached the pinnacle of its appeal in the mid-nineteenth century.[1] Occasionally an entire domestic structure, such as Lyndhurst in Tarrytown, New York, was created in the Gothic style.[2] Davis, Lyndhurst's architect, also designed architecturally based Gothic furniture for several of the rooms in the home. The average consumer, however, usually chose simply to add Gothic furniture or accessories to a single room such as the library, hall, or dining room to update the interior aesthetic.[3]

The MWPI étagère includes many of the traits characteristic of high-style nineteenth-century homes and furnishings of upstate New York. It also presents a dictionary of the Gothic vocabulary, just as the elegant Cazenovia, New York, home, Century House, from which the étagère came, offered an encyclopedic view of nineteenth-century furniture and architectural styles. Century House, built in 1841 in the Greek Revival style, was a wedding gift from merchant Jacob Ten Eyck to his daughter Mary and her husband Elisha Litchfield. In 1863 the home was remodeled when the Litchfield's daughter Elizabeth married Eli Benedict Oakley. A mansard roof and Gothic architectural details were added, and a parlor was remodeled in the rococo revival style and fitted with compatible textiles, furniture, wallpaper, and accessories.[4] Beginning in the late 1860s, the house was primarily used as a summer home. Although some rooms were updated with aesthetic-period furnishings in the 1870s, the interiors remained basically unchanged from 1863 until 1995 when the house was sold and the furniture dispersed.[5]

For several generations this étagère, which was referred to by the family as "the ice cream server," was positioned in the dining room along with a collection of furnishings that reflected a progression of nineteenth-century styles. The eclectic amalgam included a labeled New York State federal-style sideboard, a rococo revival gasolier, and a later nineteenth-century table and chairs. As the family purchased newer furniture for their New York City residence, it appears that they brought their older furniture to Cazenovia to decorate their summer home. It is therefore likely that this étagère was made in New York City.

The MWPI étagère combines a mélange of motifs. The base, which cloaks one drawer, is in the form of a table with clustered-column legs. The shelf above the tabletop is supported by carved, arcaded Gothic tracery that resembles flying buttresses. Simple tracery also encloses the mirrors behind the shelf and outlines the side panels and drawer front. The maker added naturalistic carvings of grapes, grape leaves, acorns, and oak leaves to the scrolled cross stretchers and to the broad arch between the front legs. The most outstanding—and perplexing—carved element on the étagère is the crest. Here grape clusters and leaves are encased within a Gothic arch; outside the arch, rusticated globate acorns and thick convex oak leaves sweep upward to the apex. In the center of this leafy bower, projecting from a simple circular medallion outlined by a carved chain, the enigmatic countenance of a bearded man wearing a button-brimmed hat looks at the beholder (above). The design source for the head has not been identified, but it has been speculated that the image depicts a pirate, St. James the Greater, Rip Van Winkle, or another romantic figure from literature.

ATD

70⅝ x 41¾ x 23¾ in.
Rosewood, satinwood, yellow-poplar, black walnut, glass
Original finish, but consolidated on table surface
Provenance: Hutchens family, Cazenovia, New York; MWPI.
Museum Purchase, in part with funds from the Mrs. Erving Pruyn Fund, 95.20

22

Armchair, ca. 1845–60

Maker unknown

Northeastern United States, probably New York, New York

Although in matters of taste Americans traditionally looked to England because of close political, economic, and family ties, they always regarded France, especially Paris, as the undisputed center of style. This respect for Parisian designers and artisans created periods when French influence dominated American expressions in the decorative arts. One of the most visible times of this domination came after the American and French Revolutions. The political hostility some Americans felt toward Britain, American appreciation of France's assistance during the struggle for independence, and the emigration of well-to-do Frenchmen to the United States following the French Revolution led to an increased acceptance and use of the French language and an interest in French customs and design. During the first two decades of the nineteenth century, the work of émigré French cabinetmakers and chairmakers, such as Charles-Honoré Lannuier and Joseph Brauwers of New York and Anthony Gabriel Quervelle and Michel Bouvier of Philadelphia, became highly desirable.

In the mid-nineteenth century, French fashions again became popular. Andrew Jackson Downing, one of America's most astute observers of style, noted that "modern French furniture and especially that in the style of Louis Quatorze stands much higher in the general estimation in this country than any other."[1] The "modern" French style Downing referred to is the sinuous and florid naturalistic style known today as rococo revival, the original of which developed and flourished in France when Louis XIV was on the throne between 1643 and 1715.

Thomas Webster, another writer on the subject of interior design, commented that "the style of Louis Quatorze is known . . . by its abundance of light ornamental scrollwork and foliage. Its elegance of form . . . together with its admission of every species of enrichment, as carving, gilding, painting, inlaying with coverings of the richest silks, velvets, and the choicest stuffs, admirably adapt it for the modern drawing-room. Certainly no kind of furniture equals it in the general splendor of appearance."[2] MWPI's elegant armchair captures the essence of this popular French style as it was expressed in the United States. A reasonably faithful interpretation of mid-eighteenth-century Parisian chairs, this example suggests that its American maker was conversant with the original rococo style.[3]

Protracted study of historical prototypes was one way artisans acquired knowledge to design and produce chairs of this type, but generally this kind of close study was impractical for craftsmen. For most it was easier to learn about the latest furniture fashions from published designs and pattern books. The MWPI chair is closely related in overall appearance, material, proportion, and carved detail to an engraving from the series entitled *Périodique spécial de dessins relatifs à l'ameublement*, created and published by the Parisian cabinetmaker Célestin Allard between 1850 and 1855.[4] Another possible prototype for the MWPI chair is an example made by the French upholsterer M. Langlois that was featured at the Paris Exposition in 1855 and published in the widely distributed *Le Magasin de Meubles*.[5]

The Allard engraving and the MWPI chair employ vertically oriented, cartouche-shaped backs deeply carved with genus-specific flowers (principally roses) and leaves on both sides of a large scallop shell at the center of the crest rail; the shell is repeated, in a modified form, in the middle of the seat rail.[6] Flowers were a preferred ornamental motif on carved furniture at this time, favored not only for their visual appeal but also for the many symbolic associations they evoked, including love, beauty, fidelity, truth, and sorrow.[7]

DLF

45 x 25½ x 29¼ in.
Rosewood, black walnut, ash, modern upholstery
Provenance: Emily Lowery Beardsley, Utica, New York; MWPI.
Emily Lowery Beardsley Bequest, 61.68

23

SOFA TABLE, ca. 1846

Attributed to James Miller (active ca. 1823–55)
New York, New York

WITH THE PROLIFERATION of printed English sources, such as the designs of Thomas Sheraton, the sofa table form gained acceptance in America during the first decades of the 1800s.[1] In his *Cabinet Dictionary* (1803), Sheraton described this type of table as being "used before a sofa . . . generally made between 5 and 6 feet long, and from 22 [inches] to 2 feet broad; the frame is divided into two drawers;" he added that "ladies chiefly occupy them to draw, write, or read upon."[2] In the following decades numerous English and American cabinetmakers included sofa tables in their repertoires. Although the form was less common after midcentury, two "Grecian forms of the sofa-table" are included in Andrew Jackson Downing's *Architecture of Country Houses* (1850). The line drawings depict economical variations of the table; Downing explained that "more fanciful ones" could be "easily attained." He also observed that "in towns" the sofa table was replacing the center table because "scattered here and there in a room, [sofa tables] afford various gathering places for little conversation parties—while the centre-table draws all talkers to a single focus."[3] He christened the sofa table the emblem of the evening party.

The attribution of the MWPI sofa table to James Miller is based on a surviving bill of sale (fig. 27). In 1846 James Watson Williams purchased from Miller "one sofa table" for forty-five dollars and "one hat stand" for fifteen dollars.[4] Presumably these pieces were to furnish the Utica, New York, home Williams was establishing with his bride, Helen Munson. Although the hat stand does not survive, the sofa table remained in the family's possession until 1935 when the entire family collection became a part of the Munson-Williams-Proctor Institute Museum of Art.[5]

Miller is one of hundreds of cabinetmakers whose work is nearly lost to contemporary scholars. He worked in New York City from about 1823 to 1855 and relocated his shop several times; he was doing business at 441 Broadway from 1828 to 1851.[6] Because of the limited number of pieces that can be attributed to him, MWPI's sofa table is a rare entity. It provides vital information on the quality of his craftsmanship and on the types of items produced in his shop.

In fashioning this table Miller may have been influenced by early nineteenth-century English sources. Or he may have relied on American design books—often blatant copies of English or French publications—that were issued in large cities, such as New York and Philadelphia. The discovery of an example printed in upstate New York demonstrates the broad dissemination of these design sources. The MWPI table resembles plate 74 in Sheraton's *Cabinet Dictionary* but also parallels objects illustrated in Robert Conner's *Cabinet Maker's Assistant*, published in Buffalo, New York, in 1842.[7] With simple S-curves and without drawers or leaves, Conner's pattern for a sofa table is relatively unadorned. Drawers and drop-leaves, however, were incorporated into his sketch of a library table.[8]

MWPI's table is a simple interpretation of the form. The smooth, flat horizontal and vertical surfaces display the rich grain of the mahogany veneer. The narrow drop-leaves increase the length of the table by barely twenty inches. False drawer fronts give the appearance of four drawers, two on each side of the table. In reality, there are only two deep drawers; one opens on one side of the table and the other on the opposite side. C-shaped leg braces and the two abutting-urn shapes that constitute the stretcher lighten the effect of the unassuming rectilinear top. A line of beading under the drawers and turned ornamental disks on the ends of the brackets and at the center of the stretcher are the only enriching details.

ATD

27⅝ x 52⅛ x 26 in.
27⅝ x 33⅞ x 26 in. (closed position)
Mahogany, cucumbertree (*Magnolia acuminata*),
eastern white pine, yellow-poplar, cherry, black walnut
Provenance: Proctor Collection.
Proctor Collection, PC. 422

Fig. 27. Invoice, ink on paper.
James Miller to James Watson Williams, 1846. MWPI Archives.

Mr J. Watson Williams

Bot of James Miller

one Sofa table — $45 " 00

one hat Stand — 15 " 00

Boxing and all Compts 1 00

$61 " 00

New York Nov 4th 1846 Recd payment

James Miller

No 421 B. Way

Fig. 27

 24

Sofa, Armchair, and Side Chair, ca. 1850–60

Attributed to John Henry Belter (active 1844–63)
New York, New York

John Henry Belter (1804-63) was born in the town of Iburg in the kingdom of Hanover, in the northwest corner of present-day Germany, about forty miles north of the city of Dortmund.[1] In 1833 he traveled to New York City presumably to investigate its potential as a place to live and work. He apparently liked what he found, but he may not have been a permanent resident of New York until 1844, when he was listed in the city directory as a cabinetmaker at 40½ Chatham Street.[2] In the interim Belter may have worked as a journeyman to be able to accumulate enough capital to establish a business under his own name.

Belter's move to the United States was fortuitous. He left what almost certainly would have been a life of obscurity and instead made his name synonymous with the rococo revival style. His fame was apparently deserved; he not only fashioned dramatic and comfortable furniture of good quality, he continually sought ways to improve what he was making as well. Between 1847 and 1860 he obtained four patents from the United States Patent Office. One was for a process that allowed Belter to fabricate compound-curved components by pressing layers of laminated wood in cauls. Belter termed it an "improvement in the manufacturing of furniture," from which one can presume that he did not invent the idea of using laminated wood to produce curved furniture. Indeed, he observed that "pressed work [for furniture] has [previously] been curved only in one plane so that each part forms a portion of a hollow cylinder or cone; but by my invention each portion of the pressed work, when completed, forms a portion of a hollow sphere."[3] Belter fabricated what he called "dishing forms"—his laminated work was curved both in height and in width.

The backs of the pieces of furniture in the MWPI matching suite are made of seven laminated layers of wood with alternating grain; they are curved but not dished.[4] Because a number of other mid-nineteenth-century American furniture manufacturers made laminated forms that curved in only one plane, one hesitates to attribute this seating to Belter. However, a set of rosewood seating furniture that is virtually identical in design and execution with this group exists with its original bill of sale from Belter. The bill itemizes two sofas, two armchairs, four parlor chairs, a center table, and an étagère.[5] The sofa and chairs are described in the bill as being in the "Arabasket" design. In all likelihood Belter was referring to, and phonetically misspelled, the term arabesque, "a species of . . . decoration . . . composed in flowing lines of branches, leaves, and scroll-work fancifully intertwined."[6]

The choice of juxtaposed and overlapping elements adapted from nature reflect a culture in which attitudes toward the forested wilderness were evolving. Until this time Americans had tended to regard wild nature and its native inhabitants as dangerous, as things to be tamed and conquered. However, with the "civilizing" influences of the early nineteenth century—canals, turnpikes, railroads, westward expansion, growth of

50⅞ x 68⅜ x 31 in.
Mahogany, cherry, rosewood, yellow-poplar, modern upholstery
Provenance: John or Killian Shaeffer, Pottsville, Pennsylvania;
Clara Brooks, Larchmont, New York; Mrs. Garasalo, Syracuse, New York;
Robert Palmiter, Bouckville, New York; MWPI.
Museum Purchase, 59.116

inland cities, and widespread and scientific cultivation of the land—nature became less threatening. Its bounty was welcomed into homes in the forms of potted plants and cut flowers and their counterparts in carved wood.

The MWPI suite of furniture handsomely represents this phenomenon. It is a striking and voluptuous interpretation of the design aesthetic suggested by the term arabesque. The frames are almost completely covered with a complex intertwining of carved naturalistic motifs—leaves, tendrils, roses and other flowers, grape clusters, ruffled shells, and cornucopias—that embellish a composition of intertwined voluted scrolls. The piercing of the laminated backs allows light to pass through and heightens the visual impact of the rococo motifs.

This emphasis on visual complexity did not come at the expense of comfort. Sofas, chairs, and even stools were built to withstand the considerable pressure of a network of coil springs tied under compression. Sprung bottoms, as they were termed, were developed during the early nineteenth century to increase the comfort of seating furniture and beds. Although backs were not sprung, they were often tightly stuffed with horsehair and tufted to provide cushioned support.

DLF

Armchair: 44¼ x 25 x 28¾ in. (one of a pair in MWPI collection)
Side Chair: 38⅝ x 18⅞ x 25 in.
Mahogany, black ash, cherry, modern upholstery
Provenance: Mrs. Garasalo, Syracuse, New York;
Robert Palmiter, Bouckville, New York; MWPI.
Museum Purchase, 59.119 and .121

25

ÉTAGÈRE, ca. 1850–60

Maker unknown
Probably New York, New York

ÉTAGÈRES WERE DESIRABLE ADJUNCTS to fashionable mid-nineteenth-century homes. A flattering complement to the taste and wealth of its owners, the étagère or whatnot, as it was sometimes called, was "a piece of furniture which serves occasional or incidental use, and belongs, indifferently to the dining-room, drawing-room, or parlour."[1] Although relatively simple examples are known, most étagères are heavily decorated monuments to lavish display with mirrored backs to enhance the impact of the artifacts exhibited on them. The designer and architect Andrew Jackson Downing believed that nothing bespoke a householder's taste and status as much as a "handsome etagere, of French design, suitable for the drawing room of a villa. In the centre is a handsome mirror, on either side of which are shelves for articles of virtu—bouquets of flowers, scientific curiosities, or whatever else of this kind the owner may indulge his taste in."[2]

The MWPI étagère adheres to French design precepts. Its lower section, with four voluptuously curved and carved legs, ultimately derives its overall form, scale, and naturalistic decoration from mid-eighteenth-century Parisian console tables and their nineteenth-century interpretations.[3] The upper section of this étagère does not have an eighteenth-century prototype. But, like the base, it has a curvilinear outline embellished with deeply carved grape clusters, flowers, leaves, and tendrils, and it is made of solid and laminated rosewood.[4] Rosewood was the favored wood for such ostentatious objects, because as one cabinetmaker's guide put it, it was "likely to furnish a permanently fashionable material for drawing-room furniture. Besides being intrinsically beautiful, it contrasts admirably with the materials usually employed in drapery."[5]

Étagères of this type are often attributed to the renowned John Henry Belter of New York City because of his innovative use of laminated rosewood. While New York is the probable place of origin for this étagère, it may have been made by any one of the fine furniture makers working there during the mid-nineteenth century. An étagère closely related in form, material, and design to the MWPI example, for instance, was among the many pieces of furniture by the Brooklyn cabinet-maker Thomas Brooks displayed at the Exhibition of the Industry of All Nations, commonly called the Crystal Palace exhibition, in 1853 in New York City. The catalogue of the exposition describes the étagère as having been "elaborately and elegantly carved in rosewood after the designs of G. Herter. Ornamental furniture, particularly of the kind of which this piece is an example, is represented extensively in the Crystal Palace. Our exhibitors have a tendency to ostentation, or presume that this will be the feeling on the part of visitors. We regret that some of this display had not been replaced by furniture better suited to our daily wants and necessities."[6] Other New York cabinetmakers who were capable of making furniture of this quality include Alexander Roux, John and Joseph Meeks, and Charles A. Baudouine. Indicating the widespread popularity of the rococo-revival style, similar products were made in Philadelphia by Gottlieb Vollmer, in Boston by George Croome, and as far west as Cincinnati, Ohio, by the firm of Robert Mitchell and Frederick Rammelsberg. Because of the many talented craftsmen working in this mode, accurate attribution of this and other unlabeled étagères awaits the discovery of signed or labeled examples.[7]

DLF

109½ x 69⅝ x 24¾ in.
Rosewood, black walnut, white oak, basswood, black ash, glass
Provenance: Mrs. Garasalo, Syracuse, New York;
Robert Palmiter, Bouckville, New York; MWPI.
Museum Purchase, 59.118

 26

WORKTABLE, ca. 1846

Charles Baudouine (active 1829–ca. 1854)
New York, New York

DURING THE YEARS Charles Baudouine (1808-95) operated his cabinetmaking firm, he established one of the preeminent shops in New York City.[1] The *Stranger's Guide in the City of New-York, 1852* noted that "Mr. Baudouine is one of the oldest manufacturers in N. York, and we do not hesitate to pronounce him the most enterprising and extensive one in the country. The rapidity of his rise, and his increasing reputation and fame, furnishes an excellent illustration of the onward progress of the times."[2] The quality and scope of Baudouine's products rivaled that of his competitors, such as John Henry Belter, whose shop in 1851 was only a few doors from Baudouine's establishment.[3] Although he trained in New York City, Baudouine was aware of prevailing European styles and worked in modes from the elaborate rococo revival to simple Renaissance expressions.

Earnest Hagen (1830-1913), who worked in Baudouine's shop around 1854, left a manuscript memoir, "Personal Experiences of an Old New York Cabinetmaker," which includes a detailed portrait of Baudouine's business.[4] Baudouine began his career in 1829 with a small shop at 508 Pearl Street. According to Hagen, Baudouine opened his shop "with a capital of $300, which he got from his wife, Ann Postley, who kept a milliner shop nearby."[5] By the 1850s Baudouine's growing business employed about two hundred hands, including approximately seventy cabinetmakers as well as carvers, varnishers, and upholsterers.[6] Baudouine was not only a manufacturer of furniture; he was also an importer. Hagen explained that Baudouine made annual trips to France and that he "imported a great deal of French furniture and upholstery coverings, French hardware, trimmings, and other material used in his shop."[7] Measuring "275 feet long," the luxurious Baudouine salesrooms were reportedly "one of the greatest attractions in the City."[8] R. G. Dun & Company's credit report notes that Baudouine had "a large and flourishing business" and that those who had "dealt with him for many years . . . always found him forthright and honorable in his dealings."[9]

Notable pieces of labeled Baudouine furniture illustrate the breadth of his creations and his strong reliance on French design. Objects produced in Baudouine's shop range from intricately carved étagères to conservative parlor suites.[10] Hagen's memoir describes the "gaudy and over ornate," carved, French-style furniture made in the shop and "the rosewood heavy over decorated parlor [suites] with round perforated backs" that Baudouine sold for twelve hundred dollars a set.[11] Although Baudouine apparently also worked in the Gothic style, no known pieces in this mode have been attributed to him.

After retiring from his successful career as a cabinetmaker, Baudouine invested in real estate, a venture that brought him additional prosperity. He resided on Park Avenue, and accounts of his life often observe that he traveled in a coach-and-four. At the time of his death in 1895 his estate was reportedly valued at about five million dollars.

Numerous examples of Baudouine's work survive in the collection of MWPI and are a testament to the quality of the wares his shop produced. On his frequent trips from Utica to New York, James Watson Williams often acquired furnishings for his home, and this worktable is his first documented purchase from Charles Baudouine's shop. Williams paid sixty dollars for it (fig. 28) and wrote to his fiancée on July 11, 1846, about the purchase: "After looking various places for a gift for you, I have selected at Baudouine's, a work table which I am sure must please you; no lacquer-work, nor papier mache, nor tinsel of any sort; but a neat, well-made, and convenient table of the most approved French pattern."[12]

$29\frac{1}{4}$ x $20\frac{1}{2}$ x $15\frac{5}{8}$ in.
Rosewood, mahogany, white oak, ash, glass, brass, metal
Provenance: Proctor Collection.
Proctor Collection, PC. 420

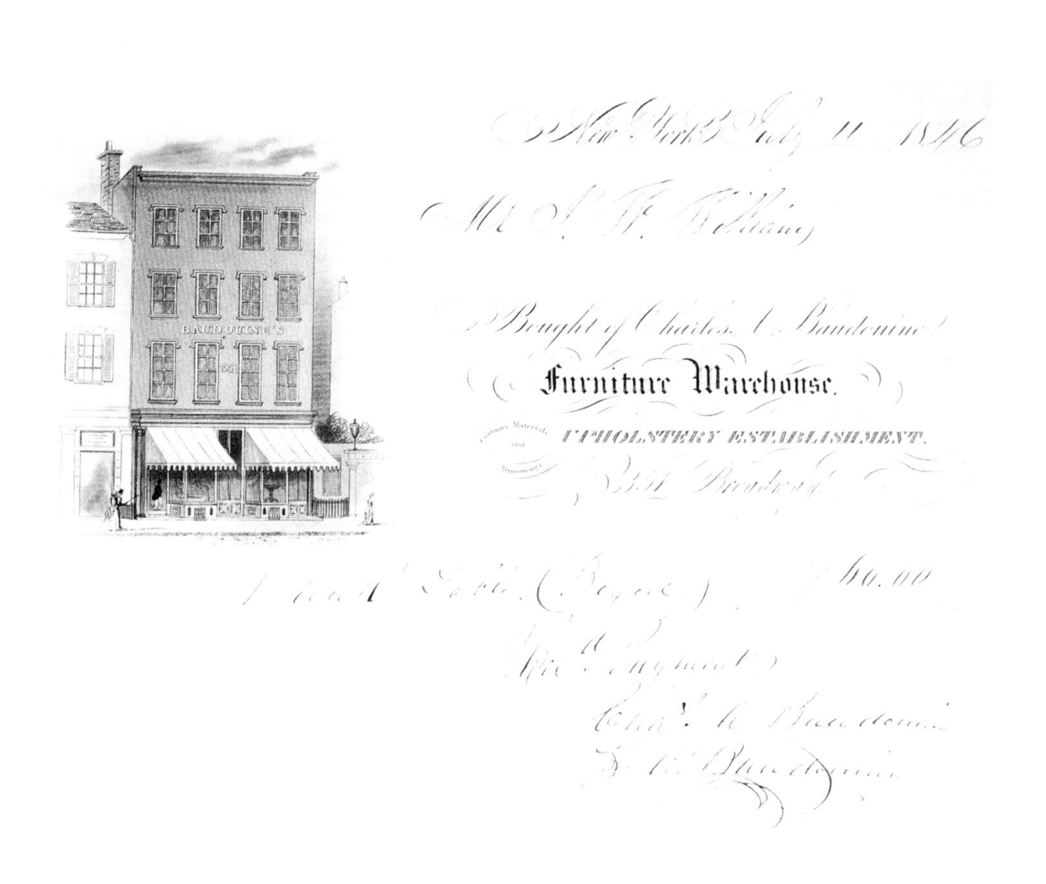

New York Feby 11 1846

Bought of Charles A. Baudouine

Furniture Warehouse.

UPHOLSTERY ESTABLISHMENT.

Broadway

40.00

Fig. 28

Williams purchased the multifunctional worktable that would serve as a sewing table as well as a writing surface. The lid, mirrored on the underside, opens for access to the interior of the table, which is fitted with a removable four-sectioned tray above a single compartment. The hinged top board of the lid, released by turning a latch adjacent to the mirror, can be adjusted to create the preferred angle for a writing surface. A "hidden" drawer, located beneath the main body of the table where the legs join the top, runs the width of the table. Not readily visible to a casual observer, this drawer can be opened only when a small lever, located next to the interior tray, is lifted and held.

Worktables were common in the mid-nineteenth century, and many designs for them were printed in English and French sources. The form and ornamentation of the MWPI table are decidedly French. Compared with another Baudouine worktable of the same period, now in the collection of Historic Hudson Valley, the MWPI table seems to represent the conventional line offered in Baudouine's shop. The Historic Hudson Valley table is more delicate and is embellished with ormolu and black lacquer. By contrast, the plain rosewood surfaces of the MWPI table are ornamented with a modest bead molding around the perimeters of the undulating form of the lid and skirt. Four curvilinear brackets, joined at a spindle cage, support the body of the table. This unit rests on a base with four S-shaped legs. The stylized acanthus leaves and volutes of the feet furnish the only carving on the piece.

ATD

Fig. 28. Invoice, ink on engraved paper.
Charles Baudouine to James Watson Williams, 1846.
MWPI Archives.

27

SETTEE, ARMCHAIR, SIDE CHAIR, AND MULTIFORM TABLE, ca. 1852

Charles Baudouine (active 1829–ca. 1854)
New York, New York

IN THE LATE 1840s and early 1850s James Williams frequently traveled to New York City to procure furnishings from the best firms for his Utica house, although the Utica city directory of 1852 lists fifty-three cabinetmakers, and Albany, also endowed with fine cabinetmakers, was much closer to home. In 1846 James purchased a worktable (cat. no. 26) made in the shop of Charles Baudouine (1808-95) for his fiancée Helen Munson. Six years later, the elegant simplicity of the worktable apparently appealing to the Williamses' conservative taste, the couple went back to Baudouine's shop for an analogous rosewood parlor suite. The May 1852 bill of sale reads:[1]

1 Suit Rosewood Furniture in Green Tapestry Viz.		
2 Tete a Tetes, 4 Chairs & 2 Fauteuils [armchairs]		340.
1 Rosewood Multiform Table		160.
Boxing 5 Boxes	$2.50	12.50
		$512.50

40¼ x 51½ x 20½ in. (one of a pair in MWPI collection)
Rosewood, ash, modern upholstery
Provenance: Proctor Collection.
Proctor Collection, PC. 423.3

Executed in a customary interpretation of the rococo revival or Louis XV style, the MWPI parlor grouping is the largest known extant suite of documented Baudouine furniture. The graceful outline of each chair is accented at the crest by a subtle arch enhanced with modest volutes. In a similarly restrained manner, the cabriole legs feature an unobtrusive cabochon on each knee, and the curved seat rail is decorated with gentle scrolls on either side of a central cabochon. In overall form each settee (tête-à-tête) resembles two joined armchairs. The settees are somewhat more complex in their decoration than the chairs: on each settee a carved stylized leaf spray fills the middle of the back, and seat rail carvings that resemble shield-shaped medallions are accented by volutes.

The two sections of the aptly named multiform table can be joined to create a center table (opposite, bottom) or used individually (opposite, top). In the configuration of a center table, the four pierced and castered inner legs cluster together to form a central "pedestal" with a striking, sinuous outline.[2] Nonetheless, the practicality of using the multiform table as a center table might be questioned because of the intrusive middle seam that is created when the tables are joined. The separated sections form matching side tables, which can be used as gaming tables by swinging the inner legs (joined to the outer legs by curved stretchers) outward until the four legs form a square. The top leaf, when lifted and resting upon the repositioned legs, reveals a felt-covered surface.

The simplicity of the tabletop with the applied carved moldings on the skirt is in keeping with the tenor of the suite, but the legs are more intricate. Each outer leg, beginning with a carved corbel at the skirt, descends in rhythmic C-scrolls. Each inner leg is pierced to follow its scroll. Several examples of this table design survive, testifying to the popularity of flexible forms of furniture at a time when parlors and drawing rooms were used for multiple purposes.[3]

ATD

Armchair: 37⅜ x 23⅝ x 24 in. (one of a pair in MWPI collection)
Side chair: 36¼ x 19 x 17¾ in. (one of four in MWPI collection)
Rosewood, ash, modern upholstery
Provenance: Proctor Collection.
Proctor Collection, PC. 423.5 and .7

Fig. 29

One table half used as card table (top): $29\frac{3}{8}$ x $46\frac{1}{2}$ x $31\frac{3}{4}$ in.
Two halves joined as center table (bottom): $29\frac{3}{8}$ x $46\frac{1}{2}$ x 32 in.
Stenciled label inside drawer of each half (fig. 29): "FROM/C. A. BAUDOUINE/335/BROADWAY/NEW.YORK"
Rosewood, ash, black walnut, unknown tropical wood, modern felt, leather
Provenance: Proctor Collection.
Proctor Collection, PC. 423.1-2

28

ÉTAGÈRE, ca. 1850–55

Attributed to Elijah Galusha (active ca. 1828–70)
Troy, New York

ELIJAH GALUSHA (1804-71) was born in Shaftsbury, Vermont, and probably had some training as a cabinetmaker before moving, in about 1825, to Troy, New York.[1] By 1828 Galusha opened a shop at 307 River Street where he produced a variety of furniture in the Empire style. His 1828 *Troy Sentinel* advertisements feature a line drawing of an Empire-style worktable with a pillar base and carved legs; the ads also note that Galusha had Pembroke and "Pillar and Claw" tables on hand in his shop. From the late 1830s through the 1850s Galusha's business grew steadily—he had eight workers in 1840 and fifteen by 1848. As his operation expanded, so did the range of objects and services his firm offered. By the 1840s, in addition to parlor and case furniture and frames, Galusha's comprehensive shop included interior decorating materials and services.[2]

Galusha, working in a conventional production mode, used traditional joinery techniques, carved embellishments from solid pieces of wood, and applied hand- and machine-carved components to flat surfaces to achieve greater depth.[3] Although he used many of the decorative elements common to the rococo revival style, the distinctive floral ornamentation in combination with machine-produced decorative detail differentiates his work from that of his contemporaries. While most other cabinetmakers favored a combination of fruit, flowers, and other naturalistic motifs, Galusha relied on carved, horticulturally accurate floral elements. Roses appear frequently on Galusha's work; sometimes they are in combination with honeysuckle (as on the pediment of this étagère) and other garden flowers of the period. Although these motifs are executed with great attention to detail (discrete flowers are recognizable), a source for Galusha's representations has not been determined.

Galusha's forms—including parlor suites, fireplace screens, armoires, bureaus, desks, and mirrors—were typical of the period.[4] Comparisons of Galusha furniture to illustrations from French furniture design publications, especially Désiré Guilmard's *Le Garde-Meuble*, indicate that Galusha may have received one or more of these periodicals or was acutely familiar with their illustrations, or he may have been influenced by the works of makers who used these publications as resources.[5] Documented Galusha furniture and the patronage he received from prosperous local customers confirm that he emulated the work of his New York City counterparts and added embellishments that distinguish his furniture from that of other manufacturers.[6]

Galusha's most stylistically energetic furniture is in the rococo revival mode.[7] The combination of decorative techniques on the MWPI étagère makes it an encyclopedic representation of his rococo revival vocabulary. Several motifs predominate—flowers such as daisies and primroses, gadrooning, and applied ripple molding. The architectural proportions of the base are enhanced by colonettes (spindles) that angle outward from the front corners, mirrored surfaces, a plethora of naturalistic ornament, and applied stock trim. The top half of the étagère, featuring two shelves supported by C-shaped brackets, culminates in an ornately carved, pierced crest. The added feature of piercing appears on only a few pieces of known Galusha furniture.

Judging from the amount of furniture in the rococo revival style attributed to Galusha, the 1850s were the most prosperous years for his cabinet shop. His 1857 credit rating notes that he was "good as gold for all you can sell him."[8] His business declined during the Civil War era but regained some of its strength in the late 1860s perhaps because of his ability to modify designs according to popular taste (see cat. no. 32). Galusha's business waned from 1866 until his retirement in 1870; he died the following year.[9]

ATD

72¾ x 44½ x 22⅝ in.
Rosewood, bird's-eye maple, curly maple, yellow-poplar, eastern white pine, black walnut, mahogany, cucumbertree (*Magnolia acuminata*), marble, glass, metal
Provenance: Foster family, Palatine Bridge, New York; MWPI.
Museum Purchase, 60.34

29

Centripetal Spring Chair, ca. 1849–58

Design attributed to Thomas E. Warren (active 1849–53)
Manufacture attributed to American Chair Company (active 1829–58)
Troy, New York

Few examples of furniture better epitomize the design tensions of mid-nineteenth-century America than centripetal spring chairs. These objects combine two competing and contradictory approaches to design in a highly original way. On the one hand, the unadorned steel C-shaped springs, the use of cast iron for structural elements, and the new postures enabled by these tilt-and-swivel chairs represent what John Kouwenhoven half a century ago called America's vernacular design tradition.[1] On the other hand, the cast-iron neo-rococo ornament, the rosewood graining on the metal back, and the extensive use of fabric upholstery, evocative of both culture and comfort, are evidence of the influence of Europe's cultivated tradition.[2] While the vernacular tradition encouraged direct, functional, and often inexpensive solutions to design problems, goods made in accordance with the cultivated tradition typically emphasized costly materials, painstaking workmanship, elaborate decoration, and reverence for the past. Most people who have written about Warren's chairs find their vernacular features the more noteworthy.[3]

The most distinctive feature of this chair is the spring mechanism, which Warren patented in this country on September 25, 1849, and in Britain on November 21, 1850.[4] That same year Warren's chairs won a prize at the Franklin Institute's twentieth annual exhibition in Philadelphia.[5] A year later they achieved international acclaim when they were described and illustrated in accounts of London's Crystal Palace exhibition. That event took place in Joseph Paxton's memorable cast-iron and glass exhibition hall, a building as technologically innovative as Warren's chairs. One of the most authoritative accounts of the fair, the Art Journal's *Industry of All Nations*, commended Warren's products, pointing out that America had "long been noted for the luxurious easiness of its chairs."[6]

In *Mechanization Takes Command*, his classic study of the role of technology in modern life, Siegfried Giedion linked Americans' midcentury propensity to experiment with new seating forms to their earlier development of the rocking chair. The lively minds of American inventors hit on the idea of combining "the oscillating motion of the rocking chair" with "the rotary motion of the revolving chair."[7] Warren's centripetal spring rockers were among the earliest examples of this experimentation to go into extensive production. Of the descendants of these rockers, tilt-and-swivel desk chairs, in their seemingly endless variations, have become the most enduring.[8]

Today Warren's chairs are familiar icons of Victorian America, but Warren himself remains obscure, as do the details of his relationship to the American Chair Company. Warren is listed in Troy directories between 1849 and 1852 as a broker and appears three times in the records of the United States Patent Office, first in 1849 for chair springs, again on July 30, 1850, for railroad car seats incorporating springs, and finally on October 18, 1853, when he patented a sheet-iron railroad car. The American Chair Company, which manufactured reclining seats for railroad cars, appears in Troy directories from 1829 to 1858.[9] Along with nearby Albany, Troy was a major center of iron production, specializing in stoves and architectural iron work. Although little is known about Warren, he seems to have been typical of many inventors of the time who worked at the intersection of emerging industries and transferred ideas from one medium to another.

The MWPI chair, like those in other collections, is attributed to Warren on the basis of its similarity to period images, particularly those published in conjunction with London's Crystal Palace exhibition. In fact, however, few surviving chairs exactly duplicate those images. The most obvious difference is the pitch of the cast-iron legs. Period images show the legs joining the central post at a forty-five degree angle. The legs on the MWPI example and most others are horizontal and parallel to the floor. It is possible that the horizontal arrangement is a later adjustment made by Warren for aesthetic or practical reasons—greater stability, for example. A similar horizontal arrangement appears on rocking and rotating chairs advertised by M. W. King & Son of New York in 1855.[10] Another possibility is that not all centripetal spring chairs were made by the American Chair Company or even authorized by Warren, for one of the truisms about patents is that they are often infringed upon.

KLA

32 x 23½ x 23½ in.
Cast iron, steel, hard maple, birch, yellow-poplar, basswood, brass, paint, reproduction upholstery
Provenance: Joan Bogart, Rockville Centre, New York; MWPI.
Museum Purchase, 86.33

30

Desk, ca. 1845–65
Hall Chair, ca. 1845–69

Edward Whitehead Hutchings (active 1832–84 or –85)
New York, New York

Edward Whitehead Hutchings (1807-89) was the proprietor of a prosperous business that offered up-to-date fashions and rivaled the most prominent New York City furniture manufacturers in the mid-nineteenth century. Hutchings, son of Samuel and Lois Whitehead Hutchings, was first listed in a New York City directory in 1832 as an upholsterer at 67 Sullivan Street; by 1835 he was listed as a cabinetmaker at 31 Thompson Street. In 1845 the Hutchings shop was located at 475 Broadway, where it remained until 1868. The firm name changed several times from E. W. and W. Hutchings to E. W. Hutchings & Company and to E. W. Hutchings & Son.[1]

By 1850 Hutchings employed seventy-five men and four women; in 1855 his workforce included 125 men and three women.[2] The business occupied at least two structures—475 Broadway and an adjoining building at 42 Mercer Street—and possibly a third at 46 Wooster Street.[3] The flourishing firm exhibited a sideboard, armchair, tête-à-tête sofa, étagère, and chair at the Crystal Palace exhibition in New York in 1853. An illustration of the sideboard reveals a fashionable buffet with richly carved decorations of classical figures, dead game, sea life, and other appropriate motifs.[4]

Hutchings' business endeavors included attempts to expand the distribution of his wares outside New York City.[5] His brother William, who had worked with the firm in New York, briefly operated a retail store in Chicago from about 1856 until 1858; Edward apparently supplied wares for this store.[6] His entrepreneurial ventures may have also included short-lived branches in New Orleans, Louisiana, about 1850, and in Mobile, Alabama, in the late 1850s.[7] If his enterprises outside New York were not prosperous, his wealthy New York clients, the longevity of his New York warerooms, and his solid credit ratings indicate a highly successful business. He expanded his

Fig. 30

trade to provide a full spectrum of interior decorating services by the 1870s. An 1872 advertisement promoted a wide variety of offerings including "Architectural Hard Wood Work, Wood Mantels . . . Frames and Wainscoting."[8] Although he enjoyed considerable commercial success, Hutchings' work was overshadowed by that of his protégés Gustave Herter and Auguste Pottier.[9] Hutchings' business continued in operation until 1884 or early 1885, at which time the firm was dissolved and its holdings were sold at auction.[10] Hutchings' sons Edward Jr. and Charles, however, continued in the furniture business into the 1890s.

The firm's quality of workmanship and stylistic preferences are set forth in the MWPI desk. It consists of two parts—a base with two drawers and a slant-top desk with an étagère top—that are joined together by four concealed pegs. The base is supported on delicate cabriole legs. Applied carved cabochons and foliage accent the front legs, but the composition is not fully articulated on the rear face of the back legs. The lower edges of the drawers and sides of the case follow a curved silhouette that is enhanced by an applied molding.

52⅛ x 36¾ x 17⅝ in.
Stenciled label (fig. 30): "FROM/E. W. HUTCHINGS/CABINET WAREROOMS/475/BROADWAY. N.Y."
Rosewood, tulipwood, satinwood, black walnut, yellow-poplar, pine, glass, metal
Provenance: Robert Palmiter, Bouckville, New York; MWPI.
Museum Purchase, 60.203

Inside the slant-top desk are two compartments, four small drawers, and two sliding trays. The drawers and trays are faced with herringbone-patterned veneer. The partitioned interior, constructed as a separate unit, slides into the desk case. Hutchings' label is located inside an interior drawer (fig. 30).

Above the desk is a shelf with a mirrored back. The uppermost shelf, above the mirror, is supported by carved, pierced brackets and is enclosed on three sides by a gallery (also carved and pierced) of flowing C-scrolls. There is little detail in the execution of this carving other than simple concaving for depth. Two urn-shaped finials, which coordinate with two on the lower shelf, cap the gallery corners.

Hutchings often drew inspiration from French design sources and advertised that he carried "the Latest and most Fashionable Style of FRENCH FURNITURE." The MWPI desk presents the same restrained rococo vocabulary and elegant lines found on forms illustrated in French periodicals published by Michel Jansen, V. Quetin, and Désiré Guilmard. Plate 62 in Guilmard's *Le Carnet de l'Ébéniste Parisien: Collection de Meubles Simples* (ca. 1845) has especially tangible similarities.[11]

Hutchings also relied on English sources for artistic stimulation. The MWPI hall chair is analogous to examples in mid-nineteenth-century English design books, such as *Designs for Furniture and Cornices* (n.d), but they may have been ultimately derived from Renaissance models.[12] The form of this chair is simple and utilitarian in outline. The shaped back is cut from a solid piece of wood and pierced in four areas. Applied moldings, forming interlocking scrolls and rounded tracery, surround a shield-shaped garnish and add dimension to what otherwise would be an austere chair back. The bottom of the chair is uncomplicated. The hinged trapezoidal seat is supported by tapering, square, Renaissance-inspired legs with incised outlines. Flat, applied ornament on and below the seat rail alleviates the plainness of the surfaces. The contrast in aesthetic merit between the desk and the hall chair illustrates the range of goods available from the Hutchings showrooms.

ATD

45¼ x 20⅛ x 17½ in.
Stenciled label: "FROM/E. W. HUTCHINGS/CABINET WAREROOMS/475/BROADWAY. N.Y."
Rosewood, black walnut, ash, hard pine, yellow-poplar, metal
Provenance: Mimi Findlay Antiques, New York, New York; MWPI.
Museum Purchase with funds from the Mrs. Erving Pruyn Fund, 85.49

29⅜ x 33 x 18¼ in.
Stenciled label (fig. 31): "J & J. W. MEEKS/MAKERS/Nº 14 Vesey St/NEW YORK"
Rosewood, satinwood, mahogany, yellow-poplar, walnut
Refinished top, central finial on stretcher and two disks on feet replaced
Provenance: New York City estate; William Doyle Galleries, New York, New York;
Joel J. Einhorn, Woodbury, Connecticut; Peter Hill, Inc., East Lempster, New Hampshire; MWPI.
Museum Purchase, in part with funds given by James and Patricia Rudi in memory of Robert Oehme, 91.30

31

Games Table, ca. 1845–50

J. and J. W. Meeks (active 1836–59)
New York, New York

The Meeks family cabinetmaking firm was one of the largest and most prolific furniture operations in New York City during the first half of the nineteenth century.[1] The firm evolved through three generations of cabinetmakers from a shop headed by a single master craftsman to a large manufacturing establishment that, by 1850, reportedly employed more than 125 people.[2] As the Meeks firm developed, its product line was diversified to include a variety of revival styles in different price categories. The firm provided broad consumer choices ranging from common "fancy chairs" and painted and grained washstands to lavishly upholstered bedsteads and ornately carved étagères. While the firm's operations were always based in New York City, the Meeks family expanded its market by distributing products to locations such as Savannah, Georgia; New Orleans, Louisiana; and Natchez, Mississippi.

Joseph Meeks (1771-1868) established the firm bearing his name in 1797. After working with his brother Edward through 1799, Joseph operated independently until 1828 and then went into business with his sons from 1829 to 1835. Upon their father's retirement, John (1801-75) and Joseph W. (1805-78) Meeks formed the partnership of "J. & J. W. Meeks," which lasted from 1836 until 1859. The R. G. Dun & Company credit report dated March 22, 1858, notes that the brothers "have been selling off for some time past, reducing their stock & trying to get out of bus'[iness]."[3] After Joseph W. Meeks retired and the J. & J. W. Meeks firm was dissolved, John Meeks worked in the furniture trade under his own name in 1859 and 1860 before entering into business with his son from 1861 to 1863.[4] The firm was operated under the direction of John Meeks Jr. (1835-92) from 1863 through 1869, closing a few months after the death of its original founder.[5]

The MWPI games table probably dates to the mid-1840s, a period when the Meeks firm produced furniture in a variety of styles. Indeed, in 1844 the *New Mirror* recommended a tour of the Meeks wareroom for "amusement": "The fancies of every age and country are represented—those of the Elizabethan era and the ornate fashion of Louis XIV. predominant [*sic*], though tables and sofas on Egyptian models are more sumptuous."[6]

As nineteenth-century craftsmen frequently borrowed from historical vocabularies with scant archaeological correctness, revival styles often became amalgamated. The MWPI games table is a product of this eclecticism, embodying both the rococo and Elizabethan idioms popular in midcentury America. Rococo revival elements are employed on the table in the C-scrolls—used as structural and decorative devices on the supports, stretcher, and legs—and in the representation of foliage and shells. Details evocative of Elizabethan Renaissance precedents include simulated strapwork and turned pendants. This dense configuration of elements manifests the period's growing preoccupation with rich and, ultimately, naturalistic carving.

Fig. 31

The rectangular top of the MWPI table has semicircular ends with carved and pierced ornamentation on the apron. Alternating squares of inlaid light and dark woods create a central game board. A drawer under the top is embellished with a beveled molding. Carved foliage, C-scrolls, and turned pendants are harmoniously united by carved strapwork to form the table supports. The stretcher is composed of carved C-scrolls with a turned finial and pendant at the center. Both pairs of legs are separated by a central carved shell and terminate in flattened disk feet.[7]

The large number of objects bearing the stenciled mark of J. & J. W. Meeks (fig. 31) exhibit a wide range in quality.[8] In contrast to the bold, veneered forms produced in the Grecian style by Joseph Meeks & Sons between 1829 and 1835, the objects J. & J. W. Meeks made during the late 1830s and early 1840s are often rudimentary in form and poorly proportioned, suggesting that the sons lowered the overall quality of their product line to decrease prices and to increase volume of production. During the late 1840s and early 1850s, however, the firm also produced a select group of armoires, cabinets, étagères, and tables (including this games table) in the rococo and Elizabethan styles that, in design and workmanship, is equal to the firm's earlier repertoire. The MWPI table is emblematic of the firm's highest level of achievement.

JP

32

Armchair, ca. 1850–70

Attributed to Elijah Galusha (active ca. 1828–70)
Troy, New York

In *The Architecture of Country Houses* (1850), Andrew Jackson Downing illustrated "*Elizabethan chairs* of modern designs, suited to the library or drawing-room" and commented that "chairs in this style, but of a great variety of designs and highly elaborate carving, may now be found in the principal warehouses in our largest cities."[1] This library chair, probably made a decade or two after Downing's popularization of the style, is the embodiment of an elaborate variation of the Elizabethan chair. For its aesthetic success the designer of this chair relied on a balance of rectilinear decorative elements, C-scrolls, and naturalistic shapes gathered within an angular outline. The turned and carved stiles terminate in finials, and the apex of the simple rounded-arch crest rail is crowned by carved openwork. The upholstered back is framed by scrolled carving that concludes with scallop shells at the lower corners.[2] The arm supports, legs, and stretchers, all turned and carved, incorporate details such as spool turnings, stylized acanthus leaves, and shallowly carved block elements.

The MWPI chair may have been made in the shop of Elijah Galusha (1804-71). This attribution is based on several factors. Although few pieces of Galusha's work from the 1860s have been documented, numerous examples of his furniture in the rococo style survive and are documented by bills of sale.[3] The aesthetic evidence these works provide is validated by a comparison of the MWPI chair with a nearly identical chair in the collection of the Shaftsbury Historical Society in Shaftsbury, Vermont, Galusha's hometown.[4] The Shaftsbury chair descended in a branch of the Galusha family, and family tradition names Elijah Galusha as its maker.[5]

The MWPI chair is part of the furniture the Williams family acquired for Fountain Elms. Although much of this is documented, no receipts have been found for items purchased from 1859 to 1873. Ascribing this chair to Galusha, however, is in keeping with the Williams family's practice of patronizing cabinetmakers in upstate New York to complement their partiality to New York City shops.

This armchair, like the MWPI's Galusha étagère (see cat. no. 28), exhibits French lineage. Related side chairs with carved crests, spindle finials, turned stiles, and turned and block-shaped legs and stretchers are illustrated in contemporary French design periodicals such as Désiré Guilmard's *Le Garde-Meuble*. A close examination of the carved features on the crest of the MWPI chair further suggests Galusha as its maker. Here, foliage with floral garnishes angles upward to support a nosegay of flowers with gathered stems that are seemingly threaded into a mock cleft in the wood. Inside the triangle formed by these components is a scallop shell with a cabochon center. Similar flower-cluster and shell motifs are found in plate 4 of Guilmard's *Album des Ornemens d'Appartemens* (n.d.).[6] One of the elements in this plate, a depiction of a bunch of flowers with the stems tied together by a ribbon bow, is replicated in numerous examples of Galusha's documented work.[7]

ATD

50⅜ x 24½ x 22⅛ in.
Rosewood, walnut, white ash, modern upholstery
Provenance: Proctor Collection.
Proctor Collection, PC. 419

33

Side Chair, ca. 1850–55

Maker unknown
Probably New York, New York

MWPI's high-back chair is a classic interpretation of the Elizabethan revival style, popular in America in the 1860s and 1870s. The carved and pierced leafy scrolls (encased in a geometric framework at the crest of the chair), twisted spindles, cabochons, and drop finials are all elements common to European and American interpretations of the style. An examination of the construction of the chair reveals a variety of manufacturing techniques. The chair is fabricated of solid rosewood. An additional layer of wood was applied at the crest to achieve the necessary depth for the execution of the hand-carved face. The foliate pattern in the crest and the acanthus leaves at the tops of the front legs are also hand carved. In other areas, however, mass-production techniques were used in conjunction with hand carving to create an overall effect of intricate artistry. The "relief carvings" at the bottom corners of the seat back and within the central tablet on the seat rail, for example, are composed of wooden elements applied to flat surfaces. The casual viewer might conclude that the chair was costly to produce, but a more detailed exploration of construction would demonstrate otherwise.

The combination of workmanship and ornamentation imply that the maker of this chair was imitating the work of upper-echelon New York City cabinetmakers such as Alexander Roux and Charles Baudouine, who produced related examples. The use of intricate foliage within an angular framework and the incorporation of a carved mask at the crest compare to furniture attributed to Baudouine.[1] However, Baudouine's works exhibit finer craftsmanship, use laminated rosewood, and rely more heavily on rococo details than this chair does.

The grotesque mask in the MWPI chair's crest rail introduces a captivating motif that is possibly a derivation of the Green Man—a male face comprising leafy fragments, sometimes rendered with horns sprouting from its head or with vegetation growing from his mouth. On this chair the countenance is encircled by leaves and disports foliage at the top of the head and side of the face. The use of the Green Man motif can be traced to ancient Rome. By the nineteenth century, designers were most familiar with the image from its use as an architectural element that was incorporated into the decorative treatments on the exteriors of cathedrals and public buildings from as early as the fifteenth century.[2] Nineteenth-century American furniture artisans were also familiar with the Green Man through pictorial sources such as Owen Jones's *Grammar of Ornament* (1856), in which several plates incorporate variations on the Green Man motif as it appeared in Roman and Renaissance ornamentation. French furniture design publications such as Désiré Guilmard's *Garde-Meuble, Album de l'exposition de l'industrie, 1844* (1845) also illustrated the Green Man motif.[3] Another possible source for this face may have been the representations of the Green Man that became part of May Day celebrations during the nineteenth century.

The symbolism of the Green Man has varied throughout the centuries, but the likeness has been generally associated with life, renewal, and the taming of nature. The Green Man may have been considered an appropriate symbol for mid-nineteenth-century society as it embraced, perhaps ambivalently, burgeoning industrialization. The image on the chair may have been an expression of man's dominance over nature or a nostalgic token of a disappearing relationship with nature.

ATD

42⅜ x 18⅜ x 17½ in.
Rosewood, ash, modern upholstery
Provenance: Private collection, Reston, Virginia; MWPI.
Museum Purchase, 96.5

34

Chair, ca. 1850

Maker unknown, Shaker Community
New Lebanon, New York

The sect known as the Shakers is a Protestant millennial group whose celibate members live in a communal environment. Members settled first in New York and New England in the last decades of the eighteenth century. By 1810 Shaker settlements also existed in Ohio, Kentucky, and Indiana.[1] Only one very small community of Shakers, located at Sabbathday Lake, Maine, remains. At the sect's height of acceptance, however, hundreds of converts were added to the Shaker "families," which were independent entities with their own leaders, farms, and businesses. Geographically contiguous "families" were united into communities that often bore the name of the nearest town.[2]

The Shakers are widely recognized for creating a style of American furniture known for its simple elegance. Their designs, a natural outgrowth of the sect's beliefs in simplicity, humility, honesty, and prudence, were the results of their attempts to harmonize their surroundings with their beliefs. Most Shaker communities included workshops where members made chairs and other pieces of furniture; throughout the nineteenth century the Shaker community at New Lebanon, New York, the largest of the Shaker villages, made chairs for its own members and to sell to other Shaker villages and the public.[3] The history of chairmaking at New Lebanon is obscure, but surviving documents show that it had begun by 1789 and continued as a cottage industry until after the Civil War, when the business was greatly expanded.[4] Although Shaker records have yielded the names of some New Lebanon chairmakers (Gilbert Avery, Benjamin Lyon, and John Bishop), students of Shaker furniture have neither been able to connect chair styles with specific makers nor to date individual chairs precisely.[5] However, in the interval between the fabrication of the earliest eighteenth-century chairs and the production of the elegant chairs of the 1850s, Shaker seating furniture can be chronologically arranged according to evolving design details.[6]

The earliest New Lebanon chairs, the lathe-turned slat-back chairs common in the eighteenth century, have turnings as stout and decorative as their "worldly" counterparts. The Shaker-chair finials or pommels on the back posts are squat or bulbous. With straight backs and rear posts that meet the floor at right angles, the chairs are practical but rigidly uncomfortable. During the next few decades, Shaker chairmakers gradually changed this generic form into a uniquely Shaker creation. By the 1850s New Lebanon chairs had thinner turnings and had become progressively lighter. Shaker craftsmen had also elongated and refined the pommels, canted the front and rear posts to make the chairs more comfortable, reduced the diameter of the chair posts to about one and one-eighth inches, and replaced the traditional seats of splint, rush, or cloth webbing with cane.[7] Chairs became so delicate that a stout person might doubt the wisdom of sitting on one.

As early as 1820 small buttons or tilters—wooden balls held in sockets by rawhide cords that were threaded through the bottom of the tilter, drawn tightly, and pegged through a hole in the back post (inset)—were incorporated into Shaker chair design. These ingenious devices swiveled to permit the sitter to tilt backward while the rear feet of the chair remained flat on the floor. This stabilized the chair and kept its feet from marring the floor when a sitter leaned back. A few extraordinarily lightweight chairs were fitted with pewter tilters, patented by the Shakers in 1852.[8] Thus tilters date the chairs, and they identify the last stage of Shaker chair design before the sect began factory production.

The MWPI Shaker side chair most closely resembles New Lebanon chairs made about 1850.[9] Its posts and stretchers are thin, but they are not as delicate as those found on chairs from the patent-tilter era. The pommels are more elongated and refined with a smoother transition along the narrow neck than what is seen on the chairs of the early 1840s, and the chair has tilters of an early design. The MWPI chair was constructed to have a splint or cloth seat rather than a cane seat.

JVG and TDR

40 x 18⅝ x 14¾ in.
Soft maple, cloth tape
Tape seat is late-nineteenth or early-twentieth century
Provenance: Robert Herron, Austerlitz, New York; MWPI.
Museum Purchase with funds from the Verne S. Swan Fund, 70.7

87 x 52¼ x 20⅜ in.
Ebonized cherry, eastern white pine, mahogany, tulipwood, amaranth, bird's-eye maple, marquetry of various woods, gilded bronze, unidentified metal, gilding
Marquetry panel on central door refinished; band of marquetry on right front leg replaced; carved "snake" heads on pediment are modern
Provenance: William Doyle Galleries, New York, New York;
Private collection; Peter Hill, Inc., East Lempster, New Hampshire; MWPI.
Museum Purchase, 92.40

 35

Cabinet, ca. 1865–75

Maker unknown

Probably New York, New York

This colorful and imposing drawing room cabinet beautifully documents and displays the assertive visual qualities of Gilded Age America. Although its manufacturer is not now known, the object is a major example of a distinctive line of Franco-American furniture purveyed by New York's leading cabinetmakers in the decade of the 1860s.[1] Léon Marcotte, Pottier & Stymus, Alexander Roux, and Herter Brothers are potential candidates for maker of this piece, or it may have been produced by one of the many lesser-known firms listed in city business directories of the period.[2] Until a systematic analysis of major examples of furniture in this manner appears, attributions remain tentative.[3]

The style of this cabinet is easily recognized but not so easily named.[4] It is characterized by an eclectic combination of classical or classicizing features filtered through Renaissance, baroque, and *néo-grec* lenses. Preceded by the richly sculptural and typically curvilinear mode of midcentury and followed by the reductive rectilinearity of the English Reform movement, the style occupies and exemplifies a pivotal historical moment. It not only demonstrates yet another efflorescence of the classical tradition but also represents the figurative high-water mark of workmanship, visual complexity, and what might be called the courtly paradigm in nineteenth-century America.[5]

Like the rest of the group of objects to which it belongs, this cabinet celebrates and emulates the scale, splendor, and high-quality workmanship associated with aristocratic French and Continental furnishings of the seventeenth and eighteenth centuries. Embodying the assumption that appropriate models for nineteenth-century living could be found in the aristocratic past, the cabinet is an example of top-down diffusion. The political implications of the style were challenged at the time of its manufacture by democrats and populists and later by English reform and arts and crafts advocates.[6]

Within the aesthetic and ideological system that produced this cabinet, more is definitely better, particularly when the many components of an object display erudition and exemplary execution. Informed historical references and paraphrases were prized and, as in architecture in the same manner, outstanding objects were those that combined forceful massing of their major features and a highly complex composition with exquisite workmanship.[7] The most notable features of the composition on this cabinet are the concave semicylindrical niches, the intricate marquetry of the central door that dominates the upper section, and the exceptional quality of the rich and diverse ornamentation that adorns most of the other surfaces.[8]

Color plays an important role here. Like many aspects of this cabinet, it is historically referential. Gold has obvious courtly associations, as does the use of marquetry and contrasting woods. Less apparently meaningful, but perhaps more significant, are the extensive ebonized surfaces of the object. Black not only provides the strongest possible foil for gilt surfaces and for light-colored woods but also evokes the origins of modern cabinetmaking. The importation of ebony into seventeenth-century Europe created a ripple effect that eventually and irrevocably transformed furnituremaking throughout the western world. Ebony was beautiful to look at but difficult to work. Furniture makers found that it was best used in thin sheets—or veneers—over secondary woods. Veneering subsequently became the basis of cabinetmaking. Because much of the early experimentation with ebony took place in France, cabinetmaking became *ébénisterie*, and cabinetmakers became *ébénistes*. The ebonized surfaces of the MWPI cabinet serve as visual links to traditional French *ébénisterie* and its reputation for excellence.[9]

Cultural change, the doctrines and dogmas of passing movements in the arts, and an increasing awareness of the ideologies often embodied in art and design have affected latter-day assessments of objects like this cabinet. Its celebration of ornament and its historical references have offended modernists, while its overt elitism has sometimes upset egalitarians. In the late years of the twentieth century, however, when traditional education in the arts and humanities is on the wane and fine workmanship in architecture and furnishings is largely a thing of the past, many people once again find the art historical references and dazzling workmanship of this cabinet profoundly appealing.[10]

KLA

 36

Cabinet, ca. 1865–70

Alexander Roux (active 1836–80)
New York, New York

Alexander Roux (1813-86) was born in Gap, France, and emigrated to the United States.[1] By 1836 he established a cabinetmaking shop on Broadway in New York City.[2] Roux's prosperous trade included domestic and imported furniture as well as interior decorating services. He steadily capitalized on his French ancestry and training by promoting himself as a "French cabinet maker" and by emulating the French styles his clientele favored.[3]

Roux formed several partnerships during his business years. Between 1847 and 1848 he worked with his brother Frédéric, who later moved to California and eventually returned to Paris.[4] Established as a Parisian *ébéniste*, Frédéric shipped merchandise to his brother in New York City. A ca. 1856 advertisement for Alexander Roux explains that he, "having established a new house . . . [in] Paris, is now prepared to take orders for French fancy inlaid Buhl and Mosaic Furniture."[5] From 1858 through 1859 Alexander was in partnership with Joseph Cabus, a former Roux foreman.[6] In 1865 Roux had a brief association with Amand A. Chatain, who had been a designer with the New York City firm of Pottier & Stymus.[7] Roux restructured his firm in 1870 when his son Alexander J. joined him. His brother Frédéric returned from Paris in 1870 or 1871 and retained an association with the business until his retirement in 1873.

Alexander Roux's shop had various locations on Broadway until 1877, when the firm's contiguous factory buildings on Mercer Street burned.[8] Fully covered by insurance, the business subsequently moved to larger facilities on 5th Avenue and 18th Street.[9] Alexander Roux retired in 1880 and died in 1886, but the firm remained in operation under the direction of his son until 1897 or 1898.

By 1850 Roux was touted as the finest cabinetmaker on Broadway. In *The Architecture of Country Houses* (1850), Andrew Jackson Downing, the cultivator of popular taste, noted, "In New York, the rarest and most elaborate designs, especially for the drawing-room and library use, are to be found at the warehouse of Roux, in Broadway." He later applauded Roux's designs as "the most tasteful" renditions of "Louis Quatorze, Renaissance, Gothic, etc., to be found in this country."[10] Downing's endorsement is affirmed by an examination of extant labeled Roux furniture. The cabinets Roux designed in the mid-1860s are among his most finely crafted items. American-made drawing room cabinets drew upon eighteenth- and nineteenth-century French antecedents and consequently are called "French cabinets." The form reprised classically derived motifs and numerous artistic formulae including carving, marquetry, ormolu mounts, porcelain and bronze plaques, and, in some cases, *pietre dure* (flat mosaic images composed of colored stones) plaques, or handpainted designs. Most of New York City's leading firms made this style of cabinet. This prepossessing form, with little utilitarian function, communicated the wealth of its owner by providing an extravagant stage for personal bibelots and art pieces.[11]

The MWPI cabinet is aesthetically and technically superior to the work of many of Roux's competitors.[12] Tripartite in arrangement, the rosewood cabinet has concave sides flanking a central door that is topped with a shape-conforming flat surface capped by a plinth. Compartmentalized decoration is segregated by the play of light against dark—ormolu mounts and incised, gilded framing highlight the ebonized and dark-colored woods.

Marquetry panels and ormolu mounts are prominent features on Roux's French cabinets. The marquetry panels of wheat (within two-dimensional columns beside the central door) and of flowers (on the concave sections), as well as the ormolu bands, rosettes, classical roundels, Ionic capitals, and frame around the painted plaque on this example, can also be found on other labeled Roux parlor cabinets. One mount on the MWPI example is marked "R" on the back.[13] It is conceivable that Roux's sizable establishment—the factory employed 120 hands in 1855 and by 1856 occupied several buildings—had the capability to produce elaborate bronze mounts.[14] Alternatively, Roux may have purchased these mounts from a specialty factory, such as P. E. Guerin in New York City, or, as was presumably the case with the marquetry panels and porcelain plaque that appear on this piece, imported the merchandise from France. The MWPI cabinet carries an impressed mark, "A. Roux," in four locations on the back (fig. 32).[15]

ATD

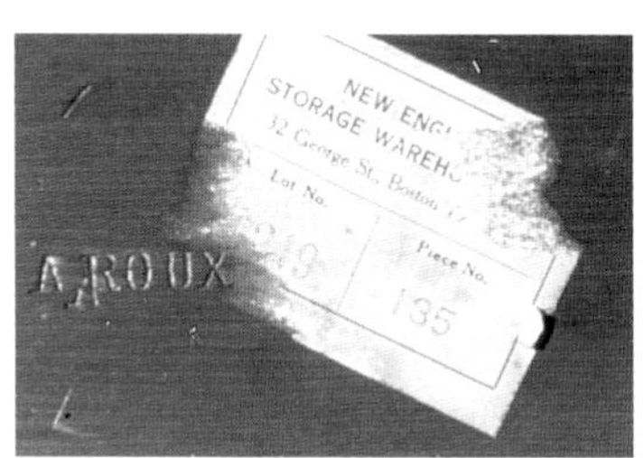

Fig. 32

49⅞ x 51½ x 18⅛ in.
Impressed stamp four times on back (fig. 32): "A. ROUX";
one mount marked with "R" on back.
Paper label on back (fig. 32): "NEW ENG[LAND]/STORAGE WAREHO[USE]/
32 George St., Boston/Lot No./[?]219/Piece no./135"
Rosewood, curly maple, black walnut, eastern white pine, cherry, yellow-poplar,
marquetry of various woods, gilded bronze, painted porcelain, gilding
Finish restored at Williamstown Art Conservation Center, 1989
Provenance: Paul M. Callahan and Jean Singer, New York; MWPI.
Gift of George and Barbara Callahan, 86.85

37

Cabinet, ca. 1865–75

Maker unknown
Probably New York, New York

It is difficult to know which is more impressive, the visual impact of this imposing cabinet or how little is known about it. The object belongs to an extended group of richly detailed case pieces presumably manufactured in East Coast cities—most likely New York—in the 1860s and 1870s.[1] Little else about its origins can be stated with certainty except that the Husted family, its one-time owners, held that the cabinet once belonged to James S. Sherman, vice president under President William H. Taft, until his death in Utica in October 1912. In concept, configuration, and a number of details, the bottom portion of this cabinet bears a strong resemblance to several other cabinets that have entered major public and private collections during the last two decades.[2]

What sets the MWPI cabinet apart is the addition of a mirrored upper section. Three tabernacle-shaped mirrors dominate the piece and give it a decidedly vertical emphasis. The effect is intensified by the turned finials atop the two smaller, flanking mirrors and by the elaborate framework that rises above the central mirror. These prominent mirrors suggest that the cabinet may have been intended for installation opposite a mantel or that it may have been the focal point of the room in which it was originally placed.

The object's considerable visual impact is due to its height and to its design, workmanship, and materials. Like other objects to which it is related, this cabinet provides a partial anthology of historical cabinetmaking techniques, including veneering, gilding, ebonizing, incising, and marquetry, and of applied decoration, which here includes metal mounts and a painted ceramic plaque. The two female figures that visually support the middle unit of the lower section are bronze, as is the male head (portraying an ancient or early medieval king?) in the circular frame in the upper section. The colorful ceramic plaque depicts a classicized scene; other ceramic inserts may have originally flanked the center mirror where empty spaces now appear. As is typical of furniture in this style, carving plays a very minor role.

Like so much of Victorian design, the style of this cabinet eludes easy definition.[3] The designer created an eclectic and engaging combination of forms and motifs, most of which paraphrase rather than quote historical antecedents. Although many of the features of the cabinets in this group echo classical or neoclassical prototypes, this cabinet's tripartite composition, coupled with its soaring central mirror, imparts a vaguely Gothic flavor. Yet the only features that might be considered Gothic are the attenuated columns adorned with incised vines of ivy and the monarch's head at the top.

The form of this cabinet is not conventional. The base section is familiar and closely resembles other horizontal-format cabinets.[4] With the mirrors added, however, the familiarity vanishes and a form with few contemporary parallels emerges.[5] Although the top and bottom sections of this cabinet seem to have been together always, the rarity of this arrangement suggests that the upper section was specially designed as an addition to a more or less stock base.

What this cabinet may indicate most clearly is that knowledge of high-style nineteenth-century furniture is today where knowledge of eighteenth-century furniture was in about 1920. We have a general sense of the terrain, but the specifics remain elusive. Enough of this furniture has been located to offer an exceptional research opportunity to the adventurous scholar who is willing to subject it to systematic analysis. Close examination of the many examples now known should make it possible to sort the objects into groups. And that, at least, might be a first step toward a better understanding of this body of highly impressive, but still lamentably under-known, furniture.

KLA

113½ x 73 x 23 in.
Rosewood, unidentified secondary woods, marquetry of various woods, glass, bronze, porcelain, gilding
Provenance: Mr. and Mrs. William G. Husted, Whitesboro, New York; MWPI.
Gift of Mr. and Mrs. William G. Husted, 87.33

54¾ x 26⅝ x 15½ in.
Rosewood, satinwood, curly soft maple, eastern white pine, cherry,
black walnut, yellow-poplar, marquetry of various woods and pewter, gilding
Provenance: Margot Johnson, Inc., New York, New York; MWPI.
Museum Purchase with funds from the Wallace Thurston Bequest, 90.56

38

MUSIC CABINET, ca. 1868–72

Herter Brothers (active 1864–1906)
New York, New York

GUSTAVE HERTER (1830-98) and his brother Christian (1839-83) established Herter Brothers in New York City in 1864.[1] Sons of an *ébéniste* in Stuttgart, the Herters were among thousands of German emigrants who came to America by way of New York City during the 1840s and 1850s. Young Gustave arrived in 1848 and quickly distinguished himself as a craftsman. Although he described himself as a "Bildhauer," or sculptor, it was as "a designer of patterns for rich furniture" that Gustave made his reputation.[2] In 1853 he was credited with the design of three important pieces displayed at the Crystal Palace Exhibition in New York. After a brief partnership with Auguste Pottier from 1851 to 1853 and a longer association with Erastus Bulkley from 1853 to 1858, Gustave started his own firm—called Gustave Herter—at 547 Broadway and expanded his practice to include the full spectrum of interior decoration. By April 1859 Christian Herter had arrived in New York and soon was working for his brother. He became a partner in the firm, newly styled as Herter Brothers, five years later.[3]

Building upon Gustave Herter's earlier success, the firm of Herter Brothers rose to preeminence among New York City cabinetmakers and decorators after the Civil War. Many of the city's wealthy citizens who became Herter clients in the 1860s—risk-taking financiers, real estate magnates, and railroad men—solicited more work from the firm around 1880. In 1870 Gustave retired and returned with his family to Germany. Christian assumed artistic control of the firm, then located at 877-879 Broadway near Union Square. In 1883 his career was cut short by his death at the age of forty-four; the firm, however, continued in operation until 1906.

Throughout the early 1870s Herter Brothers worked in the Parisian style of Second Empire France. Carving, much esteemed during the 1850s, was eschewed during the 1860s in favor of rich surface decoration achieved with veneers, contrasting woods, painting, and gilding. The firm's work is distinguished by its formally inventive interpretation of the prevailing style and by a distinctive and consistent vocabulary that, in the absence of marks (as in the case of the MWPI music cabinet), identifies the maker. The lyre on the door, the Ionic capitals atop each of the legs (reiterated in the plaque above the door), and the rectangular spiral (incised and gilded to emphasize each corner of the base) are elements derived from Second Empire decoration that were absorbed into the Herter lexicon. The firm's excellent craftsmanship is noteworthy. The frame-and-panel construction, seamless rosewood veneers, and memorable marquetry of this cabinet exemplify the high quality that is typical of Herter furniture.

The MWPI cabinet can be dated between 1868 and 1872. Its weighty presence and the configuration of the legs and feet suggest that it was made when Gustave was still involved with the firm, before 1870. Similar marquetry lyres, applied plaques, and stop flutes appear in contemporaneous Herter commissions including several rooms for the LeGrand Lockwood mansion in Norwalk, Connecticut, of about 1867-69.[4] However, the linear marquetry patterns on this music cabinet appear on cabinets associated with Thurlow Lodge in Menlo Park, California, decorated between 1872 and 1873 after Gustave left the firm. The band under the cornice—meandering vines interrupted by shield-shaped rosewood insets that display a frilly variation of the French fleur-de-lys in pewter—is unusual among Herter Brothers' distinctive marquetry patterns.[5]

The MWPI music cabinet illustrates how Herter Brothers' mastery of coloristic effects heightens the architectonic character of its furniture. Gilding emphasizes the structure of the rosewood carcass. Gilded stop flutes on the engaged columns flanking the door draw the eye upward, while the gold decoration on the apron stretches tautly across the horizontal edge of the base and balances the marquetry band above. Gilding also outlines the panel on each side of the cabinet and the capitals and turned legs that support the base on which the cabinet sits. Light-colored marquetry incorporating yellow, olive green, and red woods and the brilliant yellow satinwood of the interior—revealed when the door is open—contrast dramatically with the plum-colored rosewood.[6]

This type of cabinet-on-stand, with a spindle gallery and marquetry veneers, became popular in Europe in the seventeenth century.[7] The vertical and rectangular orientation of this one-door cabinet distinguishes it from the horizontal or square formats (usually with double doors) of its historical antecedents and from other cabinets-on-stand made by the Herter firm. Despite the universal importance of music in American homes during the nineteenth century, music cabinets are rare in Herter Brothers' oeuvre.[8]

CHV

 39

Armchair, ca. 1869

George Hunzinger (active 1860–98)
New York, New York

George Jacob Hunzinger (1835-98), the designer and maker of this eccentric armchair, was born September 12, 1835, in Tuttlingen, Germany, into a family that for two centuries had included cabinetmakers. In 1849 Hunzinger began an apprenticeship in the family shop and in 1853 went to Geneva, Switzerland, to serve as a journeyman.[1] Hunzinger emigrated to New York City in 1855 and settled in Brooklyn within the growing German immigrant population. He first appears in the Brooklyn directory in 1860, where he is listed as a cabinetmaker at 117½ Court Street. Little is known about Hunzinger's first years in America, but his obituary states that he worked with Auguste Pottier (1823-96) before opening an independent shop in 1860 on Centre Street in Manhattan. During the next two decades Hunzinger worked at eight different locations in lower Manhattan before building a factory in 1879 at 323-327 West 16th Street.[2]

Hunzinger was a successful manufacturer responsible for all the designs produced by his firm. At the time of Hunzinger's death his obituary noted that, stylistically, his furniture designs belonged to no school. Indeed, it is difficult to categorize his furniture according to the terms commonly used to describe nineteenth-century revival styles. The abstract qualities of Hunzinger's designs can be explained by a novel, prescient source of aesthetic inspiration. Hunzinger was one of the first American furniture makers whose designs were inspired by the means of production—the machine. The crisply turned members and geometric details of Hunzinger's pared-down furniture resemble parts of the very machines that produced them.

Hunzinger's designs not only looked forward to the machine age; his concepts of marketing and production anticipated modern practices. Between 1860 and 1899 Hunzinger secured twenty-one technical patents for ingenious extension, swivel-top, and nesting tables; folding and reclining chairs; convertible beds; general structural innovations; and novel applications of new and existing materials.[3] He utilized these inventions as marketing tools, stamping each piece of furniture with his name and the appropriate patent date. In addition, he offered consumers a wide range of prices and presentations. The same chair could be purchased in a variety of finishes and stains including maple, cherry, walnut, ebony, and gilded wood. Offering upholstery of different qualities and prices was another strategy Hunzinger used to increase his market share.[4] Although he primarily made "fancy" chairs that were intended to be used singly or as mismatched pairs, Hunzinger also produced a limited number of occasional tables, daybeds, and settees.[5]

The proper left back leg of this idiosyncratic armchair bears the impressed mark (inset) "Hunzinger, N.Y." and the patent date. This patent is for the diagonal side brace that connects the back stiles with the midpoint of the side seat rail and then becomes the front leg. According to the patent application letter that defends this invention, the addition of a diagonal brace increased the strength of the chair. In using the diagonal brace to form the front leg and to cantilever the seat, Hunzinger altered traditional chair design.[6] His innovation in chair construction preoccupied furniture designers in the early twentieth century. While the cantilevered seat implies calculated balance, the construction also suggests change; the chair looks as if it could fold, but it is, in fact, fixed. The implied metamorphosis energizes the design.

This chair is an important example of late nineteenth-century protomodernism, yet its design is not entirely ahistorical and can be understood in the context of stylistic revivalism. The abbreviated structural form, the implied capacity to fold, and the textile back slung between the stiles are features found in chairs inspired by ancient and neoclassical folding chairs.[7] The baluster-shaped vertical supports at the front of the chair and the turned and applied buttons have classical and Renaissance associations. Although devoid of any naturalistic decoration or ancient motifs, the classical allusion of the form suggests that this chair is an example of the *néo-grec* style, another of the episodic resurgences of classicism that punctuated the nineteenth century.

BRH

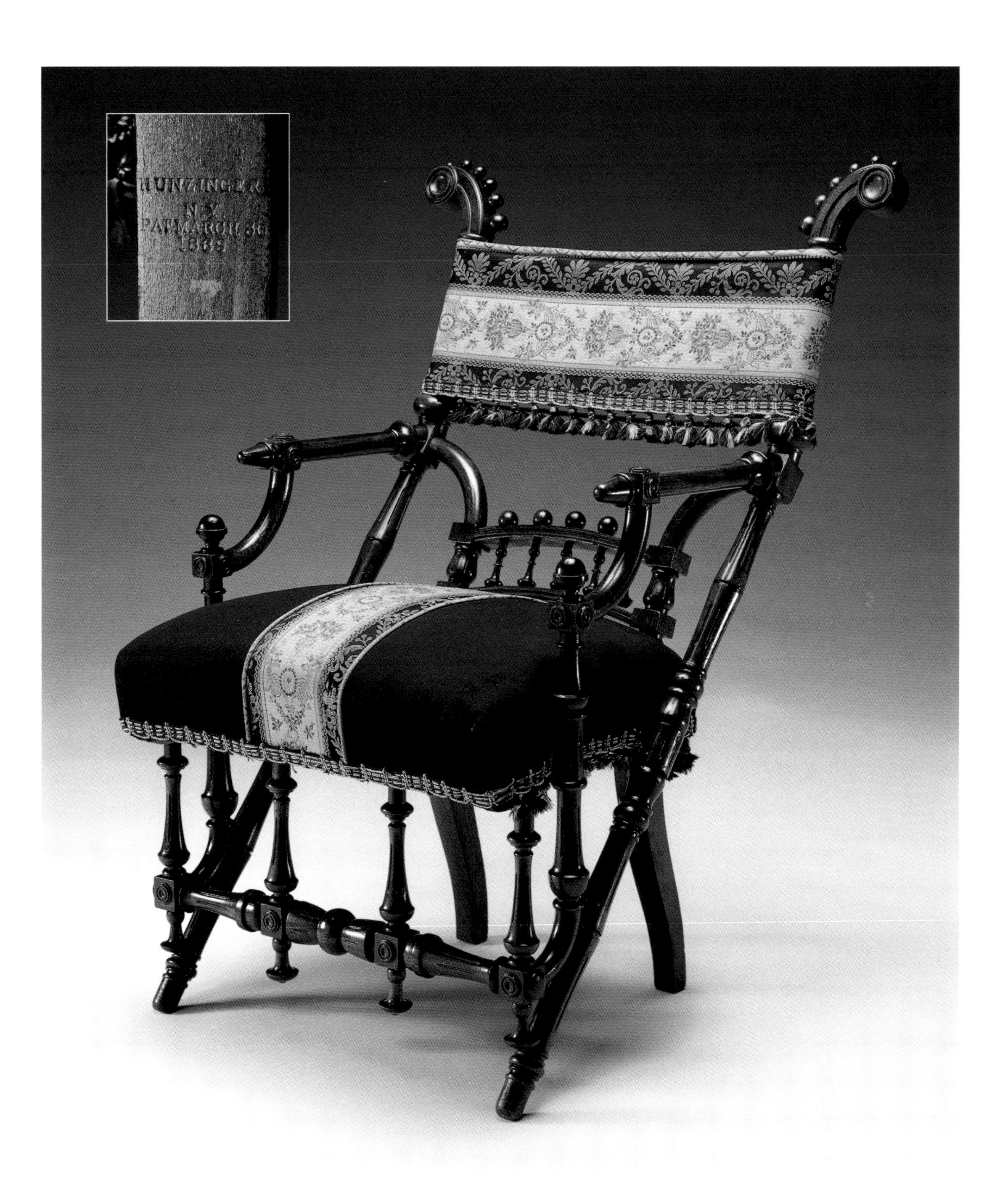

35½ x 26⅜ x 25 in.
Impressed mark: "HUNZINGER/N.Y./PAT.MARCH 30/1869"
Walnut, black ash, modern upholstery
Small losses, modern upholstery
Provenance: Hamish Hog Antiques (Helen Hersh), Brooklyn, New York;
The Brooklyn Museum of Art, Brooklyn, New York; MWPI.
Museum Purchase, in part with funds from the Mrs. Erving Pruyn Fund, 93.21

35⅛ x 57¾ x 23½ in.
Marked: "C. F. PALMER UTICA N.Y. MFG'R/FERN/
PHOENIX/IRON/WORKS/UTICA/N.Y." and "FERN"
Cast iron, modern paint
Provenance: Private collection, Utica, New York; MWPI.
Museum Purchase, 84.16.1

40

Settee, ca. 1870–80

Phoenix Iron Works (active ca. 1863–1906)
Utica, New York

In the mid-nineteenth century, cast iron was elevated from a utilitarian metal to an aesthetic form. Ease of manufacture and assembly made it an ideal industrial material for buildings and furnishings. The use of cast iron, a favored material for outdoor furniture, was also part of a wider Victorian movement to tame nature through "civilizing" artifacts. The MWPI settee, a product from a once-thriving regional industry, attests to the nineteenth-century desire to tame the outside world through furnishings.

Mass-production techniques and improvements in foundry manufacturing methods made cast-iron furniture affordable for middle- as well as upper-class Victorian consumers. The process of casting iron required an original wood model designed by a skilled craftsman, or another cast-iron piece from which castings were directly made.[1] This latter process permitted manufacturers to copy a competitor's creations quickly, and thus the market became flooded with favored designs. This example, for instance, is in the popular "fern and blackberry" motif manufactured by several firms.[2] Although some designs were patented, opportunistic businessmen were not deterred from copying them.[3] Unfortunately, the majority of craftsmen did not patent their designs, and these artisans remain undocumented.[4] Competing foundries could credit their products, however, by casting the firm name directly into the cast-iron seats. The maker of the MWPI settee promoted his work by casting "C. F. PALMER UTICA N.Y. MFG'R/FERN/PHOENIX/IRON/WORKS/UTICA/N.Y." into the diaper-patterned seat.[5]

Designers strove to make industrially produced cast-iron furniture appear to be a product of nature.[6] Cast-iron furniture evolved from mid-nineteenth-century designs of naturalistic, rustic forms in imitation of bound branches and twigs to rigid and controlled styles that expressed the desire to domesticate nature. The design of the MWPI settee is derived from the popular Victorian houseplant and implies the dominance of artifice over nature.[7] On the MWPI example the fern-leaf motif forms the main structure of the back. The fern-and-blackberry design first appeared in American trade catalogues in the 1870s.[8] Of European origin, the pattern has arcing fern foliage, suspended blackberry clusters, and symmetrically arranged fronds contained within the crest rail in a naturalistic yet highly controlled fashion. The legs suggest a cabriole shape by curving inward and back while ending in small ball feet. The back, sides, and legs of the settee are one continuous casting, while the seat is cast separately and bolted into place. A wrought-iron brace supports the seat and prevents the legs from splaying.

Chauncey Palmer (1807-84) was born in the Oneida County, New York, town of North Bridgewater, and received his training in woodworking and cabinetmaking prior to moving to Utica in 1828. He soon began a partnership with Lewis Lawrence and opened the first wood planing mill in Utica.[9] In 1853 Palmer established an independent foundry containing a machine shop and iron-railing works at 55 Blandina Street. His business was twice destroyed by fire. In 1863 Palmer rebuilt his foundry and changed the name from C. Palmer & Company to Phoenix Iron Works, in reference to the mythological bird that rose from its own ashes. Advertisements illustrate that in addition to cast-iron seating, Phoenix Iron Works manufactured urns, garden statuary, fountains, fencing, architectural castings, and hardware.[10] Under the direction of Chauncey's son Cyrus (1830-1906), the foundry continued to prosper and to expand its line of wares until Cyrus's death.[11]

DSB

41

Pedestal and Worktable, ca. 1870

Kilian Brothers (active 1856–ca. 1920)
New York, New York

The pedestal and the worktable are exemplary of the workmanship and stylistic approach of the New York City firm Kilian Brothers.[1] Both pieces are illustrated in the company's album of photographs of about 1870 (figs. 33 and 34).[2] Kilian Brothers manufactured high-style, yet affordable, goods that suited the aesthetic sensibilities of a middle-class clientele. A report on the firm's display at the Centennial Exhibition in Philadelphia (1876) characterized the firm's products: "As extensive use of machinery is made in their manufacture, the goods are recommended for cheapness, being within reach of people of moderate means who have a taste for the ornamental."[3]

Theodore (b. 1828 or 1829) and Frederick (b. 1831 or 1832) Kilian, German emigrants, formed "Kilian and Brother" in 1856 or 1857 and adopted the name "Kilian Brothers" in 1858. In 1860 or 1861 they were joined by a third brother, William (b. 1834 or 1835).[4] This prosperous family business owned and occupied at least three buildings, utilized steam-powered machinery by 1869, and employed as many as 110 people in 1870.[5] Kilian Brothers held a patent for a folding chair and at various times sold mantelpieces and operated a carpet-cleaning business in addition to manufacturing and retailing furniture. After the death of its founders, the enterprise was managed by other family members, presumably the sons of William and Theodore, until 1919.

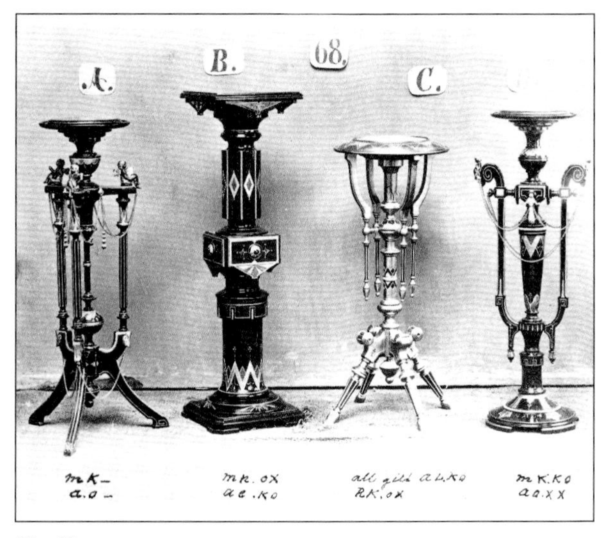

Fig. 33

The MWPI pedestal is composed of a turned body that is flanked by two handle-like appendages. Mass production and high fashion, united by vivacious ornamentation, enliven the simple form. The polychrome decoration of gold, blue-green, red, and black is a characteristic interpretation of what was believed at the time to be a classical palette. Painted and gilded incising create palmettes, bands, stripes, and geometric patterns in accordance with Greek and Egyptian motifs from Owen Jones's *Grammar of Ornament* (1856). The application of rich colors to the abstracted geometric patterns accentuates the angularity of the composition. A bronze-colored and vert metal putti crowns the termination point of each appendage and contrasts with the woodwork colors. The fusion of these decorative devices creates a successful interpretation of the *néo-grec* style, which reached its apogee in America during the 1870s.

That numerous firms, such as Clarke Brothers of Brooklyn and James W. Cooper of Philadelphia, carried similar pedestals attests to the popularity of the form. Kilian Brothers, active in both retail and wholesale markets in and outside New York City, could have

39 x 14 x 12½ in.
Walnut, bronze, patinated metal, gilding, paint
Provenance: Margot Johnson, Inc., New York, New York; MWPI.
Gift of Mrs. Arnold Gingrich, by exchange, 92.2

Fig. 33. Page from an album of furniture photographs, Kilian Brothers, ca. 1870. Courtesy, The Winterthur Library: Joseph Downs Collection of Manuscripts and Printed Ephemera, no. 72x360.37, col. 305.

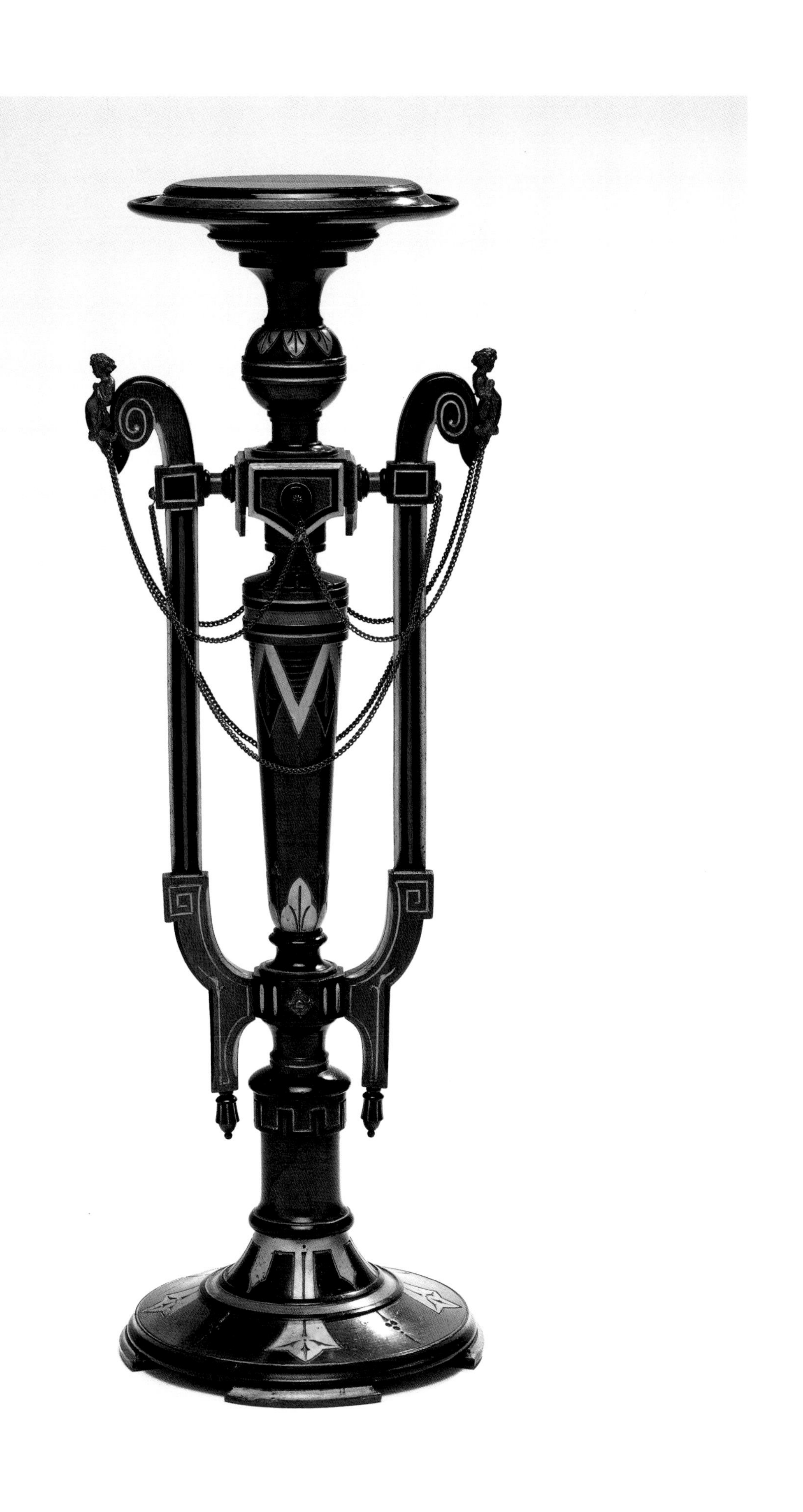

manufactured some of the pedestals depicted in other makers' catalogues.

The simple hinged box of this worktable is supported by four angular legs that terminate in abstract hoof feet. The delicate legs, mounted with Renaissance-inspired figureheads, are embellished with black highlights and incised green and gold lines. The box section features burled veneer panels on all sides, two of which are decorated with bronze roundels of classical figures and with incised green lines. The hinged lid, with a mirror on its under-side, opens to disclose a divided tray that can be removed to allow access to a small compartment. This worktable and the pedestal have identical mounts and similar color schemes.

Kilian Brothers utilized interchangeable decorative parts to offer a broad variety of forms and levels of ornamentation at little additional cost. For example, Kilian Brothers' 1872 price list records three variations of this worktable—a plain model selling for sixteen dollars; a "finished and richly ornamented" example priced at twenty-four dollars; and the same table with a "marquetrie top, black & gilt" for twenty-eight dollars.[6] The top of the MWPI worktable has a marquetry panel flush with the rest of the top, which differs from the raised, round panel on the model featured in the circa 1870 catalogue.

As with other parlor accessories illustrated in the firm's catalogue, the designs of the pedestal and worktable are indebted to English and French antecedents. The forms refer to candlestand and pedestal designs often reproduced in nineteenth-century design publications. Illustrations in V. Quetin's *Le Magasin de Meubles* in the 1870s, for example, present colorful jardinieres with ormolu mounts, chain ornamentation, and delicate leg supports.[7] The MWPI worktable and pedestal are fanciful objects that exhibit the makers' knowledge of the prevailing fashion, yet they are functional. As chic accessories for updating an interior, they served to demonstrate an owner's awareness of the latest trends.

ATD

Fig. 34

31 x 13¾ x 13¾ in.
Mounts marked "2459"
Black walnut, mahogany, birch, maple, marquetry of various woods, bronze, glass, gilding, paint
Provenance: 19th-Century America (Priscilla St. Germain), Lafayette, Louisiana; MWPI.
Museum Purchase, in part with funds from the Sarah T. Norris Fund, 93.15

Fig. 34. Page from an album of furniture photographs, Kilian Brothers, ca. 1870.
Courtesy, The Winterthur Library: Joseph Downs Collection
of Manuscripts and Printed Ephemera, no. 72x360.37, col. 305.

42

ARMCHAIR, ca. 1870–75

Attributed to M. & H. Schrenkeisen (active 1859–1903)
New York, New York

Fig. 35

THIS ARMCHAIR IS PART of a relatively large group of related seating furniture with individual examples differing from one another primarily in their carved details.[1] The chair and matching sofa (not shown) have been attributed to the shop of John Jelliff (1813-93) in Newark, New Jersey, but the extraordinary similarity of these pieces to the "Grand Duchess" suite photographically illustrated in the 1872 catalogue of the New York City firm of M. & H. Schrenkeisen suggests that the latter firm probably made them.[2] With its incised and gilded detailing, female head on the crest rail, and pendant drops, the MWPI chair is virtually identical to the example in the Schrenkeisen catalogue (fig. 35). The only significant difference is the substitution, on the MWPI chair, of scrolled arm supports in place of ones terminating with female heads. This variation is not surprising given the options available to retailers ordering from Schrenkeisen. Parlor suites, for example, were available "plain or carved" or with "extra heavy carving," and furniture frames could feature oil or varnish finishes with or without gilded detailing. Clients could specify whether they wanted upholstery and, if so, what they preferred for stuffing and fabric and tufting patterns.

Parlor suites—generally consisting of a sofa, two armchairs, and four side chairs—ranged in price from $17.50 for unembellished, unupholstered frames to the elaborate "Grand Duchess" suite covered in silk for $266 wholesale, a considerable sum in the 1870s.[3] It is likely that the retailer doubled these prices to cover his overhead and profit. Therefore, furniture like the MWPI chair—featuring two expensive, labor-intensive options of diamond tufting and gilded detailing—was beyond the reach of all but wealthy consumers.[4]

M. & H. Schrenkeisen was an important New York City cabinetmaking firm during the last half of the nineteenth century. Henry Schrenkeisen (d. 1887) worked as a cabinetmaker from at least 1851, but company catalogues state that the firm was founded in 1859, the year the carver and cabinetmaker's shop of John M. Schrenkeisen, possibly the father of Henry and Martin, opened at 39 Attorney Street.[5] M. & H. Schrenkeisen apparently emerged as a major force in the New York furniture trade in 1863 when Martin Schrenkeisen (d. ca. 1900), who moved the workshop to 65 Suffolk Street, is first listed in city directories. Two years later the concern was listed as M. Schrenkeisen & Brother; in 1867 the name changed to M. & H. Schrenkeisen and remained so for thirty years; after that it was called Schrenkeisen Company until 1903.[6]

Martin, whom contemporaries noted stood "high as to character & integrity," seems to have been the driving force behind the success of the business.[7] Under his leadership the company expanded dramatically and increased in value from approximately $125,000 in 1871 to $500,000 in 1885.[8] During this period M. & H. Schrenkeisen also grew in physical size and reputation. The firm moved into larger factory and showroom space twice by 1874, when R. G. Dun & Company termed it "one of the best houses in New York." Schrenkeisen pieces won a medal at the Centennial Exhibition in Philadelphia in 1876.[9] In spite of the praise the firm received in its day, M. & H. Schrenkeisen is hardly known today. The fact that the company sold wholesale to retailers probably means that it did not label its furniture, thus making identification difficult.

New York's furniture trade was exceptionally complicated in the nineteenth century with scores of firms making everything from specialized furniture parts to entire matching suites.[10] The Schrenkeisen company appears to have been of the latter type, manufacturing and upholstering a variety of furniture forms in several styles. Trade catalogues illustrate that the company was still producing furniture for the rococo revival taste in the late 1860s, but it soon phased out this mode in favor of what is now broadly called the Renaissance revival style.[11] MWPI's chair is in this style and reveals how little this style drew, in reality, from Renaissance design. In fact, nineteenth-century observers would have considered this piece to be in the French taste because of its affinity with contemporary French design. This French orientation is also reflected in the names of the parlor suites listed in the 1871 Schrenkeisen price list—"Grand Duchess," "Pompadour," "Marie Antoinette," and "Napoleon." By the late 1870s Schrenkeisen moved away from these heavy, French-inspired styles toward the lighter designs of the aesthetic movement.[12]

CV

43½ x 32 x 28¼ in.
Matching sofa (not shown): 77¾ x 47¼ x 35 in.
Rosewood, ash, eastern white pine, gilding, reproduction upholstery
Provenance: Mildred Bisselle Fewlass Estate, New York Mills, New York; MWPI.
Gift of the Mildred Bisselle Fewlass Estate, 86.82.2

Fig. 35. *"Grand Duchess" Chair.* Detail from *Supplement to Illustrated Catalogue of Parlor Furniture Manufactured by M. & H. Schrenkeisen, Warerooms: No. 17 Elizabeth Street, near Canal, Factory, Nos. 328, 330, 332 & 334 Cherry Street, New York City*, 1872. Courtesy, The Winterthur Library: Printed Book and Periodical Collection.

43

CHAIR, ca. 1873–80

Maker unknown
Possibly San Francisco, California

BY THE LATE 1860s Americans were moving toward a new design mode—set in motion in England—known as the aesthetic movement. One component of this reform initiative was the inauguration of "Modern Gothic," a reinterpretation of the architecturally accurate Gothic style that had been popular at midcentury. The design vocabulary of modern Gothic furniture features simple functional forms with straightforward construction. Ornamentation is subordinate to the object, appropriate to the form, and honest to the material. Publications such as Bruce Talbert's *Gothic Forms Applied to Furniture, Metal Work, and Decoration for Domestic Purposes* (1867) and Charles Locke Eastlake's *Hints on Household Taste in Furniture, Upholstery, and Other Details* (1868) attempted to refine the public aesthetic by publishing furniture designs in the modern Gothic style. Advocates of the modern Gothic mode endorsed the use of adornment that was derived, but not directly copied, from nature. Abstracted natural motifs, promulgated in English designer Christopher Dresser's publications, were easily adapted to modern Gothic objects and became an insignia of the style.

The broad, weighty frame of the MWPI upholstered armchair encloses a deep box seat and square back. At the tops of the legs, center of the seat rail, and termination points of the curved back stiles, the light-colored maple framework is contrasted by darker, applied, stylized rosettes of shallowly carved walnut. The overall frame features incised, geometric lines; abstracted renderings of leaves; and applied semicircular emblems of radiating petals.

The architectural properties of this chair are lightened by the rich color and pattern of the original upholstery.[1] A polychromatic, jacquard-woven, silk-and-cotton fabric around the midsection and sides of the chair is divided by bands of deep purple silk velvet. The aesthetic-style pattern of the multicolored material features blocks enclosing motifs such as sunflowers, geometric figures, and stylized botanical elements. Analysis shows that the fabric color was originally more vibrant with a golden brown ground and figures in purple, pale blue, black, cream, and red.[2] The fabric, a rare survival, is probably an example of what was termed "raw silk upholstery" in the 1870s and 1880s; the 1878 catalogue of McDonough, Wilsey & Company, a Chicago furniture-manufacturing firm, explained that "the most fashionable goods used for covering Parlor Work at present are Bourettes or Raw Silks," the latter described as "of unspun silk, dyed and woven in every color and pattern."[3] M. & H. Schrenkeisen of New York City also endorsed the use of figured, raw silk furniture coverings; its 1879 catalogue pictures two rocking chairs with upholstery similar to that on this chair—figured "'raw silk,' with Plush Top and Front."[4]

In addition to the importance of its historic upholstery, the MWPI chair has a celebrated provenance. The chair, along with nine matching pieces en suite, was sold at the 1942 auction of the contents of Sherwood Hall in California, part of the estate of Mary (Mrs. Timothy) Hopkins.[5] Built between 1872 and 1873, Sherwood Hall was originally fitted by Herter Brothers of New York City.[6] Herter Brothers probably shipped most of the furniture from its New York warerooms, but the firm may also have relied on local California craftsmen for some aspects of the work, or the entire suite may be a later addition to the furnishings of the home. Recent wood analysis reveals that western Pacific cedar was used in the construction of the seat-cushion frame; this fact, along with a California provenance, suggests that the chair may have been the work of a San Francisco shop.[7] It is also possible that the chair frame was shipped to California from the East Coast before it was upholstered. Acquired by Universal Studios in 1942, this chair and its matching pieces were used as movie props before the suite was sold at auction in 1991.[8]

ATD

38⅛ x 26¼ x 28¼ in.
White oak, walnut, Port-Orford (western Pacific) cedar, consolidated original upholstery
Provenance: Mrs. Timothy Hopkins Estate, Menlo Park, California; Butterfield & Butterfield, *Sherwood Hall: The Estate of the Late Mary E. Hopkins (Mrs. Timothy Hopkins)*, sale cat. (San Francisco, California, Oct. 5, 1942), lots 297–306; Universal Studios, California; Butterfield & Butterfield, *American and European Furniture and Decorative Arts in Los Angeles*, sale cat. (Los Angeles, California, June 17, 1991), lots 543-548; David Petrovsky, New York, New York; MWPI.
Museum Purchase, 96.24

 44

DESK, ca. 1876

A. Kimbel & J. Cabus (active 1862–82)
New York, New York

THE NEW YORK CABINETMAKING and decorating firm of A. Kimbel & J. Cabus was founded during the Civil War and earned its greatest renown during the 1870s with its furniture in the modern Gothic style. The MWPI desk is not marked, but it is firmly documented by a photograph of a nearly identical desk in a rare album that descended in the family of one of the company's partners, Anthony Kimbel (1822-95). The photograph is inscribed in ink with the number "378" and bears the firm's oval ink stamp.[1]

Anthony Kimbel was born in Mainz, Germany, to a distinguished family of furniture dealers, cabinetmakers, and decorators. His father, Wilhelm (1786-1869), and his uncle Anton Bembé (1799-1861) provided Anthony with his early training. After further apprenticeships, including one in Paris with Alexandre-Georges Fourdinois, Anthony Kimbel emigrated to New York about 1847. From 1848 until 1851 he was a designer in Charles Baudouine's cabinet shop, and in 1854 Kimbel established his own company, Bembé & Kimbel, with financial backing from his German uncle. Eight years later he became partners with Joseph Cabus (1824-98), who had been born in Calmutier, France, and emigrated to New York City with his family between 1832 and 1836.[2] For several years Kimbel & Cabus was located at 928 Broadway, the former site of Bembé & Kimbel, but after 1873 the showrooms were at 7 and 9 East 20th Street in the fashionable district surrounding Union Square. The business was evidently prosperous, but Kimbel & Cabus dissolved in 1882.[3]

During the 1860s Kimbel & Cabus essayed the French *néo-grec* style in the form of large parlor cabinets with central medallions.[4] During the 1870s the firm shrewdly developed a distinctive version of the much-vaunted modern Gothic, or reform, style based on examples set by British designers such as Bruce J. Talbert and by proselytizers of design reform such as Charles Locke Eastlake. The Philadelphia Centennial Exhibition in 1876 provided the perfect forum for the introduction of this style to American consumers. In its innovative booth Kimbel & Cabus created a drawing room with furniture and woodwork of ebonized cherry, which was seen by thousands of visitors and commended by the press. The exposure assured the success of the company and its product line.

The MWPI desk epitomizes the firm's interpretation of the modern Gothic style. Big, bold, and black, it conveys the essential tenets of design reform in its rectilinearity, its allusions to "honest" construction (spindle gallery, open shelves, and trestle feet), and its recalling of medieval design with strapwork hinges. The black finish, imitating Japanese lacquerware, reflects the 1870s vogue for the arts of Japan, a latter-day medieval culture much revered in the West. The desk is constructed of cherry and is entirely ebonized on the interior as well as the exterior—an economic choice that could be philosophically and aesthetically rationalized. Design reform in furniture insisted on the production of well-conceived but affordable goods, and ebonizing, a less expensive alternative to using fine cabinet woods, became a hallmark of the movement. Kimbel & Cabus also manufactured furniture in rosewood, walnut, mahogany, and oak in styles inspired by British, French Second Empire, Asian, and even Tyrolean models. The firm was capable of producing cabinetwork equal to that made by any of its contemporaries, but it is best known for successfully translating the precepts of the design reform movement into commercially viable products.[5]

Economy of means and materials is evident in the decoration of this desk. Simple incising and low-relief carving, including conventionalized plant forms and geometric designs, subtly enhance the surface. Four carved lion heads, stylized to such a degree that they are barely legible as such, are arrayed across the middle of the desk. Paper decorations incorporating Gothic revival motifs are applied to the cupboard doors and fall front. Apparently overprinted in black on brown paper, these appliqués appear on a number of Kimbel & Cabus case pieces and seating furniture and were probably meant to suggest the refined, more labor-intensive, marquetry veneers that embellish other ebonized furniture of the 1870s and early 1880s. Motifs such as the paired birds and mice on the upper cupboard doors were copied directly from Christopher Dresser's *Studies in Design* (1874-76), an important contemporary British pattern book.[6] On occasion the firm used more expensive decorative elements such as ceramic tiles, imported porcelain plaques, painted and gilded panels, and inlaid woods to enrich its furniture.[7]

CHV

64½ x 45½ x 16⅝ in.
Ebonized cherry, yellow-poplar, probably gilded copper, paper, modern leather writing surface
Provenance: Neal Auction Company, sale cat. (New Orleans, Louisiana, Sept. 1991);
Margot Johnson, Inc., New York, New York; MWPI.
Museum Purchase, 92.34

45

Rocking Chair, ca. 1875

Designed by Grove M. Harwood and Robert Wood
Manufactured by Henry I. Seymour Chair Manufactory (active 1851–85)
Troy, New York

This astonishingly simple rocking chair was patented February 23, 1875, by Grove M. Harwood and Robert Wood and was made by the Henry I. Seymour Chair Manufactory of Troy, New York.[1] The construction of the chair is economical, consisting only of eighteen round-profile members. Five of the components were steamed and bent: an inverted U-shaped member forms the continuous back stiles and crest, two others form the continuous S-shaped arms and front legs, and two more form the sleighs, or runners.[2] The remaining thirteen nearly identical narrow dowels form the seat rails, cross bars, and the square stretcher system. To create a seamless silhouette, the parts were joined by countersunk and hidden screws or were doweled. The chair combines stylistic traditions borrowed from the Shakers and innovative manufacturing techniques borrowed from Thonet Brothers of Vienna.

The Henry I. Seymour Chair Manufactory had its office at 171 River Street in Troy and its factory at Erie and Auburn Streets in West Troy. The firm was owned and operated by brothers Henry I. and George R. Seymour.[3] From 1854 through 1858 the Seymours were in partnership with Robert M. Taylor in the Taylor, Seymour Company.[4] Henry I. Seymour and Company is listed beginning in 1859, and George Seymour is listed as a partner in the firm until 1865.[5] In 1871, a year after Henry's death, George was listed as "agent" for the Henry I. Seymour Chair Manufactory and as "manager" of the newly renamed Seymour Chair Company in 1878. On August 6, 1885, George O. Catlin and George R. Collins became owners of the Seymour Chair Company and renamed it the Troy Chair Company.

Not a great deal is known about the designers of the MWPI chair. Robert Wood first appears in the West Troy directory in 1857 as a "chairmaker." Between 1866 and 1869 his name is absent from the directories, but beginning in 1869 he is listed as "foreman, chair factory," presumably at the Seymour firm.[6] Grove Harwood is recorded as an attorney and an insurance agent in Troy from 1855 and is never identified as a chairmaker.[7]

Although the Seymour firm produced conventional furniture for a middle-class market, it seems to have had a penchant for copying the successful ideas of others.[8] This rocker is stylistically indebted to Shaker design and has often been incorrectly attributed to Shaker craftsmen.[9] In addition to adapting Shaker models, the Seymour firm borrowed several of the Shakers' innovative marketing ideas. The firm produced its chairs in graduated sizes, offered a variety of wood stains, and presented a selection of woven tape colors.[10] The tape seems to be the same type as that used on authentic Shaker chairs. It is not certain where the tape was purchased or if the seats and backs were woven in the Seymour factory. Shaker work-order books from the 1880s note that Shaker workshops repaired Seymour rockers.[11]

The incorporation of bent members on Seymour's Shaker-inspired rocker is indebted to another firm, Thonet Brothers, whose patent on bentwood furniture expired in 1869. Almost immediately, European companies began making exact copies of the firm's most successful products, but Seymour was the first manufacturer in the United States to grasp the profitability of imitating Thonet's creations.[12] On May 31, 1870, Seymour secured a patent for two bentwood side chairs that overtly plagiarized Thonet's most famous designs. The MWPI rocker is not, however, a slavish copy of either of its precursors; rather, it is a successful fusion of two disparate sources.

BRH

36⅜ x 20¾ x 27½ in.
Elm, hard maple, original cloth-tape back, reproduction cloth-tape seat
Provenance: Private collection, Hamilton, New York; MWPI.
Museum Purchase, 86.68

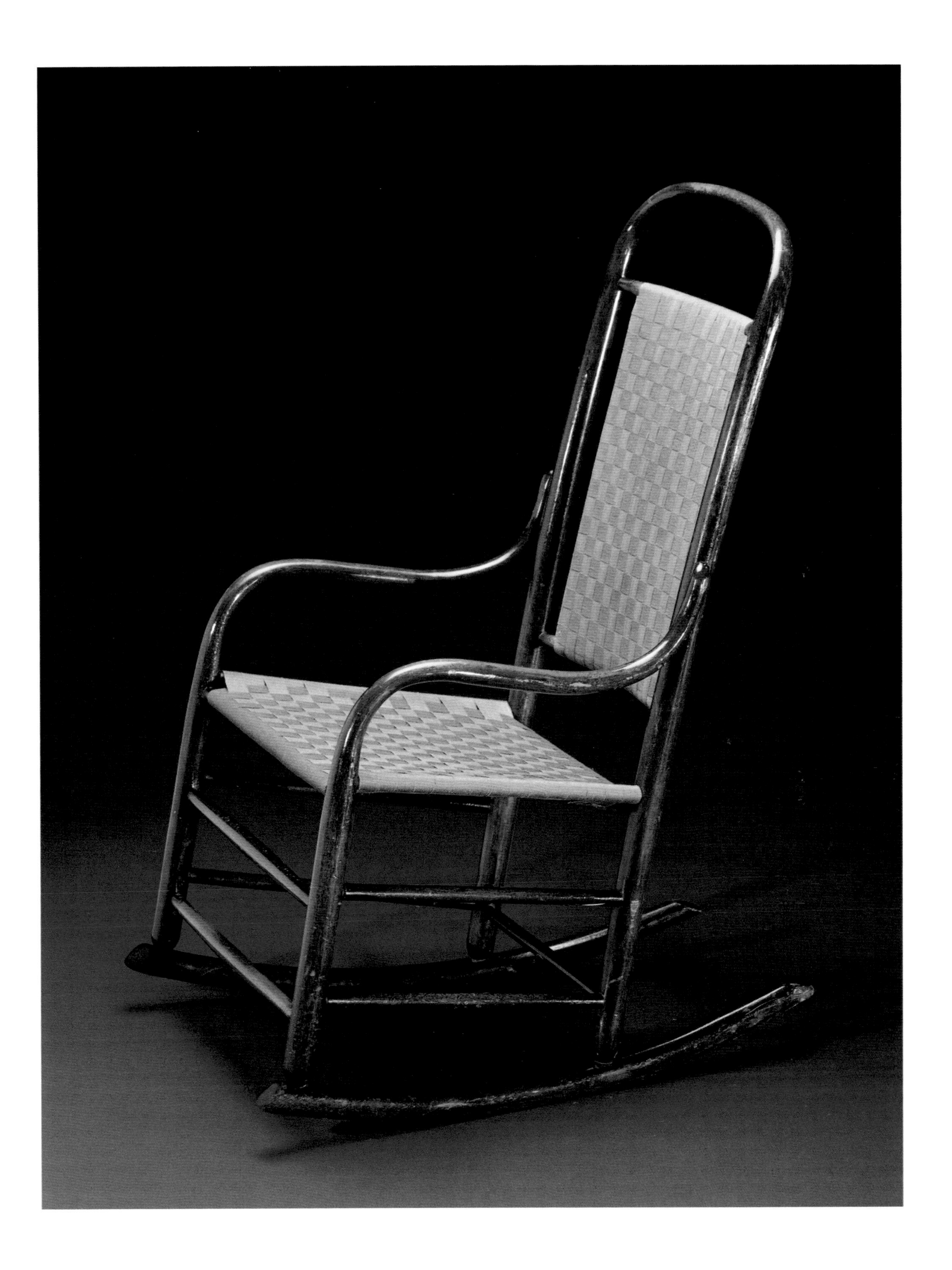

 46

Worktable, ca. 1875–85

Maker unknown
Probably New York, New York

The rich assortment of colors, textures, and materials employed on this worktable coalesce in a visually intoxicating, yet fundamentally utilitarian, object. The form of the worktable is straightforward. The top has two hinged lids that open to reveal mirrored backs and satinwood interiors. The body of the table incorporates three drawers (two opening on one side and one on the other) that are fitted to hold spools of thread. A barrel-shaped drawer offers ample space for the storage of fabrics or works in progress.

The table is designed to be viewed in the round; therefore no surface is left unadorned. The puissant surface is enriched by alternating, sinuous bands of parquetry composed of small shell-shaped brass and slate-colored pieces accented by drops of reddish-hued resin. The pattern is repeated on the inside and outside of the arched legs and along the top edge of the barrel-shaped drawer. Inlaid wood forms intricate ribbons, shields, and abstracted flower shapes. Mother-of-pearl and metal inlays enhance some of the forms.

Other costly materials project opulence. Brass trim and turned spindles contrast with the warm purplish-red of the amaranth tabletop, which is circumscribed by a carved entablature. Perhaps the most luxuriant feature of the table is the barrel-shaped drawer. The interior and exterior of the drawer were originally enveloped in brocaded blue silk velvet (surviving in perfect condition in the interior).[1] The semicircular drawer sides drop slightly below the arches of the legs. Even this small surface is ornamented with an abstracted floral motif executed in brass and mother-of-pearl inlay.

The form of the MWPI table and the motifs applied to it were inspired by British designs of the period. The worktable, or lady's sewing table, appears in a variety of styles in eighteenth- and nineteenth-century published sources. The utilization of flat surfaces with two-dimensional ornamentation follows some of the dicta established by British design reformers such as Charles Locke Eastlake. The use of opulent materials, however, contradicts Eastlake's opposition to superfluous ornament. The mosaic of motifs incorporated into the presentation is inspired by several artistic trends. The shield form and paw feet are derived from classical vocabulary, the floral elements recall Anglo-Japanesque patterns, and the polychrome parquetry is an exotic feature.

The level of workmanship required to execute this table places it on a par with examples from the shops of Herter Brothers, Pottier & Stymus, Herts Brothers, and George Schastey and indicates that it was produced for a wealthy client.[2] Although the maker of the MWPI worktable remains unknown, the drawer pulls are identical with those on several pieces from the original furnishings of a house at 4 West 54th Street, New York, New York, decorated between 1881 and 1884 for Arabella Worsham Huntington and purchased by John D. Rockefeller Sr. in 1884. In addition to the identical pulls, the use of costly materials on the MWPI worktable parallels a similar use of choice materials for the furniture produced for the Huntington-Rockefeller house.[3] Scholars have debated the significance of two letters sent to John D. Rockefeller Sr. that mention the furnishings and interior decoration of the house. In the first letter, dated January 21, 1884, the New York City cabinetmaker George A. Schastey (active 1869-97) stated, "I have furnished the house 4 West 54th St. and can give you all the information you may desire, should you contemplate buying." Later that year, Schastey wrote, "We desire to state that the interior woodwork and decoration of your new residence (#4 W. 54th St.) was designed and executed by us."[4] However, some of the interior work has also been attributed to Pottier & Stymus, the firm that employed Schastey before he opened his own enterprise by 1873.[5] An August 18, 1885, *New York Times* article describes Schastey & Company's building on 53rd Street. The article also cites the striking furniture made by the firm from amaranth inlaid with mother-of-pearl, silver, and brass. The only other indications of Schastey's cabinetwares are an illustration of his submission to the Centennial Exhibition (1876) in Philadelphia and an early twentieth-century sales catalogue from the Schastey firm that pictures furniture in arts-and-crafts-influenced designs.[6]

ATD

29¾ x 40⅜ x 24¼ in.
Amaranth, satinwood, walnut, mahogany, poplar, brass, pewter or lead, mother-of-pearl, glass, unknown colored resin, original and reproduction textiles
Provenance: Canadian collector to Sotheby's, *19th Century Furniture, Decorations and Works of Art*, sale cat. 6734 (New York, Sept. 12, 1995), lot 200; MWPI.
Museum Purchase by exchange with gifts from Jane B. Sayre Bryant and David E. Bryant in memory of the Sayre Family, and from the H. Randolph Lever Bequest, 96.2

47

STAND, ca. 1880–85

Attributed to Bradley & Hubbard Manufacturing Company (active 1875–ca. 1940)
Meriden, Connecticut

DURING THE LAST QUARTER of the nineteenth century, Meriden, Connecticut, was a center for mass-produced silverplated and base metalwares. Faddish "art brass goods," including lamps, mirrors, small tables, stands, easels, umbrella stands, trays, jewel caskets, and handkerchief boxes, were produced by companies such as Bradley & Hubbard Manufacturing Company, Charles Parker Company, Meriden Britannia Company, and Matthews & Willard Company, all located in or near Meriden.[1] Surviving company catalogues illustrate furniture forms ranging from elaborate tables constructed of tubular brass with "gold and steel finish"—offered with a combination of porcelain tops, hammered metal surfaces, and cast and applied ornaments—to understated stands with unadorned tubular leg supports and marble tops enclosed by simple brass frames.[2]

The stand in the MWPI collection is featured on the back cover of Bradley & Hubbard Manufacturing Company's circa 1880 catalogue.[3] Bradley & Hubbard, established in 1854 in West Meriden, marketed its goods in catalogues and in New York, Boston, and Chicago retail outlets.[4] The company's display at the Centennial Exhibition in Philadelphia communicated the scope of its production—"gas and lamp chandeliers . . . bronze and other styles of jewel-cases, inkstands, match-safes . . . jardinieres, stand with painted vases, and cardtables in gold, silver, and other bronzes."[5]

The MWPI stand well represents the character of decorative furniture produced by art metal companies in the 1870s and 1880s. Most of these wares incorporated the design motifs associated with the aesthetic movement, a reform campaign that sought to elevate the status of everyday objects by fusing art and labor in the creation of utilitarian wares.[6] Advocates of the movement promoted various artistic expressions such as modern Gothic (see cat. nos. 43, 44) and Anglo-Japanesque (see cat. no. 49). Most aesthetic-style furniture, however, shares basic characteristics—simple, architectural, often angular outlines and two-dimensional naturalistic ornamentation.

Expressive of an owner's sense of fashionable taste, this stand—with a combination of stylish design and ornamentation, color, and reflective surfaces—served as an accent piece, adding richness to a high-style interior. The MWPI stand is a typical mass-produced American interpretation of aesthetic principles. In an attempt to make a utilitarian item a work of art, it parades sundry ornamentation. Individual elements—machine-stamped parts formed from brass sheets and a tubular brass framework—screw together to create the stand. Sharp angles are counterbalanced by polychromatic ceramics, textured details, and light-diffusing surfaces. The geometric reductions of plant life to two dimensions parallel the rigid structure of the stand, while the botanical motifs contrast with the reductionist characteristics of mass production.

The floral enhancements illustrate the influence of naturalistic design popularized by English ornamentalist Christopher Dresser (1834-1904). Floral images, impressed into brass, decorate the frame around the tile top, the cylindrical and semispherical sections of the body, and the feet. The smooth, raised floral depictions are set against a stippled, matte ground to capitalize on the illuminating character of brass. A four-paneled pierced basket supports the pedestal top; four free-standing brass flowers branch out just below the top. The naturalistic motifs, appropriate for a plant stand, are echoed in the stylized design on the polychromatic ceramic elements.

The obscured mark on the base of the cylindrical ceramic element indicates it was made by the Longwy Faience Company (active 1798 to present) in Longwy, France, and imported into the United States. Other examples of this type of stand utilize a variety of ceramics from various makers.[7]

ATD

33¾ x 18½ x 13½ in.
Impressed on underside of ceramic cylinder: "Longwy"
Brass, ceramic
Provenance: Margaret Caldwell, New York, New York; MWPI.
Museum Purchase, in part with funds from the Sarah T. Norris Fund, 96.6

48

SIDE CHAIR, ca. 1880

Attributed to Kilborn Whitman & Company (active 1876–96)
Boston, Massachusetts

BY 1880 THE LONGTIME HEGEMONY of certain northeastern cities in the American furniture trade was gradually diminishing. Nevertheless, Boston still ranked first in labor productivity and fifth—behind New York City, Chicago, Philadelphia, and Cincinnati—in aggregate production.[1] At this time there were more than a hundred Boston furniture firms. One of the firms that successfully performed both manufacturing and selling (wholesale and retail), albeit on a moderate scale, was Kilborn Whitman & Company.[2] All but forgotten today, in its own era Whitman-produced merchandise appears to have been widely available.[3] The firm's documented oeuvre was above average in aesthetic conception and craftsmanship, and in some cases, such as the chair in the MWPI collection, the results were exceptional.[4]

Kilborn Whitman & Company, established in 1876, was managed throughout its twenty-year existence by Kilborn Whitman. The business occupied a succession of addresses on Canal and Merrimac Streets in Boston's North End, the site of many similar operations.[5] Before creating the firm, Whitman had worked for about a decade with Beal & Hooper (active 1850-76), a prestigious local decorating and furniture-making concern, and for almost four years with Arthur W. Palmer in the wholesale trade.[6] In October 1876 Whitman and Charles A. Jones organized Kilborn Whitman & Company using the former Palmer & Whitman facilities.[7] The inclusion of several Whitman items in J. Wayland Kimball's *Book of Designs: Furniture and Drapery* (1876), an illustrated compendium of work from "Leading Manufacturers" in New York City, Boston, and Philadelphia, was an auspicious beginning for the young company.[8]

From the outset Whitman offered catalogues to wholesale customers.[9] About 1880 the firm issued a thin but handsome catalogue containing 145 photolithographic images of sofas, chairs, lounges, stools, tables, and stands.[10] The last page of this work pictures an unupholstered seat frame that exactly matches the MWPI chair.

Stylistically the MWPI chair displays an eclectic mixture of influences that places it firmly in the Eastlake "art furniture" genre. The overall form is simple and traditional. The baluster-like front legs, somewhat mirrored in the "miniature arcade" on the back, are of Northern Renaissance inspiration. The use of geometric and floriform incising and the curved brackets below the seat rail and the arcade were viewed, in the 1880s, as modern Gothic. The stylized leaves and flowers featured on the carved crest panel have Oriental precedents.[11] Upon analysis, each of these motifs has a *raison d'être,* and the end result is a fusion of charm, delicacy, and strength, perfectly appropriate to the object's function as an easily movable "accent" in the parlor, boudoir, or bedroom. The gilded finish on the MWPI chair, more expensive than a "natural" or an ebonized surface, implies the formality of a parlor setting.[12]

The design sources for the MWPI chair are speculative. Similarities of form and detail can be found in images of furniture appearing in the 1870s trade catalogues of the London furniture makers Collinson & Lock, James Shoolbred & Company, and William Watt, and in works describing the international exhibitions held in London (1862), Paris (1867 and 1878), and Philadelphia (1876).[13] The products of trendsetting, contemporary New York City firms such as Herter Brothers, Pottier & Stymus, and Kimbel & Cabus also might have provided inspiration.[14] And widely circulated "good taste" manuals—Charles Locke Eastlake's *Hints on Household Taste* (1868) and Clarence Cook's *House Beautiful* (1877)—may have influenced the company's designs. Plate IV of Eastlake's *Hints,* for example, pictures a carved ebony chair similar to the Whitman design.[15] Regardless of its origins, the MWPI chair is an imaginative work whose inherent qualities easily express Eastlake's tenets of simplicity without "extravagant contour or unnecessary curves" and simultaneously satisfy Cook's belief that a well-designed chair is "at the same time handsome and useful."[16]

EPD

32 x 16⅞ x 18 in.
Beech, birch, cherry, gilding, replacement upholstery
Conserved at Williamstown Art Conservation Center, 1998
Provenance: Thomas G. Schafer, Utica, New York; MWPI.
Gift of Thomas G. Schafer, 87.1

49

Side Chair, ca. 1881–82

Herter Brothers (active 1864–1906)
New York, New York

Perhaps more than any other form, small side chairs reveal the sophisticated design talents of Christian Herter and his associates during the 1870s and early 1880s. Because they were lightweight and easy to move, such chairs were popular in European and American drawing rooms, bedrooms, and boudoirs throughout the nineteenth century, and they frequently appear in period photographs of interiors Herter Brothers designed. Chairs related to the MWPI example, for instance, include models in Jacob Ruppert's drawing room pictured in *Artistic Houses* (1883-84), a rosewood chair with floral marquetry on the crest rail that descended in the family of Cornelius Vanderbilt II, and an ebonized variation of the chair that belonged to Jay Gould.[1]

Around 1880 Herter Brothers commenced the decoration of several important New York City houses—William H. Vanderbilt (1879), Darius Ogden Mills and J. Pierpont Morgan (both 1880), Mrs. Robert Leighton Stuart (1881), and Jay Gould (about 1882)—that featured gilded or gold-spangled furniture in the drawing rooms. Considering the number and scope of these commissions, surprisingly few pieces of gilded Herter furniture have come to light.[2] The MWPI chair is identical in form and ornamentation to chairs in the photograph of Mary Stuart's drawing room published in *Artistic Houses*; the inlaid ivory garland entwined by a ribbon on the crest rail is clearly visible on one of four Stuart chairs.[3] In *Artistic Houses* Herter Brothers is credited with the fabrication of all the embroideries, plasterwork, woodwork, furniture, and other decorations in the room, and the architect William B. Bigelow, in charge of the Herter Brothers design department at the time, was identified "in connection with their qualities of design and execution."[4]

Mrs. Stuart's drawing room, completed by the spring of 1883, was typical of most of the drawing rooms Herter Brothers decorated in the early 1880s. It was characterized by ubiquitous stylized surface patterns—*de rigueur* during the aesthetic movement—that used the colors and delicate floral patterns of eighteenth-century French interiors. The author of *Artistic Houses* described the room as having "enameled bass-wood . . . picked out in different colors of gold and in pale colors to harmonize with the wall-coverings and the paintings of the ceiling . . . [and presenting] a general tone of ivory." "The furniture," the narrative continues, "corresponding in finish with the room, shows ivory enamel and gilt, and the upholstery is of the same materials as the wall-coverings, namely, Louis Quinze damask, with a cherry ground."[5] The photograph in *Artistic Houses* suggests that, with the exception of the crest rails, the Stuart side chairs were entirely gilded, as seen in the MWPI example. The chairs were upholstered in a pale-colored silk that was embellished with flowers to harmonize with the rest of the furnishings in the room.[6]

Even if the maker of this chair were not known, the butterfly-shaped hand-hold (an allusion, perhaps, to a popular aesthetic movement motif), curved crest rail, flaring stiles, and tapering front legs (each of which is encircled by a pronounced "cuff" above a flaring conical foot) would suggest the authorship and date. The gentle outward sweep of the stiles is reminiscent of the gilded chairs Christian Herter designed for the Vanderbilt drawing room (1879-82), although the slight backward arch of these supports was already evident in chairs the firm produced earlier. The unusual turned legs and the shaped backrest of the MWPI chair, which seems suspended between the stiles by parenthetical voids, are also Herter Brothers hallmarks of the early 1880s.[7]

CHV

34⅛ x 16⅞ x 19 in.
Impressed on underside of rear seat rail, "891"; inscribed in blue crayon on seat rail, "891 Gilt" and "Store"; stamped on brass plate mounted beneath front seat rail, "DE H"
Gilded hard maple, walnut, ash, inlaid ivory, modern upholstery
Regilded at the Williamstown Art Conservation Center, 1989
Provenance: Lyndhurst Corporation, New York, New York; MWPI.
Museum Purchase, in part with funds from the Sarah T. Norris Fund, 82.41

29½ x 29¼ x 23 in.
Stamped: "TIFFANY & C$^{\underline{O}}$/MAKERS"
Electroplated silver over copper, mahogany
Provenance: Private collection, New Jersey; Sotheby's, *Fine Americana*, sale cat. 6392 (New York, Jan. 28, 1993), lot 64; Margot Johnson, Inc., New York, New York; MWPI.
Museum Purchase, 93.29

50

Tilt-top Table, ca. 1885–93

Designed by Frank Shaw
Tiffany & Company (active 1837–present)
New York, New York

In 1837 Charles L. Tiffany founded Tiffany & Company as a stationery and fancy goods store. As the country's economy expanded, he adapted his merchandise selection to meet the demand for luxury goods. Although chiefly known for its fine sterling silver, Tiffany & Company began offering electroplated items in the 1850s; it was not until after the Civil War, however, that the firm began to promote this aspect of its business.[1] The company maintained its reputation for high-quality wares in all aspects of its work, including its plated goods.

In 1868 Charles Tiffany went into partnership with Thomas Shaw, a talented silversmith knowledgeable in the art of electroplating. Shaw was joined a few years later by C. C. Adams, and the company's name became Adams, Shaw & Company.[2] In 1877 the business moved to Newark, New Jersey. With the departure of Adams in 1881, the name became Thomas Shaw Silversmiths. By 1883 Shaw's business had been absorbed into Tiffany's, and all plated wares were produced in the New Jersey workshop.

The MWPI table is electroplated silver over copper and, using this process, is the most ambitious piece executed by the company.[3] The table was part of Tiffany's extensive exhibit of electroplated items at the World's Columbian Exposition in Chicago in 1893 (fig. 36).[4] Work on this table began many years prior to the exposition. According to *The Jeweler's Review*, "The table was designed and partly chased by the late Frank Shaw, a son of Mr. Thomas Shaw. . . . but the young man died without completing [it] and it was finished in time for the [Chicago] fair by other chasers in the shop."[5] Frank Shaw died in 1885, which indicates that the table had been in production for nearly a decade.[6] The MWPI table probably was intended for the 1889 exposition, but Frank Shaw's death precluded its inclusion.

In a catalogue of Tiffany's exposition exhibit, the MWPI table is listed as "Table. Ornamental Table, richly chased all over with flowers, vines, ferns, and other repoussé work ornamentation."[7] The elaborate floral decoration on the table is executed in repoussé, a form of relief chasing. Undulating ferns, roses, forget-me-nots, morning glories, chrysanthemums, daisies, dogwood, and numerous other blossoms adorn the tabletop; the catalogue described the design as "a veritable battle of the American flora, in which battalions of roses, vines, buds, ferns and others of the horticultural kingdom are scattered all over the field."[8] This "garden" continues onto the canted sides and frames the "picture." The design is softened by cast scroll motifs applied at the corners. The table rests on a pedestal support. On each side of the base, acanthus leaves adorn the feet and sweep upward to a lush botanical spray.

Fig. 36

During the 1870s Tiffany & Company produced silverware embellished with motifs inspired by the arts of Japan, a phase which lasted until 1883 when the firm began making silver objects decorated with naturalistic foliage. This new style was first presented in the firm's exhibit at the Exposition Universelle in Paris in 1889. Tiffany's display showcased objects decorated with American flora—including a tea and coffee service with repoussé carnations, pansies, and ferns that, in its decorative conception, bears a resemblance to the flora on the MWPI table.[9] Tiffany & Company assembled an extensive library of books on the decorative arts to serve as reference material for its designers. An inventory of the books in this collection lists a two-volume set of *Native Flowers and Ferns of the United States* and a portfolio of ninety-six photographs of ferns; either or both may have been source material for the decorative motifs on the MWPI table.[10]

American silver furniture is extremely rare. Tiffany & Company made only two silver tables, both of which it exhibited at the 1893 Chicago exposition. With the exception of the mahogany board that has the tabletop and tilt mechanism affixed to it, the MWPI example is made of metal, while the body of the other, a toilet table, is made of amaranth fitted with a sterling silver tabletop, mirror, and six-branch candelabrum.[11]

JZ

Fig. 36. The Tiffany & Company display at the World's Columbian Exposition, 1893, from *The Jeweler's Review*. Courtesy Tiffany & Co.

51

Occasional Chair, ca. 1880

Maker unknown
United States

This chair is a rare, apparently intact, survival that effectively demonstrates the international influence of high-style French upholstery design, its dissemination far from large fashion centers during the nineteenth century, and the longevity of some of its visual conventions in the United States. Because of its fragile condition the interior structure of the chair cannot be analyzed, but it has a wooden frame and a spring seat and back.[1] The color combination, the quality of the needlework strip, and the use of heavy silk satin as the primary cover fabric suggest that this piece may date from the last quarter of the nineteenth century. The design, however, was not new; it dates from the Second Empire (1852-70), a period of great innovation in French upholstery design and technique in both drapery and seating furniture.[2]

In the late 1830s the name *confortable* was first applied to overstuffed chairs with springs. By the Second Empire, forms of overstuffed seating proliferated to include, among others, *poufs* (overstuffed backless seats), *fauteuils de cercle* (barrel chairs), *crapauds* ("toad" chairs of squatty proportions), and *méridiennes* (napping couches). So, too, did styles profilerate. Some *confortables* were actually loose interpretations of classic seventeenth- and eighteenth-century modes, swaddled in fabric and stuffing, while others were clearly intended to be "Oriental." "Turkish" furniture forms, which invited sensual, relaxed postures different from the deportment required in formal social life, appeared in France as early as the late seventeenth century.[3] Nineteenth-century versions, however, display a virtuosity in fabric treatment and trimming that seems to echo French dressmaking. Pleated and buttoned tufting, which was both decorative and stabilizing to deep layers of stuffing materials, was another important element of the Second Empire's upholstery aesthetic.

Denise Ledoux-Lebard's brief catalogue of Second Empire furniture forms and decor illustrates a "tufted chair with inverted back" close in appearance to the MWPI example.[4] No self-respecting French upholsterer of the time would have been satisfied with such a boring moniker, however. The seventeenth number of V. L. Quetin's *Le Magasin de Meubles* (ca. 1860), the *Album de Sièges*, published a number of designs for "*sièges riches*" (opulently upholstered chairs) and "*sièges de fantaisies*" (fancy chairs, intended for use as single accents to the decor). The "*Chaise . . . genre Bébé*" in plate 55 is particularly close to the MWPI chair. Although it lacks the continuous sweep of back and seat, the design does include a roll and *macarons* with tassels at the crest of the slanted back.[5]

This type of overstuffed chair probably made its first widely noted appearance in America when a "Turkish fauteuil" covered in "white brocade silk" was exhibited at the New York Crystal Palace in 1853.[6] The MWPI example may have been made as a single accent chair, but it was more likely to have been sold with a settee and one or more armchairs as part of a "Turkish" parlor suite.[7] Turkish suites were produced by the mid-1870s, but they were never highly popular in the middle-class market perhaps because of their expense, their relative fragility compared with more substantial forms with wood frames, and the social ambiguities of their apparent invitation to relax in formal rooms.[8]

The use of silk satin as upholstery fabric on the MWPI chair seems ridiculously impractical, but it appeared in American interiors by the early 1840s on French-style furniture and resurfaced periodically throughout the nineteenth century as a frank extravagance.[9] Contrasting strips of needlework running from crest to seat front appear in French upholstery design by the 1820s, but they (along with imitations printed on velvet, woven of silk and wool, or even depicted illusionistically in the weave of the upholstery fabric itself) became one of the most beloved conventions of fancy upholstery in America after 1870.[10]

KCG

35¼ x 25½ x 32½ in.
Ash, black walnut, original silk and needlework upholstery
Provenance: Mrs. Edith Stark Brownell Shortliffe, Sauquoit, New York; Dr. Ernest C. Shortliffe, Hamilton, New York; MWPI.
Gift of Dr. and Mrs. Ernest C. Shortliffe, 85.3

52

Dressing Table and Chair, ca. 1890

Maker unknown, possibly R. J. Horner & Company (active 1886–ca. 1915)
New York, New York

THIS WHIMSICAL YET ELEGANT imitation bamboo dressing table and chair are evidence of the popularity of Oriental furnishings among late nineteenth-century consumers. After the opening of Japan to foreign trade in 1854, the flow of Japanese goods into the United States created an intense interest in Asian taste and products. American furniture makers responded by adapting Japanese designs and motifs to their product lines.[1] At the 1876 Centennial Exposition in Philadelphia, authentic Japanese bamboo furniture and decorative arts were introduced to a broad spectrum of the American public. Over the next two decades, a mania for Japanese arts permeated much of American popular culture.

Although a few furniture companies had direct access to Asian bamboo furniture prior to the Centennial, enterprising urban merchants began importing bamboo furniture in significant quantities after the exposition.[2] In 1878 the influential arbiter of American domestic taste, Clarence Cook, spread the fashion for bamboo furniture when he endorsed the New York City importer and merchant A. A. Vantine as a retail source for Asian bamboo furniture. In the Vantine emporium, Cook noted, "there is always a supply of bamboo furniture,—settees, lounges, stools, chairs of various styles,—made in China or Japan and capital stuff it is to fill up the gaps in the furnishing of a country house for a summer."[3]

Cook described only imported Asian seating furniture, but by advocating the style, he encouraged American manufacturers to produce their own variations. Advertisements in the *New York Times* indicate that R. J. Horner & Company (see cat. no. 53) was dealing in bamboo and imitation bamboo furniture as early as 1886 and was recommending it for use in the garden and country house.

To create faux bamboo case pieces, American firms used maple, turned and stained to look like bamboo. MWPI's maple dressing table uses "bamboo" turnings as support elements—stretchers and legs—and as ornamentation to frame the exterior structure and the highly figured drawer fronts and side panels. Similarly, bamboo turning lines the inner edge of the mirror. The turned discs set in the fretwork gallery and the pointed finial terminals across the top of the mirror and on its side posts make no pretense at bamboo but do complement and enliven the overall effect. The back of the chair both imitates bamboo and includes two other design elements associated with Japanese taste—brackets and a diagonal splat embellished with circular ornaments.

A number of other examples of imitation bamboo furniture, also made of maple stained dark in evenly spaced turnings, survive in museum collections.[4] Although few examples are signed or labeled by their makers, imitation bamboo furniture is often associated with R. J. Horner & Company because of a few marked examples, including a desk and an accompanying chair in the High Museum of Art, Atlanta, Georgia. The High Museum's desk shares many characteristics with the MWPI dressing table—both are made of yellow-stained maple and use yellow-poplar as a secondary wood, have evenly spaced and dark-stained turnings on the bamboo support elements, and have imitation bamboo front legs terminating in canted feet. Like the spindle railing flanking the mirror on the MWPI dressing table, the railing framing the shelf-top of the High Museum desk has a single central turning on each spindle. The High Museum desk's drawers have simple turned knobs rather than the intriguing pulls (knobs with turned faux bamboo sticks running through them) on the MWPI dressing table.

Clarence Cook's 1878 words about the use and availability of bamboo furniture appear in the chapter of his book devoted to living rooms (instead of parlors). Most surviving imitation bamboo furniture consists of small desks, chairs, beds, or dressing forms, however, and would seem to indicate that such furniture was preferred for bed chambers. Horner advertisements suggest that imitation and natural bamboo became increasingly popular in the 1880s and 1890s and remained in production at least through the end of the nineteenth century.

DCP

Dressing table: 58½ x 42½ x 20½ in.
Bird's-eye maple, hard maple, yellow-poplar, glass
Chair: 36¼ x 17¾ x 17¼ in.
Hard maple, cane seat
Provenance: Margot Johnson, Inc., New York, New York; MWPI.
Museum Purchase, 94.13.1-2

53

DESK, ca. 1895–1910

R. J. Horner & Company (active 1886–ca. 1915)
New York, New York

Fig. 37

ROBERT J. HORNER (ca. 1855-1922), originally a retailer of lace and curtains, may have made professional contacts within New York City's booming furniture and interior decorating trades that influenced his decision to begin manufacturing furniture. From 1884 to 1887 city directories list his business as "curtains" at 460 Broadway, but in 1888 R. J. Horner & Company, "furniture," located at 63 West 23rd Street, appears in a city directory. The opening of the Horner furniture store took place two years earlier, according to an advertisement in the November 4, 1886, issue of the *New York Times*.[1]

Marked changes in some of the city's leading furniture firms—retirements, deaths, dissolutions, reorganizations—and growth in middle- and upper middle-class markets provided opportunities for new furniture makers and retailers like R. J. Horner & Company.[2] Just two years after it opened, Horner's business was listed among the top furniture makers and retailers in New York City with a minimum of $100,000 in capital.[3]

Initially Horner's 23rd Street retail store had a factory on the top floor, but by 1897 the firm gained a second address, undoubtedly a separate factory. A November 4, 1909, advertisement in the *New York Times* noted that "designs and estimates [are] furnished for all kinds of woodwork" at the firm's factory at 147-149 West 25th Street and that the renovated 23rd Street showrooms were "one of the sights of New-York . . . specimen rooms are presented as examples of modest furnishing at a very small outlay, also as examples of high-class decorative furnishing without extravagant expenditure." Since at least the 1870s furniture retailers had used room settings to inspire customers and to compete with the growing interior decorating trade. Horner sought to attract a broad segment of the market by displaying its reasonably priced wares in "specimen rooms" that combined furniture with rugs and accessories.

In 1912 the retail store moved to a fashionable uptown address, 20 West 36th Street. By 1915 Horner had merged with George C. Flint and Company, and Robert J. Horner Jr. became secretary of the Flint and Horner firm. In 1916 neither of the Horners nor Flint are listed as officers of the firm.[4]

The MWPI desk was probably made between about 1895 and 1910, before R. J. Horner & Company moved uptown. The fall-front desk is a simple, even conservative, interpretation of mid-eighteenth-century French rococo prototypes. The rectilinearity of the desk is relieved by the application of carved scroll-and-leaf decoration to the slant top, by the scalloped apron with a large semicircular arch at the center, and by tapering cabriole front legs. Beading and leaf-carved decoration outline the apron's curves, and matching applied scroll-and-leaf carvings flank the large central arch. The lower section of the desk has a top drawer (running the full width of the desk) and two small side drawers beneath it. Each drawer has its original cast-brass pulls, adaptations of eighteenth-century French rococo designs. Other hardware includes a brass gallery crowning three sides of the top of the desk and an elaborate escutcheon. The fittings of the desk interior are simple—two brass-knobbed drawers, two writing instrument holders, and a shelf with five pigeonholes. The writing surface is veneered in highly figured maple.[5]

Advertisements document that R. J. Horner & Company imported, made, and sold furniture in eighteenth-century and Renaissance styles, and surviving products show that the company also adapted American colonial and federal-period furniture. Encouraged by the tastemakers Edith Wharton and Ogden Codman and their influential book, *The Decoration of Houses* (1902), wealthy Americans collected antique French furniture or bought modern adaptations. In creating this interpretation in maple, a wood not usually associated with eighteenth-century Parisian *ébénistes*, Horner demonstrated its awareness of the current taste for antique furniture but made no serious attempt to duplicate an eighteenth-century prototype. Most American consumers wanted new furniture that provided the appearance of furniture from an earlier period, not line-for-line reproductions.[6]

DCP

41¼ x 32 x 18⅛ in.
Paper label on back (fig. 37): "FROM/R. J. HORNER & CO., /Furniture Makers/
AND IMPORTERS/61, 63 & 65 WEST 23D STREET, NEW YORK CITY."
Bird's-eye maple, elm, basswood, birch, brass
Provenance: Mr. and Mrs. Thomas R. Proctor home, 312 Genesee Street,
Utica, New York (demolished 1959); MWPI.
Proctor Collection, PC. 596.1

33⅝ x 40½ x 20¼ in.
Soft maple, cloth tape
Provenance: Robert Herron, Austerlitz, New York; MWPI.
Museum Purchase, 70.8

54

Settee, ca. 1895

Shaker Community, South Family
New Lebanon, New York

By 1850 Shaker communities were well-established and respectable parts of the American landscape, and Shaker agricultural and manufactured products were noted for their high quality. In New England and New York, Shaker families had reached their peak membership by midcentury, and many had excess capital.[1] At New Lebanon, New York, Shakers invested this capital to change their cottage-industry chair business into a commercially competitive chair factory. The earliest sign that members were enlarging the chair business came when the Second Family Shakers printed its first price list for chairs in the 1850s. Between 1860 and 1863 the Shakers made production more efficient by standardizing the sizes of their chairs.

In 1863 the New Lebanon chair business was placed under the supervision of thirty-year-old Robert M. Wagan. For the next decade Wagan slowly improved the business, but old equipment and reliance on seasonal waterpower limited annual production to about six hundred chairs. In 1872, under Wagan's direction, the community spent twenty-five thousand dollars on a chair factory with new machinery powered by steam. Shakers as well as non-Shakers from the surrounding towns worked in the factory.[2] "Br. Robert is enterprising," observed Henry C. Blinn, a leader from the Shaker community at Canterbury, New Hampshire. "He says anything will sell that is carried into the market."[3] To take advantage of those markets, Wagan published a series of catalogues illustrating the various sizes and models of chairs available from the community.[4] The Shakers also sold chairs to retailers such as Marshall Field and Company in Chicago, Illinois. By 1885 production and sales had more than quadrupled. Wagan died in 1883, and the management of the chair business passed to William Anderson, who continued the business at roughly the same level into the twentieth century.

The variety of Shaker chair styles available to customers was considerable. The commercially made chairs were fabricated in eight sizes ranging from "0," a child's chair, to "7," the largest adult chair. Chairs could be ordered with or without arms, with or without rockers, with acorn-shaped finials, and with rails from which to hang padded cushions. Customers could choose wood slats or woven cloth-tape backs, select from four different finishes, and pick from a number of colors of webbing and plush cushions. The Shakers were willing to accommodate a customer's request for special modifications, even to the point of making chairs in older styles.

Shaker-made settees are extraordinarily rare—they were not included in the Shakers' chair catalogues but were created out of the standard line of chairs. It is not known whether the impetus for this innovation was developed by the Shakers, by one of their wholesale customers, or by a special order from an individual, but they seem to have first been made in the mid-1890s. A railroad receipt dated April 5, 1895, records the shipping of two settees from the Shakers to Marshall Field and Company.[5] The sales of a few other settees are recorded about this time, and the July 1895 issue of the Shakers' monthly magazine, *The Manifesto*, mentions that there "continues a constant demand for the famous Shaker chairs, sofas, [and] footrests."[6]

Settees were made from standard armchair parts, but extra long front and back stretchers were used to create a double seat. In order to bear the weight of an additional person, the stretchers that carry the woven seat and back are thicker than those on the chairs. The length of the back posts and depth of the seat suggest that the MWPI settee was made from parts of two different standard chairs. The back and front posts are probably from the size "3" side chair. To provide a deeper seat, the Shakers apparently used side stretchers and arms from the size "6" chair. Fewer than a half-dozen Shaker settees survive; some of them are somewhat larger, which suggests that all may have been made to order.

JVG and TDR

55

Armchair, 1896–ca. 1920

Joseph P. McHugh & Company (active 1878–ca. 1920)
New York, New York

The entrepreneurial disposition and business acumen of Joseph P. McHugh (1854-1916), self-proclaimed originator of "mission"-style furniture, helped bring the arts and crafts alternative to an American mass market.[1] Launched by British reformers such as John Ruskin (1819-1900) and William Morris (1834-96), the arts and crafts movement was a reform initiative that encompassed an entire philosophy of interior design. In a reaction to industrialization and to the poor quality of mass-produced goods, proponents of the movement advocated handcraftsmanship, the use of natural materials, and construction in which joints plainly showed. The arts and crafts movement influenced American design from the last quarter of the nineteenth century through the 1920s. In the United States, unlike in England, production of arts and crafts-style furniture was commercially successful because many manufacturers adapted the style without subscribing to the ideology of the movement.

Although overshadowed by more prominent individuals such as Gustav Stickley, Joseph P. McHugh was the first American manufacturer of affordable arts and crafts goods. McHugh's intense marketing of the movement's concepts and the encyclopedic range of his mission furniture forms helped set standards for consumers of American arts and crafts objects. Differing from his English counterparts, it was McHugh's business sense, rather than doctrine, that motivated his involvement in the arts and crafts market.

McHugh began his career working for his father Patrick in the late 1870s and opened his own shop in 1882. In 1884 he located his business, The Popular Shop, at 42nd Street and 5th Avenue in New York City, where it remained until the 1920s. McHugh's holistic approach to interiors led him to expand the shop's stock from window shades and dry goods to all kinds of interior fittings and to include the production and marketing of three furniture lines—mission, willow, and colonial revival.

McHugh's most popular furniture line was the mission style he began to produce between 1894 and 1897. The first forms he offered—settee, armchair, and side chair—were based on simple rush-seated chairs made for the Swedenborgian sect's Church of the New Jerusalem (completed in 1895) in San Francisco. McHugh christened his straight forms "mission," alluding to the region where the design concept originated. Subsequent pieces were the creations of the firm's chief designer, Walter J. H. Dudley (1862-1947). McHugh's marketing strategy was so successful that the trade soon began to speak of mission furniture as a distinct style and adopted the name as a generic term to embrace all arts and crafts furniture. Extensive marketing, accompanied by the rhetoric of the arts and crafts movement, achieved international recognition and acclaim for McHugh mission furniture and contributed to the acceptance of the arts and crafts vogue among middle-class Americans.

The MWPI armchair is an example of one of the first mission forms McHugh produced. The mortise and tenon construction, simple lines, and use of natural materials conform to the dicta of the arts and crafts movement. The massive proportions, rectilinearity, and stylized shape of the feet illustrate Walter Dudley's reliance on English precedents, such as the work of Arthur Heygate Mackmurdo (1851-1942). Although McHugh deliberately cultivated the aesthetic sanctioned by reformers, he readily used machines (as his competition did) to produce affordable furniture lines. McHugh, however, advertised his work as handcrafted, which most likely referred only to the application of the seating materials and finish.

McHugh's marketing intuitiveness, expressed in his promotion of cohesive interior decoration, inspired the company's range of furniture finishes and seating materials. His mission furniture could be purchased with a stained or painted finish, including "Toa" brown, weathered gray, and plain varnish. More adventuresome clients could choose from "a dainty willow-green . . . sealing wax red with black markings and a smoked black with grain brought out in deep brown."[2] The original forest green finish of the MWPI chair was one of the colors McHugh aggressively promoted and advertised as "foremost in favor as a color effect" for interiors, paneling, and furniture. The finish provides a warm hue without obscuring the natural wood grain.

ATD

36⅛ x 24⅛ x 18¾ in.
White ash, rush, green stain
Provenance: Cathers and Dembrosky, Inc., New York, New York; MWPI.
Museum Purchase with funds from the Mrs. Erving Pruyn Fund, 90.55

Notes

With Style and Propriety

1. James Watson Williams to his wife, Helen Munson Williams, Mar. 22, 1850, James Watson Williams Papers (hereafter cited as JWW), Cor.235.65, Oneida County Historical Society (hereafter cited as OCHS), Utica, N.Y. Unless otherwise noted, all Williams and Proctor family papers are in the collection of OCHS.
2. Samuel was a sharp businessman who managed a blast furnace in Clinton, N.Y., and later was a director of Western Union. When he died in 1881 the bulk of his estate went to his sister, Helen.
3. For a complete discussion of the planning and construction of Fountain Elms, see Carol Gordon Wood, *From Drawing to Dwelling: The Planning and Construction of Fountain Elms* (Utica, N.Y.: Munson-Williams-Proctor Institute, 1989). Fountain Elms was among the earliest Italianate-style houses built in Utica. When erected, it was the last house on a city gas line.
4. James Watson Williams died in 1873. Shortly thereafter, Helen and her daughters Rachel and Maria commissioned a marble fountain based on James's drawings and installed it on the front lawn between two elm trees. The family subsequently referred to the house as Fountain Elms, and they used the name on their stationery. In most correspondence, however, family members commonly referred to the home as "318," its house number. Because of conservation concerns, the original fountain was installed indoors in 1995 at one of the entrances to Fountain Elms.
5. Correspondence, receipts, and account books relating to Fountain Elms are in the MWPI Archives. Architectural elevations are in the MWPI Museum of Art collection.
6. While in New York City to secure furnishings for Fountain Elms, James regularly corresponded with his father-in-law. James even sent Alfred Munson carpet samples for his approval. James Watson Williams to Helen Munson Williams, Apr. 1, 1850, JWW Cor.235.87.
7. James Watson Williams to Helen Munson Williams, Apr. 4, 1850, JWW Cor.235.70.
8. James Watson Williams to Helen Munson Williams, Apr. 4, 1850, JWW Cor.235.70. Fountain Elms has simple ceiling moldings, most of which are believed to be original. The original mahogany balustrade and interior doors and their hardware, equally restrained, are also intact.
9. James Watson Williams to Helen Munson Williams, Apr. 4, 1850.
10. Despite James's assertion, the cost of wallpaper, including its installation, would have been more expensive than paint. The final cost of construction, including some of the furnishings, was about $15,000. There are three account books for the construction of the house, which was not completed until 1854, so an exact reckoning of costs is difficult.
11. The carpeting was purchased in January 1852 from Alexander T. Stewart and Co., New York, N.Y. See invoice in MWPI Archives. Brussels carpeting, which has a flat-loop pile, was one of the more expensive types of floor coverings then available. A "Tapestry Venetian" was a patterned, flat-pile carpeting, slightly more fashionable than the common striped variation. Venetian carpeting was durable and generally recommended for stairs and bedrooms. For a discussion of these types of carpeting, see Gail Caskey Winkler and Roger Moss, *Victorian Interior Decoration: American Interiors 1830-1900* (New York: Henry Holt and Company, 1986), pp. 34 and 85-88.
12. See Barbara Franco, "New York Furniture Bought for Fountain Elms by James Watson Williams," *Antiques* 104, no. 3 (September 1973): 462-67.
13. For an example of a mid-nineteenth-century étagère and a discussion of the form and its use, see cat. no. 25.
14. James Watson Williams to Helen Munson Williams, Nov. 30, 1853, JWW Cor.235.81. "Hutchin's" refers to the shop of Edward W. Hutchings. See cat. no. 30 for a discussion of Hutchings.
15. James Watson Williams to Helen Munson Williams, Apr. 1, 1854, JWW Cor.235.87.
16. James Watson Williams to Helen Munson Williams, Apr. 2, 1854, JWW Cor.235.88.
17. James Watson Williams to Helen Munson Williams, Dec. 30, 1854, JWW Cor.235.91. Several early twentieth-century photographs of the interior of Fountain Elms show hanging étagères. These items are not in the museum collection.
18. Whereas the Williamses spent $512.50 on their Baudouine suite, an elaborate Belter set would have cost as much as $1200. See cat. no. 24.
19. Helen owned stock in railroads, mills, coal, and iron companies. She also owned rental properties and held municipal and government bonds. At the time of her death, her estate was valued at more than 5 million dollars.
20. Maria Watson Williams diary, December 1863-March 1864, entry dated Feb. 20, 1864, Maria Watson Williams Proctor Papers (hereafter cited at MWWP), Dia.1.1. When this room was converted into a dining room, Helen furnished it with eighteen chairs from Pottier & Stymus of New York City. Early twentieth-century photographs provide visual evidence of dining room and music room alterations. These spaces continued to be used in these capacities until the house became the Institute's Community Arts Building in the late 1930s.
21. Maria Watson Williams, "Inventory of Valuables Purchased by Mrs. J. Watson Williams at Different Times, with Date of Purchase and Value at Time of Purchase. March 3, 1888" (Manuscript, OCHS); photocopy, MWPI research files. Also see invoices from Wood Carpet to Williams, Aug. 24, 1877, and Jan. 18, 1878, Helen Munson Williams Papers (hereafter cited as HEMW), Bil.119.1-.2. Axminster was a patterned, loop-pile carpeting that was used in conjunction with a coordinating border. In the 1870s "Axminsters remained the most expensive domestically produced carpets of the period." Winkler and Moss, *Victorian Interior Decoration*, p. 152. For her Axminster carpeting, Helen paid $376.88 for 83 yards and $161.69 for 49 yards of border. By comparison, she paid only $130 for 65 yards of Brussels carpeting.
22. Invoice from Herter Brothers to Helen Munson Williams, June 5, 1877, HEMW Bil.46.1. Lampas is a figured cloth of silk and cotton.
23. Invoice from Herter Brothers to Helen Munson Williams, June 5, 1877, HEMW Bil.46.1.
24. Invoice from A. T. Stewart and Co. to Helen Munson Williams, Feb. 14, 1876, HEMW, Bil.107.1.
25. Invoice from L. Marcotte and Co. to Helen Munson Williams, May 22, 1877, HEMW Bil.66.1. Gimp is a ribbon-like fabric used to trim upholstered furniture.
26. Receipt from American Art Galleries to Helen Munson Williams, June 9, 1883, HEMW Bil.3.2. See also Williams to Thomas E. Kirby, Esq. (of the American Art Association), New York, Aug. 20, 1883, HEMW Cor.135.1-.2 and 55.1. Other Asian ceramics are listed in the 1888 "Inventory of Valuables" and are accounted for by bills of sale.
27. "The late nineteenth-century popularity of ceramics collecting . . . was part of the revival of interest in the decorative arts known as the Aesthetic movement. In ceramics . . . oriental porcelains were the most favored among collectors." Doreen Bolger Burke et al., *In Pursuit of Beauty: Americans and the Aesthetic Movement* (New York: Rizzoli and the Metropolitan Museum of Art, 1986), p. 199.
28. For a full discussion of Helen Munson Williams in the context of nineteenth-century art collectors, see Anna Tobin D'Ambrosio, "The Vision of a Victorian Collector: Helen Munson Williams," *Nineteenth Century* 18, no. 1 (Spring 1998): 10-16.
29. This regional art organization, established in 1864, was an adjunct of the annual Mechanics' Association Fair and offered exhibitions in Utica through the late 1870s. For additional information, see James L. Yarnall and William H. Gerdts, comps., *The National Museum of American Art's Index to American Art Exhibition Catalogues from the Beginning through the 1876 Centennial Year* (Boston: G. K. Hall & Co., 1986), 1: 36.
30. James Watson Williams to Alfred Munson, July 17 (no year), JWW Cor.215.1; Alfred Bierstadt to Helen Munson Williams, Mar. 21, 1883, and Helen Munson Williams to Bierstadt, Mar. 24, 1883, HEMW Cor.7.1 and 118.1; and Mrs. Samuel [Sarah] Morse to Helen Munson Williams, Apr. 20 (no year), HEMW Cor.67.1.
31. Darby spent a considerable amount of time at Fountain Elms. In their diaries Rachel and Maria note that he gave them art lessons. Helen and James Williams introduced him to local society.
32. Helen Munson Williams to Hermann Schaus, Nov. 13, 1879, HEMW Cor.148.3. Helen writes, "But for some time I had wished to own a Diaz, and on my friend Mr. Darby's recommendation, I accompanied him to see the smaller one."
33. This is the wife of the merchant from whom the Williamses purchased carpeting in 1852 and 1876.
34. This New York City exhibition was organized to raise funds for the construction of the base for the Statue of Liberty. For further information, see Maureen C. O'Brien, *In Support of Liberty: European Paintings at the 1883 Pedestal Fund Art Loan Exhibition* (Southampton, N.Y.: Parrish Art Museum, 1986).
35. Daniel Cottier to Helen Munson Williams, Feb. 1, 1878, HEMW Cor.21.1.
36. Williams to Cottier, Feb. 9, 1878, HEMW Cor.125.2.
37. Williams to Cottier, Feb. 11, 1878, HEMW Cor.125.3.
38. With a few exceptions, the paintings Helen acquired are in the MWPI Museum of Art collection.
39. Edwin F. Holmes, an internationally recognized authority on thimbles and the author of *A History of Thimbles* (New York: Cornwall Books, 1985), has evaluated this collection.
40. "We saw several other pictures . . . but above all a large picture of Jules Bréton that would do nicely on the stairs. . . . This picture was made as a companion

to the 'Communicants' on which Mamma tried to bid at the Morgan sale. . . . They [Knoedlers] hold it at $20,000, but thought that $15,000 might buy it." Rachel Williams Proctor, New York City, to Maria Williams Proctor, Utica, ca. 1896, Rachel Munson Williams Proctor Papers (hereafter cited as RMWP), Cor.25.25; photocopy of the letter in the MWPI artist files. This painting was exhibited at the Universal Exhibition in Paris in 1889 and at the World's Columbian Exposition in Chicago in 1893.

41. Rachel Williams Proctor to Maria Williams Proctor, 1896, MWWP Cor.24.27.

42. Abigail Camp Dimon, "History of the Munson-Williams-Proctor Institute, Part I" (Typescript, ca. 1948), pp. 91-92, MWPI Archives. A rococo-style wallpaper is evident in the parlor, music room, and dining room in photographs of Fountain Elms taken before Rachel's death in 1915. Two small fragments of flocked wallpaper from Fountain Elms, one most likely from post-1938 renovations, are in the museum's collection. No records of the interior alterations made by Frederick and his second wife, Alice Millard Proctor (1863-1937), whom he married in 1919, are extant. They lived in Fountain Elms until Frederick's death in 1929, at which time Alice Proctor retired to Pippen Hill, about four miles south of Utica, the home that had also been the summer residence of Rachel and Frederick Proctor. She was allowed to take some of the second-floor furnishings of Fountain Elms.

43. Dimon, "History of the Munson-Williams-Proctor Institute," p. 102.

44. Dimon, p. 90a.

45. L. Earl Rome, director, Rhode Island School of Design, to G. Alder Blumer, Providence, June 13, 1929; Blumer to Maria Williams Proctor, Utica, June 15, 1929, MWWP Cor.71.18-.19. Apparently Blumer corresponded with Rome on Proctor's behalf and asked about the operations of Pendleton House and other homes used as museums. Maria Williams Proctor's library included a copy of Luke Vincent Lockwood, *The Pendleton Collection* (Providence: Rhode Island School of Design, 1904).

46. Although the 1850 architectural drawings show a bedroom and nursery on the first floor, it is not certain that the space was ever used in these capacities.

47. According to letters in the MWPI Archives, the Gothic-inspired paper was specifically designed for the project. The coordinating carpeting (since removed), also a special design, was inspired by a motif and the colors in a volume of *Journal of Design and Manufactures* (London: Chapman and Hall, 1849-52).

48. Lambrequins are window valances made of a flat piece of fabric and hung at window cornices. See Winkler and Moss, *Victorian Interior Decoration*, p. 52.

49. For the restoration of Fountain Elms, see Richard B. K. McLanathan, "History in Houses, Fountain Elms in Utica, New York" *Antiques* 79, no. 4 (April 1961): 356-63. Archival materials pertinent to the restoration of Fountain Elms shed little light on the historic bases for textile, carpeting pattern, and color choices. In the 1850s Fountain Elms, for example, was furnished with Brussels carpeting, whereas Wilton carpeting (with a cut-loop pile) was used in the 1960s alterations. Similarly, ornate Belter furniture was used instead of the Williamses' original, and more conservative, Baudouine suite.

50. Today, collectors and dealers commonly refer to the pattern of Belter furniture featured in the Fountain Elms parlor room setting as the "Fountain Elms" pattern.

51. One exception is the subcollection of materials known as the Proctor Collection, the objects left to the museum by the family. It reflects three generations of collecting and includes European and American materials used in Fountain Elms and in Maria and Thomas Proctor's house.

52. The ca. 1690 armchair was acquired by the Wadsworth Atheneum. The *kast* (a large clothespress, architectural in form) is now in the collection of the Museum of Fine Arts, Boston.

Catalogue Number 1

1. This pattern appears in all three editions of Sheraton: see Elizabeth White, comp., *Pictorial Dictionary of British Eighteenth Century Furniture Design: The Printed Sources* (Woodbridge, Eng.: Antique Collectors' Club, 1991), p. 94, plate XXXVI; Morrison H. Heckscher, "English Furniture Pattern Books in Eighteenth-Century America," in *American Furniture 1994*, ed. Luke Beckerdite (Milwaukee, Wis.: Chipstone Foundation, 1994): 199-200; and Peter M. Kenny, Frances F. Bretter, and Ulrich Leben, *Honoré Lannuier: Cabinetmaker from Paris* (New York: Metropolitan Museum of Art, 1998), p. 143. While the *Drawing-Book* may have provided the inspiration for similar chairs, it is equally plausible that they were patterned after examples made in New York City or chairs made by New York City craftsmen who traveled to other cities. A set of dining chairs documented to have been made by James Woodward (d. 1839), a Norfolk, Va., cabinetmaker, has the same pattern as the MWPI side chair. Woodward advertised in 1795 that he had "procured at considerable expense, the best workmen from *Philadelphia and New York*, and from *Europe*, which will enable him always to have on hand AT HIS MANUFACTORY *On the Main Street, near the New-Theatre*, A great variety of elegantly finished Cabinet Work"; quoted in Charles L. Venable, *American Furniture in the Bybee Collection* (Austin: University of Texas Press, 1989), pp. 74-77. Another example, a side chair in the Philadelphia Museum of Art (accession no. 1995.80.1), is labeled by the Troy, N.Y., partnership of Graff and Hayden. No New York City example has been documented to a specific maker or shop.

2. As reprinted in Charles F. Montgomery, *American Furniture: The Federal Period* (New York: Viking Press, 1966), p. 103.

3. The phenomenon of price books is discussed in Montgomery, *American Furniture*, pp. 19-26, and in Benjamin Hewitt, Patricia E. Kane, and Gerald W. R. Ward, *The Work of Many Hands: Card Tables in Federal America, 1790-1820* (New Haven, Conn.: Yale University Art Gallery, 1982), pp. 39-54.

4. For another design executed with carving and inlay, see Barry A. Greenlaw, "A New York Sideboard in the Colonial Williamsburg Collection," *Antiques* 105, no. 5 (May 1974): 1160-61, fig. 7; and *Antiques* 146, no. 3 (September 1994): 223.

5. William Duncan, *The New-York Directory, and Register for 1794* (New York: Thomas and James Swords, 1794), p. 8.

6. Although chairs with inlaid backs are uncommon, a number of variations are published. Some, such as the MWPI chair, have plain crest rails. See Montgomery, *American Furniture*, p. 111, no. 59; Christopher P. Monkhouse and Thomas S. Michie, *American Furniture in Pendleton House* (Providence: Rhode Island School of Design, Museum of Art, 1986), pp. 179-80, no. 122; and Philip D. Zimmerman, "The Livingstons' Best New York City Federal Furniture," *Antiques* 151, no. 5 (May 1997): 721, 723, plates XI, XIa. Others have five-pointed stars flanking the crest-rail tablet, while the most fully developed incorporate an archway in the crest. See *Antiques* 28, no. 4 (October 1935): 164; Edwin J. Hipkiss, *Eighteenth-Century American Arts: The M. and M. Karolik Collection* (Cambridge, Mass.: Harvard University Press for the Museum of Fine Arts, Boston, 1941), pp. 170-71, no. 108; Elisabeth Donaghy Garrett, "The Manhattan Apartment of Mr. and Mrs. Robert Lee Gill," *Antiques* 111, no. 5 (May 1977): 966, plate VI; J. Michael Flanigan, *American Furniture from the Kaufman Collection* (Washington, D.C.: National Gallery of Art, 1986), pp. 122-23, no. 42; and David B. Warren, Michael K. Brown, Elizabeth Ann Coleman, and Emily Ballew Neff, *American Decorative Arts and Paintings in the Bayou Bend Collection* (Houston, Tex.: Museum of Fine Arts, Houston, 1998), p. 97, no. F154.

Catalogue Number 2

1. Other examples are located at the Peabody Essex Museum, Salem, Mass.; the Winterthur Museum, Garden and Library, Winterthur, Del.; the Metropolitan Museum of Art, New York City; the Baltimore Museum of Art; and the New-York Historical Society. Two single examples and three matched chairs from a single set are in private collections. See also Christie's, *Highly Important Americana from the Collection of Stanley Paul Sax*, sale cat. (New York: Jan. 16-17, 1998), lot 526.

2. Nina Fletcher Little was the first to discover this inscription. It reads, "Made by John Seymour, for the Hon. Nathaniel Silsbee [Salem], about 1790. When he built his house." The chair, which Little later owned, is now at the Peabody Essex Museum.

3. John Cranch, Axminster, Devon, to his uncle Richard Cranch, Braintree [Quincy], Mass., Sept. 27, 1784, Cranch Papers, Boston Public Library Rare Book and Manuscript Division (MS Eng 483, box 4 of 4). They left Axminster, where they had lived since 1768, via the nearby port of Lyme Regis.

4. Discussed in Laura Sprague, "John Seymour in Portland, Maine," *Antiques* 131, no. 2 (February 1987): 444-49. This is the definitive work on the Seymours' period in Maine.

5. John II is identified as a "Breeches Maker" in parish records of St. Edmund Parish, Exeter, Devon, at the time of his marriage to Mary Curtis on June 14, 1765, and as a "Leather Cutter" at his second marriage to Jane Brice on Jan. 1, 1770. Parish Records, St. Lawrence Parish, Exeter; Devon Record Office, Exeter, Devon, England; transcripts in the Devon and Cornwall Record Society Library at the Westcountry Studies Library, Exeter.

6. Full details of the Seymours' lives and cabinetwork will be published in *John and Thomas Seymour, Cabinetmakers: Devon Culture and Craft to America* by Robert Mussey and Anne Rogers Haley, forthcoming in 2001. An accompanying exhibition by the same title will be presented at the Peabody Essex Museum.

7. Sprague, "John Seymour in Portland," pp. 444-49. A high percentage of independent, rural, English tradesmen pursued two (and often more) trades to support their families. Falmouth, in the "Eastern Territories" of Massachusetts, was in desperate

need of skilled and versatile tradesmen after the Revolutionary War.
8. Sprague, "John Seymour in Portland," pp. 444-49. Falmouth was bombarded and left in ruins by the British in 1775. In 1786 John Seymour III did a sketch of the rebuilding of the town, then renamed Portland, showing the town and its harbor. The drawing also included a representation of the house the Seymours rented from Thomas Robison. Although the original sketch is lost, the view survives in a later copy, which demonstrates that at the age of twenty-one Seymour aspired to be more than a house and ship painter.
9. The copy of this edition of Sheraton, owned by John Seymour III's brother Thomas, the Boston cabinetmaker, is in the collection of the Museum of Fine Arts, Boston.
10. See Laura Sprague, "Fit for a Noble Man: Interiors and the Style of Living in Coastal Maine," in *Agreeable Situations: Society, Commerce, and Art in Southern Maine, 1780-1830*, ed. Laura Sprague (Kennebunk, Me.: The Brick Store Museum, 1987), pp. 107-21.

Catalogue Number 3

1. Benjamin A. Hewitt, Patricia E. Kane, and Gerald W. R. Ward, *The Work of Many Hands: Card Tables in Federal America, 1790-1820* (New Haven, Conn.: Yale University Art Gallery, 1982), pp. 61, 67, 86. Charles F. Montgomery, *American Furniture: The Federal Period* (New York: Viking Press, 1966), pp. 30-31. I am grateful to Barbara McLean Ward for her assistance in understanding the Hewitt method. The MWPI table lacks an early history that might help pinpoint its place of origin.
2. Hewitt, Kane, and Ward, *Work of Many Hands*, pp. 88-89, 91-96.
3. See Montgomery, *American Furniture*, pp. 330-31, no. 302 (accession no. 60.332), and James F. Jensen, "Eighteenth- and Early Nineteenth-Century American Furniture at the Honolulu Academy of Arts," *Antiques* 113, no. 5 (May 1978): 1088, plate I; 1095, fig. 16 (accession no. 3819.1). I am grateful to Wendy A. Cooper of Winterthur Museum, Garden and Library and Jennifer Saville of the Honolulu Academy of Arts for generously providing detailed information about the tables in their collections.
4. See Hewitt, Kane, and Ward, *Work of Many Hands*, p. 91, with reference to varying techniques employed on tables with the label of Joseph Short of Newburyport.
5. The apparent mate is illustrated in *American Antiques from Israel Sack Collection* (Washington, D.C.: Highland House Publishers, 1976-92), 2: 496, no. 1023. I am grateful to Albert Sack and the anonymous owner of this table for their assistance. A similar table, described as "the finest Hepplewhite card table produced in New England," is illustrated in Albert Sack, *Fine Points of Furniture: Early American* (New York: Crown Publishers, 1950), p. 281.
6. On Tucker, see "Queries and Opinions," *Antiques* 17, no. 5 (May 1930): 458, 460; Richard H. Randall Jr., "Works of Boston Cabinetmakers, 1795-1825: Part II," *Antiques* 81, no. 4 (April 1962): 412-15; Montgomery, *American Furniture*, p. 483, no. 223; E. Page Talbott, "The Furniture Industry in Boston, 1810-1835" (M.A. thesis, University of Delaware, 1974), p. 70. Tucker's estate inventory is on file in the Suffolk County probate records, docket 28479, Suffolk County Court House, Boston, Mass. I am grateful to Jane Port for her assistance in gathering data on Tucker. The Decorative Arts Photographic Collection at the Winterthur Museum, Winterthur, Del., also has a record of a tambour desk with Tucker's label in addition to records of the card tables and looking glass cited above.
7. Brock Jobe, ed., *Portsmouth Furniture: Masterworks from the New Hampshire Seacoast* (Boston: Society for the Preservation of New England Antiquities, 1993), pp. 182-85, no. 34; Mabel Munson Swan, "Stephen Badlam, Cabinet and Looking Glass Maker," *Antiques* 65, no. 5 (May 1954): 383.
8. *The Victorian Cabinet-Maker's Assistant* (1853; reprint, New York: Dover Publications, 1970), 2d division, p. 48.
9. See Gerald W. R. Ward, "Avarice and Conviviality: Card Playing in Federal America," in Hewitt, Kane, and Ward, *Work of Many Hands*, pp. 14-38; and (in revised form) *Antiques* 141, no. 5 (May 1992): 794-807.

Catalogue Number 4

1. George Hepplewhite, *The Cabinet-Maker and Upholsterer's Guide* (London, 1794; reprint, New York: Dover Publications, 1969), p. 12, plate 62.
2. Edwin J. Hipkiss, *Eighteenth-Century American Arts: The M. and M. Karolik Collection* (Cambridge, Mass.: Harvard University Press for the Museum of Fine Arts, Boston, 1941), cat. no. 67.
3. See Benjamin A. Hewitt, Patricia E. Kane, and Gerald W. R. Ward, *The Work of Many Hands: Card Tables in Federal America, 1790-1820* (New Haven, Conn.: Yale University Art Gallery, 1982), cat. no. 29; and Benjamin A. Hewitt, "Regional Characteristics of Inlay on American Federal Period Card Tables," *Antiques* 121, no. 5 (May 1982): 1166, 1169, 1171. Another Pembroke table is at the Chipstone Foundation; see Oswaldo Rodriguez Roque, *American Furniture at Chipstone* (Madison: University of Wisconsin Press, 1984), pp. 302-3, no. 141; see also an example, then in a private collection, illustrated in *The Collection of Samuel Dale Stevens (1859-1922)* (North Andover, Mass.: North Andover Historical Society, 1971), p. 15. Other card tables are discussed in J. Michael Flanigan, *American Furniture from the Kaufman Collection* (Washington, D.C.: National Gallery of Art, 1986), pp. 176-77, no. 69. See also tables catalogued in the Decorative Arts Photographic Collection, Winterthur Museum, Winterthur, Del., (hereafter DAPC), 71.685 and 66.330 (both attributed to Weaver), and a privately owned card table (Museum of Fine Arts, Boston, files).
4. DAPC, 72.468.
5. For Weaver's labels, see Robert P. Emlen, "Henry Barber and the Newport Sideboards," *Newport History* 56 (Fall 1983): 122-33; the newspaper ad is illustrated as fig. 3. The copper plate for one of Weaver's labels survives in the collections of the Newport Historical Society.
6. The Pembroke tables at the Museum of Fine Arts, Boston, and in the Chipstone collection, for example, vary in construction and differ from the MWPI table. The writer is grateful to Luke Beckerdite for his examination of the construction of the Chipstone table.
7. Biographical information on Weaver is from Ruth Ralston, "Holmes Weaver, Cabinet- and Chairmaker of Newport," *Antiques* 41, no. 2 (February 1942): 133-35; Ralph E. Carpenter Jr., *The Arts and Crafts of Newport, Rhode Island, 1640-1820* (Newport, R.I.: Preservation Society of Newport County, 1954), pp. 24, 26; Ethel Hall Bjerkoe, *The Cabinetmakers of America* (Garden City, N.J.: Doubleday and Co., 1957), pp. 229-30; Joseph K. Ott, "Lesser-Known Rhode Island Cabinetmakers: The Carlisles, Holmes Weaver, Judson Blake, the Rawsons, and Thomas Davenport," *Antiques* 121, no. 5 (May 1982): 1158-59, in addition to many of the sources cited above. Weaver's labeled clock cases and chests of drawers are recorded in DAPC along with other objects attributed to him.
8. Nancy Goyne Evans, *American Windsor Chairs* (New York: Hudson Hills Press in association with the Henry Francis du Pont Winterthur Museum, 1996), p. 715, records a spurious Holmes Weaver brand on Windsor chairs; see also DAPC, 66.691.
9. A representative body of Newport Pembroke tables is illustrated in Michael Moses, *Master Craftsmen of Newport: The Townsends and Goddards* (Tenafly, N.J.: MMI Americana Press, 1984). See also *Girl Scouts Loan Exhibition of Eighteenth and Early Nineteenth Century Furniture and Glass . . . for the Benefit of the National Council of Girl Scouts, Inc.* (New York: Anderson Art Galleries, 1929), no. 688.

Catalogue Number 5

1. Charles Storrs, comp., *The Storrs Family* (New York: privately printed, 1886).
2. *The Connecticut Gazette and the Universal Intelligencer* (Hartford), Jan. 11, 1784.
3. Henry N. Flynt and Martha Gandy Fales, *The Heritage Foundation Collection of Silver* (Deerfield, Mass.: The Heritage Foundation, 1968), pp. 319-20, 332. It is unknown whether Shubael Storrs went with Jacob Sergeant to Hartford, Conn., in 1795 or remained in the Springfield shop under the eye of his relative Thomas Sergeant (1773-1834). The clocks inscribed "Storrs/Utica" have led some authors to believe that Nathan Storrs also worked in Utica. This, however, was not the case; Nathan Storrs retired in 1833 and died in Northampton, Mass., on July 31, 1839.
4. Moses Mears Bagg, *The Pioneers of Utica* (Utica, N.Y.: Curtiss and Childs, 1877), pp. 268-69; George B. Cutten and Minnie W. Cutten, *The Silversmiths of Utica* (Hamilton, N.Y.: George B. Cutten, 1936), pp. 59-81. Storrs married Chloe B. Makepeace at Utica in 1820 and trained his nephews Charles Storrs (1800-1839) and Eli A. Storrs (b. 1808) who came to Utica from Mansfield, Conn., about 1820. He also trained his son, Henry Southworth Storrs (1826-62).
5. *Utica Sentinel*, Mar. 27, 1821.
6. The clock mechanism is an eight-day movement with anchor recoil escapement and rack-and-snail strike. It has a thirteen-inch enamel dial fitted with a pictorial lunar dial at the top, a seconds dial above the pierced hands, and a calendar dial below. The case is ornamented with matched mahogany veneers, complex composite stringing, and pictorial inlays. The clock is surmounted by a scrolled pediment and supported by bracket feet. The scrolls of the pediment are restored, and two of the three original finials are missing.
7. A similar clock by Storrs is in the collection of the Metropolitan Museum of Art. It was owned in Herkimer, N.Y. (just east of Utica), as early as 1828. A third clock with a pagoda hood, signed "Storrs/Utica," is also known. See *Antiques* 109, no. 5 (May 1976): 880.

8. The clock later descended in the Sherman family of Utica.

9. The expensive eagle inlay cannot predate 1796, but may have been applied at any time after that year.

10. The pictorial eagle inlay is probably the work of a Boston specialist. Similar eagles with eighteen stars are found on two Boston and two Providence, R.I., card tables, ca. 1800, in the Yale University Art Gallery, New Haven, Conn. Related inlays appear on tables in the Diplomatic Reception Rooms of the United States Department of State and in the Henry Ford Museum, Dearborn, Mich.; another was formerly in the private collection of Eddy G. Nicholson. See David L. Barquist, *American Tables and Looking Glasses in the Mabel Brady Garvan and Other Collections at Yale University* (New Haven, Conn.: Yale University Art Gallery, 1992), pp. 197-201; Benjamin A. Hewitt, Patricia E. Kane, and Gerald W. R. Ward, *The Work of Many Hands: Card Tables in Federal America, 1790-1820* (New Haven, Conn.: Yale University Art Gallery, 1982), pp. 84, 139-41; *American Antiques from Israel Sack Collection* (Washington, D.C.: Highland House Publishers, 1976-92), 6: 1446, 8: 2268; Clement E. Conger and Alexandra W. Rollins, eds., *Treasures of State: Fine and Decorative Arts in the Diplomatic Reception Rooms of the U.S. Department of State* (New York: Harry N. Abrams, 1991), pp. 212-13, 216-17; and Christie's, *Collection of Eddy G. Nicholson*, sale cat. (Jan. 27, 1995), lot 1148. For examples of Albany area neoclassical tall clocks, see Norman S. Rice, *New York Furniture before 1840 in the Collection of the Albany Institute of History and Art* (Albany, N.Y.: Albany Institute of History and Art, 1962), p. 52.

Catalogue Number 6

1. Talbot F. Hamlin, *Benjamin Henry Latrobe* (New York: Oxford University Press, 1955).

2. *The London Chair-Makers' and Carvers' Book of Prices* (London: Committee of Chair-Manufacturers and Journeymen, 1802); Thomas Sheraton, *The Cabinet Dictionary* (London, W. Smith, 1803; reprint, New York: Praeger Publishers, 1970); Thomas Hope, *Household Furniture and Interior Decoration* (London: Longman, Hurst, Rees, and Orme, 1807; reprint, New York: Dover Publications, 1971). Hope's volume was advertised in the Jan. 4, 1819, issue of the *New York Evening Post.* Rudolph Ackermann, *The Repository of Arts, Literature, Commerce, Manufactures, Fashions and Politics* (London: R. Ackermann, 1809-28). Copies of *The Repository* were advertised in the Nov. 11, 1819, and Feb. 27, 1821, issues of the *New York Evening Post* as being available at the Minerva Circulating Library and Book and Stationery Store and at Goodrich's Library, respectively.

3. Charles F. Montgomery, *American Furniture: The Federal Period* (New York: Viking Press, 1966), pp. 117-21.

4. In 1808 Latrobe supplied a suite of Grecian furniture for William Waln's Philadelphia house, for which Latrobe was the architect. The suite is among the earliest and most visually appealing American furniture in this style. The following year he designed a related suite intended for the White House. For further information on these important commissions, see Jack L. Lindsey, "An Early Latrobe Furniture Commission," *Antiques* 139, no. 1 (January 1991): 208-19. In Boston, Samuel Gragg's "elastic" chair, patented in 1808, reproduced the *klismos* shape and occasionally incorporated animal paw feet; see Patricia E. Kane, "Samuel Gragg: His Bentwood Fancy Chairs," *Yale University Art Gallery Bulletin* 33, no. 2 (Autumn 1971): 26-37.

5. This set of chairs is recorded in Sotheby's, *Fine Americana*, sale cat. (Sept. 26, 1981), lot 441. The MWPI side chairs are reproduced in Joseph Aronson, *The Encyclopedia of Furniture* (New York: Crown Publishers, 1965), p. 103, no. 309.

6. The well-known watercolor depicting Phyfe's Fulton Street cabinet shop and showrooms incorporates a similar side chair, one with a lyre back, being shown and discussed in one of the doorways. A detail is reproduced in Morrison H. Heckscher, "Duncan Phyfe, Revisitus," *Antiques* 151, no. 1 (January 1997): 238. Another similar chair appears in a sketch attributed to Phyfe and is reproduced in Montgomery, *American Furniture*, pp. 126-27, no. 72a. Montgomery states that such a chair could be ordered with an upholstered slip seat for $23 or with a cane bottom and an accompanying cushion for $25. The only known lyre-back chairs that can be associated with Phyfe's shop are a set believed to be those listed on Phyfe's 1816 bill to James Lefferts Brinckerhoff, a New York City merchant, and discussed by Jeanne Vibert Sloane in "A Duncan Phyfe Bill and the Furniture It Documents," *Antiques* 131, no. 5 (May 1987): 1106-13.

7. Marilyn A. Johnson found that Phyfe's New York contemporaries recognized him as an arbiter of style and that other cabinetmakers analyzed and carefully copied items produced in Phyfe's shop. See her "John Hewitt, Cabinetmaker," *Winterthur Portfolio* 4 (1968): 185-205. Phyfe purchased finished cabinet goods from Fenwick Lyell between 1805 and 1809; see Elizabeth L. Frelinghuysen, "Lyell, Slover, Taylor, Phyfe, et al.," *Antiques* 97, no. 1 (January 1970): 119-20. His business dealings with other New York craftsmen can be inferred from an account noted by Daniel Turnier, a cabinetmaker, in his bound copy of the 1810 New York price book (with 1815 additions) now in the library of the Bayou Bend Collection. For additional information on Duncan Phyfe, see Michael K. Brown, "Duncan Phyfe" (M.A. thesis, University of Delaware, 1978) and Deborah D. Waters, "Is it Phyfe?," in *American Furniture 1993*, ed. Luke Beckerdite (Milwaukee, Wis.: Chipstone Foundation, 1993): 63-80.

Catalogue Number 7

1. A removable padded cushion, upholstered in haircloth, softens the seat and blocks drafts. The cushion originally would not have been tufted. Typically, a round bolster fit into the curve at the higher end of the sofa.

2. See, for example, the sofa designed by Henry Holland for Southill House, ca. 1795-1800, illustrated in John Morley, *Regency Design, 1790-1840: Gardens, Buildings, Interiors, Furniture* (New York: Harry N. Abrams, 1993), p. 372.

3. Morley, *Regency Design*, p. 376.

4. The couch at the Metropolitan Museum descended in the family of Robert Gill and remained near Fishkill, N.Y., from 1833 until 1940 when it was given to the museum. According to family history Duncan Phyfe made Gill's furniture, but no documentary evidence corroborates this claim. See Joseph Downs, *Bulletin of the Metropolitan Museum of Art* 36, no. 1 (January 1941): 7-8. The Metropolitan Museum's couch is illustrated in Dean A. Fales Jr., *American Painted Furniture, 1660-1880* (New York: E. P. Dutton, 1972), p. 161. Its reproduction horsehair upholstery is based on a small piece of plain black haircloth that remained from the original fabric. The couch at the Museum of Fine Arts, Boston, is illustrated in Jonathan L. Fairbanks and Elizabeth Bidwell Bates, *American Furniture, 1620 to the Present* (New York: Richard Marek Publishers, 1981), p. 279.

5. Furniture curators and conservators have debated what techniques were used to achieve the precise gilded designs found on the MWPI couch and others of comparable quality. While the similarity between designs suggests that craftsmen used stencils or some method of transfer, the lack of symmetry in the motifs has led experts to conclude that a degree of handwork was involved. The author would like to thank the following colleagues for their input on this issue—John Courtenay, Donald L. Fennimore, Robert D. Mussey Jr., Cynthia Van Allen Schaffner, John L. Scherer, Catherine Hoover Voorsanger, and Deborah Dependahl Waters.

6. Furniture scholar John A. Courtenay recently discovered the name of a New York City engraver on the hand-gilded nameplate of a New York pianoforte, suggesting that a specialist may have been involved in creating these decorations. John Courtenay, telephone conversation with the author, May 17, 1997.

Catalogue Number 8

1. Herbert L. Smith, *Private Sale of Important Antiques from the Randall Mansion, Cortland, N.Y., Beginning Friday, November 15, 1935;* photocopy, MWPI research files. One of the pier tables and one of the center tables are pictured in the photographs that illustrate the sale notice. One of the pier glasses made by Isaac Platt of New York—in the MWPI collection (see cat. no. 9)—is pictured hanging over the pier table. The matching pier table and one of the center tables were offered for sale by Robert Thomas and Robert Seifert in 1975; see *Antiques* 107, no. 4 (October 1975): 628.

2. Mrs. Wilson was the wife of John F. Wilson (d. 1911), the adopted son of Wilhelmina Randall, William and Betsey (Bassett) Randall's unmarried daughter.

3. According to the sale notice, "The house has been continuously occupied by important families since 1828 and appreciative and loving hands have watched over it and its contents. Every piece offered is in fine, usable condition. Seldom does the opportunity come to acquire important pieces like these that have been continuously owned by the same family and graced the house from which they are sold for more than a century" (Smith, *Private Sale*). The pier and center tables were among the contents of the drawing room and were valued at a total of $400. Photographs in the Cortland County Historical Society, taken sometime between 1910 and 1935, show the pier tables in situ on opposite sides of the room and the center tables placed directly in front of the double fireplaces. The William Randall house was torn down in 1943; the Roswell Randall house, sold in 1870, is now Cortland's Masonic Temple.

4. Edward D. Blodgett, "William Randall House One Hundred Years Old," *The Cortland Standard*, June 8, 1928.

5. Blodgett, "Randall House."

6. A similar pier table in the Georgia Governor's Mansion was illustrated in Katherine Gross Farnham, "Georgia's New Governor's Mansion," *Antiques* 94, no. 6 (December 1968): 856.

7. Cynthia Moyer, "Conservation Treatments for Border and Freehand Gilding and Bronze-Powder Stenciling and Freehand Bronze," in *Gilded Wood Conservation and History*, ed. Deborah Bigelow, Elizabeth Cornu, Gregory J. Landrey, and Cornelius Van Horne (Madison, Conn.: Sound View Press, 1991), p. 332.

8. Moyer has described the lithopone and pin-prick processes in discussing her method for reproducing a freehand-gilded lyre decoration: "Transfer paper (white 'carbon' paper) was . . . laid, dusted side down, on the finish surface, and over it . . . I traced the outline [of the motif] with a ball-tip stylus. This produced a white line on the finish surface that served as a guide [for hand painting]. . . . (Another technique would have been to puncture the outline at intervals with a fine needle-tip stylus and then dust the lithopone powder through the holes. This creates a pattern of dots that serves as a guide for painting the oil size.)"; see Moyer, "Border and Freehand Gilding," p. 335. See also John Courtenay, "Freehand Gilding in Philadelphia Empire Furniture, 1820-1840: Possible Design Sources" (M.A. thesis, Smithsonian Furniture Conservation Training Program, 1998).

Catalogue Number 9

1. Platt's biographical and business history is recorded in Betty Ring, "Check List of Looking-glass and Frame Makers and Merchants Known by Their Labels," *Antiques* 119, no. 5 (May 1981): 1190-91. Ring described seven different labels found in the Decorative Arts Photographic Collection at the Winterthur Museum, Winterthur, Del., four of which give Platt's address as 196 Broadway (1815-18). The other three labels locate him at 128 Broadway (1820-21), 138 Broadway (1821-24), and 178 Broadway. She mentioned two additional girandole mirrors with Platt labels in private collections, one with the 196 Broadway address and the other with the 128 Broadway address. The documented frames by Platt span many different styles, from rococo to federal to classical.

2. Henry Hall, *America's Successful Men of Affairs* (New York: New York Tribune, 1895-96), pp. 508-9.

3. Robert C. Smith, "Architecture and Sculpture in Nineteenth-Century Mirror Frames," *Antiques* 108, no. 2 (February 1976): 355.

4. See David L. Barquist, *American Tables and Looking Glasses in the Mabel Brady Garvan and Other Collections at Yale University* (New Haven, Conn.: Yale University Art Gallery, 1992), pp. 337-38, for a discussion of a looking glass with split turnings and foliate corners.

5. Smith, "Architecture and Sculpture in Nineteenth-Century Mirror Frames," p. 355.

6. Herbert L. Smith, *Private Sale of Important Antiques from the Randall Mansion, Cortland, N.Y., Beginning Friday, November 15, 1935*; photocopy, MWPI research files. Photographs taken between 1910 and 1935, now in the Cortland County Historical Society, show the mirrors hanging above the pier tables on opposite sides of the drawing room. See cat. no. 8 for a history of the Randall family and the Randall Mansion furnishings. This mirror was illustrated in Richard B. K. McLanathan, "Fountain Elms in Utica, New York," *Antiques* 79, no. 4 (April 1961): 357, and in Smith, "Architecture and Sculpture in Nineteenth-Century Mirror Frames," p. 355. Edgar de N. Mayhew loaned the mate of the MWPI pier glass to the exhibition "Classical Taste in America, 1815-1845," and it is illustrated in *Classical America, 1815-1845* (Newark, N.J.: Newark Museum, 1963), no. 65. The Mayhew mirror was offered for sale by Peter Hill in 1967 and is illustrated in his advertisement in *Antiques* 92, no. 5 (November 1967): 633.

7. Photocopy of part of an unknown legal document dated June 20, 1935, relating to Marion B. Wilson's estate. Attached to the document is a partial inventory of the contents of the house; photocopy, MWPI research files.

8. For a complete history of the house and its furnishings, see Douglas R. Kent, "Hyde Hall, Otsego County, New York," *Antiques* 92, no. 2 (August 1967): 187-93.

9. As quoted in Kent, "Hyde Hall," p. 189.

10. Kent, "Hyde Hall," p. 189.

11. Kent, "Hyde Hall," p. 190.

Catalogue Number 10

1. In preparation for the exhibition "Art and The Empire City," scheduled to open at the Metropolitan Museum of Art in 2000, Barbara Laux has conducted extensive research on Holmes and Haines. I would like to thank her and Catherine Voorsanger for generously sharing information about the firm with me. See also John L. Scherer, *New York Furniture at the New York State Museum* (Alexandria, Va.: Highland House Publishers, 1984), no. 58.

2. The sideboard was sold at auction by C. G. Sloan & Co., sale cat. 805 (Washington, D.C., May 19-21, 1989), lot 2531. What appears to be the same sideboard was sold at Neal Auction Co., *Estates Auction*, sale cat. (New Orleans, La., April 16-17, 1994), lot 612. The current location of the drop-leaf table is unknown. The two-drawer stand is in the collection of the New York State Museum, Albany; see Scherer, *New York Furniture*, p. 61. A pier table in the collection of the Geneva (N.Y.) Historical Society bears the label "H. & H./No. 58"; see Decorative Arts Photographic Collection, no. 89.288, Winterthur Museum, Garden and Library, Winterthur, Del., and Lorraine Welling Lanmon and H. Merrill Roenke Jr., "Rose Hill, near Geneva, New York," *Antiques* 136, no. 1 (July 1989): 151. A labeled pier table in the collection of the Metropolitan Museum of Art (accession no. 1978.586) is identified as "No. 146." The numbers on the labels may signify the order in which the tables were manufactured. According to family history the pier table at the Metropolitan Museum was made for the Piermont family of Brooklyn, whose house was destroyed by fire in 1826. After the fire the table and several other pieces of furniture were moved to lower Manhattan; they remained there until 1852 when they were taken to Garrison, N.Y. If this history is accurate, the table can be dated ca. 1825. A third bureau, closely related to the two labeled dressing bureaus (MWPI and Museum of Fine Arts, Boston, accession no. 67.1229), is in a private collection.

3. One attributed bureau is in the collection of the New York State Museum, Albany; another was sold at Braswell Auctions, South Norwalk, Conn., on an unknown date. See an advertisement for the sale in the MWPI research files. For a third, see Christie's East, *Furniture and Decorative Arts Including Ceramics*, sale cat. (New York, Jan. 20, 1998).

4. Donald L. Fennimore, "Gilding Practices and Processes in Nineteenth-Century American Furniture," in *Gilded Wood Conservation and History*, ed. Deborah Bigelow, Elizabeth Cornu, Gregory J. Landrey, and Cornelius Van Horne (Madison, Conn.: Sound View Press, 1991), p. 149. Two of the unlabeled examples include stenciled decoration on the columns.

5. Cynthia Moyer, "Conservation Treatments for Border and Freehand Gilding and Bronze Powder Stenciling and Freehand Bronze," *Gilded Wood Conservation and History*, p. 332.

6. For a discussion of the Kinnan and Mead bureau, see Wendy A. Cooper, *Classical Taste in America, 1800-1840* (New York: Abbeville Press for the Baltimore Museum of Art, 1993), pp. 219-20.

Catalogue Number 11

1. Susan Williams, *Savory Suppers and Fashionable Feasts: Dining in Victorian America* (New York: Pantheon Books, 1984), p. 51. Inventories of this period suggest that dining room furnishings usually included a table, a sideboard, a cellaret, one or more looking glasses, portraits, polished fireplace equipment, and, sometimes, a clock.

2. Elisabeth Donaghy Garrett, "The American Home: Part V: The Dining Room," *Antiques* 126, no. 4 (December 1984): 912.

3. It is possible that there was a third section of this table or that there were additional leaves to extend the top. The New York State Museum, Albany, owns two tables from this period that have three pedestal sections.

4. "Claw" is nineteenth-century terminology for what today is commonly referred to as "paw."

Remarkably few pedestal dining tables appear in published sources; the MWPI dining table is one of the most frequently cited examples. It is illustrated in Berry Tracy, *Classical America, 1815-1845* (Newark, N.J.: Newark Museum, 1963), no. 62, and in Helen Comstock, *American Furniture: Seventeenth, Eighteenth, and Nineteenth Century Styles* (New York: Viking Press, 1962), no. 599. Center tables with either carved or cylindrical pedestal supports resting on shaped plinths with naturalistically carved, elongated paw feet are more frequently illustrated. See *Nineteenth Century America: Furniture and Other Decorative Arts* (New York: Metropolitan Museum, 1970), no. 53, and Page Talbott, *Classical Savannah: Fine and Decorative Arts, 1800-1840* (Savannah: Telfair Museum and University of Georgia Press, 1995), no. 89.

5. Examples of New York tables that combine gold decorative elements include D-shaped card tables in the collections of the New York State Museum and the Museum of the City of New York (accession no. 40.372.2).

6. The hand-painted and stenciled decorative elements on the MWPI table are described in detail in Margery Miller, "A Look at Stenciled Furniture at the Munson-William-Proctor Institute," *The Decorator: Journal of the Historical Society of Early American Decoration* 29, no. 1 (Fall 1974): 12-13. Miller has noted that the stenciled decoration on this particular table was "obviously done by one of the more highly skilled craftsmen of his day." It is "artistically far above the usual. First, there is the use of freehand bronze and stumping along with multiple stencils. The two peaches, for example, seem to be composed of only one stencil each. The division of the cheeks of the fruit shows no evidence of a mechanical separation. Each section has been modeled freehand . . . with the addition of fine stumping to help mold the forms. The petals of the small flowers at the top have been built up from a single, repeated unit with stumped highlights and stamens while the stems of the grape clusters seem to be entirely stumped in with no evidence of a stencil at all. The leaves enclosing the pattern offer further example of a master touch. There is no duplication: each has been fashioned from a separately cut theorem, and their veining delicately defined with a curved edge."

CATALOGUE NUMBER 12

1. An extant piece with a label identical with that on the MWPI settee is in the collection of the New York State Museum, Albany.

2. Bates's first name has not been verified, but the cooper Jeremiah Bates—the only Bates name consistently listed in the Albany directories—is a likely partner. I am grateful to Mary Alice MacKay and Wesley G. Balla from the Albany Institute of History and Art for assisting me with this research.

3. Trade card, Joseph Downs Collection of Printed Ephemera, Winterthur Museum, Garden and Library, Winterthur, Del. Also cited in *Albany Argus and Daily City Gazette*, Jan. 5, 1819. In 1819 the Bates and Johnson establishment was located at 71 State Street.

4. *Albany Argus and Daily City Gazette*, Jan. 5, 1819, MWPI research files.

5. *Albany Argus and Daily City Gazette*, Apr. 6, 1827, MWPI research files.

6. *List of Patents Granted by the United States from April 10, 1790 to December 31, 1836* (Washington, D.C.: The Commissioner of Patents, 1872), p. 331, lists Johnson's patent as 1827. The notation also cites Johnson as residing in Albany. One explanation is that Johnson may have applied for the patent as early as 1819 while residing in Albany but was not granted the patent until 1827.

7. *Albany Argus and Daily City Gazette*, Apr. 6, 1827, MWPI research files.

8. *Albany Argus and Daily City Gazette*, Apr. 6, 1827, MWPI research files.

9. *American Masonick Record and Albany Literary Journal*, 1829, MWPI research files.

10. *New York Traveller and Spirit of the Times*, Dec. 8, 1832, p. 3.

CATALOGUE NUMBER 13

1. Edgar Miller, *American Antique Furniture* (Baltimore: Lord Baltimore Press, 1937; reprint, New York: Dover Publications, 1966), no. 1553. The table was owned at this time by Alexander Brown, a descendant of the original owner, merchant and banker Alexander Brown, for whom it was made about 1815. Miller points to the griffin decoration on the skirt as being similar to the creatures illustrated in Thomas Sheraton's *Cabinet-Maker and Upholsterer's Drawing Book* (1803); see p. 638, n. 5.

2. Weidman's article, "The Painted Furniture of John and Hugh Finlay," appeared in *Antiques* 118, no. 5 (May 1993): 744-55. This article expanded upon Weidman's previously published works in the exhibition catalogue *Classical Maryland, 1815-1845: Fine and Decorative Arts from the Golden Age* (Baltimore: Maryland Historical Society, 1993) and in *Furniture in Maryland, 1740-1940* (Baltimore: Maryland Historical Society, 1984).

3. *Federal Gazette and Baltimore Daily Advertiser*, Nov. 8, 1805, quoted in William Voss Elder III and Jayne E. Stokes, *American Furniture, 1680-1880, from the Collection of the Baltimore Museum of Art* (Baltimore, Md.: Baltimore Museum of Art, 1987), p. 47. The Abell chairs are also discussed in William Voss Elder III, *Baltimore Painted Furniture, 1800-1840* (Baltimore, Md.: Baltimore Museum of Art, 1972), pp. 45-47, 61.

4. Weidman, "Painted Furniture of John and Hugh Finlay," p. 745.

5. The Metropolitan Museum of Art purchased nine of these chairs in 1965 from an antique dealer in Baltimore. MWPI received this chair by exchange in 1977. Other chairs from the Metropolitan Museum's set are now owned by the High Museum, Atlanta (one); the Baltimore Museum of Art (two); and the George M. Kaufman collection (one). The Metropolitan Museum retained four. Two other chairs from the original set are in a private collection.

6. Weidman, "Painted Furniture of John and Hugh Finlay," p. 748.

7. See Léon de Groër, *Decorative Arts in Europe, 1790-1850* (New York: Rizzoli, 1985), pp. 12, 19. Mme. Elisabeth, whose home was at Montreuil, near Versailles, was the younger sister of Louis XVI. The furniture in the house is said to have been designed by Dugourc, Grognard, and Meunier and dates to 1790 or before. For chairs with broad tablets, continuous rear legs and back stiles, and boxed seat frames, see plate 4 in Thomas Hope, *Household Furniture and Interior Decoration* (London, 1807).

8. According to conservation analysis, the front legs, a front seat corner, and one end of the front rail have been inpainted. The crest rail has minimal inpainting. See Williamstown Regional Art Conservation Laboratory, Inc., "Furniture Examination Record" (December 1989), MWPI research files. For additional information on the conservation of another chair from this set, see Peter L. Fodera et al., "The Conservation of a Painted Baltimore Sidechair (ca. 1815) Attributed to John and Hugh Finlay," *Journal of the American Institute for Conservation* 36 (1997): 183-92. The designs of Percier and Fontaine were published in *Recueil de décorations intérieures*, issued serially beginning in 1801 and as a book in 1812.

CATALOGUE NUMBER 14

1. Thomas Sheraton, *The Cabinet Dictionary* (London, 1803), p. 145.

2. Compare, for instance, this pair of chairs with the formal set of Philadelphia *klismos* chairs pictured and discussed in Jack L. Lindsey, "An Early Latrobe Furniture Commission," *Antiques* 139, no. 1 (January 1991): 208-19.

3. All these craftsmen can be found in Philadelphia city directories and are listed in Deborah Ducoff-Barone, "Philadelphia Furniture Makers, 1800-1815," *Antiques* 134, no. 5 (May 1991): 982-95 and in "Philadelphia Furniture Makers, 1816-1830," *Antiques* 145, no. 5 (May 1994): 742-55.

4. See the unpaginated advertising supplements in *Desilver's Philadelphia Directory* (Philadelphia: Robert Desilver, 1837), *A. M'Elroy's Philadelphia Directory* (Philadelphia: A. M'Elroy, 1839), and *A. M'Elroy's Philadelphia Directory* (Philadelphia: A. M'Elroy, 1846).

5. The billhead is reproduced in Carl W. Drepperd, *Handbook of Antique Chairs* (Garden City, N.Y.: Doubleday, 1948), p. 166.

6. The decorative vertical banister between the crest rail and stay rail of the MWPI chairs is not pictured on the McDonough billhead. That is a significant difference. However, this feature would have been an option. Such banisters are found on fancy chairs with Philadelphia and Baltimore origins. See, for instance, the chair attributed to Philadelphia chairmaker John W. Patterson, pictured and discussed in Nancy Goyne Evans, *American Windsor Chairs* (New York: Hudson Hills Press in association with the Henry Francis du Pont Winterthur Museum, 1996), p. 144. A Baltimore counterpart attributed to John and Hugh Finlay is pictured in Gregory R. Weidman, "The Painted Furniture of John and Hugh Finlay," *Antiques* 143, no. 5 (May 1993): 754, plate XIX. A number of extant chairs that are identical with the MWPI pair, except for variations in the banisters, are pictured in Charles F. Montgomery, *American Furniture: The Federal Period* (New York: Viking Press, 1966), p. 456, fig. 466; Jonathan L. Fairbanks and Elizabeth Bidwell Bates, *American Furniture, 1620 to the Present* (New York: Richard Marek Publishers, 1981), p. 374; an Elizabeth R. Daniel advertisement in *Antiques* 109, no. 4 (April 1976): 667; and Robert Bishop, *Centuries and Styles of the American Chair* (New York: E. P. Dutton, 1972), p. 293, fig. 467.

The scrolled vases used at the tops of the legs of the MWPI chairs and similar chairs are also present in formal mahogany furniture such as a sideboard pictured in Wendy A. Cooper, *Classical Taste in America, 1800-1840* (New York: Abbeville Press and the Baltimore Museum of Art, 1993), p. 132, fig. 92, that is signed by Philadelphia chairmaker Joseph B. Barry and dated 1813.

CATALOGUE NUMBER 15

1. Images of pedestals in Greek and Roman interiors can be seen in Gisela M. Richter, *The Furniture of the Greeks, Etruscans and Romans* (London: Phaidon Press, 1966), figs. 312, 317, 660.

2. Rudolph Ackermann, *The Repository of Arts, Literature, Commerce, Manufactures, Fashions and Politics* (London: R. Ackermann, 1809-28), 6, no. 32 (Aug. 1, 1818): facing page 121. The tripod, a slender columnar form on three legs, had a lineage equally as ancient as the pedestal and, though typically identified as a different form by writers on interior design and furniture, seems to have served interchangeably with the pedestal.

3. One of a pair of pedestals made in Boston, Mass., about 1818 is illustrated in Page Talbott, "Boston Empire Furniture," *Antiques* 107, no. 5 (May 1975): 876, 885. One of another pair made in Baltimore, Md., about 1820 is illustrated in Wendy A. Cooper, *Classical Taste in America, 1800-1840* (New York: Abbeville Press for the Baltimore Museum of Art, 1993), p. 40.

4. For a discussion of English pattern books in American subscription libraries, see Donald L. Fennimore, "American Neoclassical Furniture and its European Antecedents," *American Art Journal* 13, no. 4 (Autumn 1981): 49-65.

5. Redner's piano case is illustrated in Donald L. Fennimore, "Gilding Practices and Processes in Nineteenth-Century American Furniture," in *Gilded Wood Conservation and History*, ed. Deborah Bigelow, Elizabeth Cornu, Gregory J. Landrey, and Cornelius Van Horne (Madison, Conn.: Sound View Press, 1991), p. 398.

6. The suite, which originally consisted of twenty-three pieces, is now dispersed. The Philadelphia Museum of Art owns the desk and bookcase and the Winterthur Museum, Garden and Library owns the bed, bedsteps, dressing bureau, washstand, and pair of wardrobes. Only the desk is signed by Jones.

7. The bed, bedsteps, dressing bureau, washstand, and two wardrobes are pictured and described in Sotheby's, sale cat. 5810 (New York, Jan. 26, 1989), lot 1463.

8. Inventory and appraisal of the goods of Elijah

Vansyckel, Mar. 8, 1855, Register of Wills, Philadelphia City Hall, Philadelphia, Pa.

CATALOGUE NUMBER 16

1. For tables of this type, see Morrison H. Heckscher, *American Furniture in the Metropolitan Museum of Art* (New York: Random House and the Metropolitan Museum of Art, 1985), pp. 178-82.
2. For a table of this type, see Charles F. Montgomery, *American Furniture: The Federal Period* (New York: Viking Press, 1966), pp. 345-46, no. 321.
3. Thomas Webster, *An Encyclopaedia of Domestic Economy* (New York: Harper and Brothers, 1845), p. 258.
4. John Claudius Loudon, *An Encyclopaedia of Cottage, Farm, and Villa Architecture and Furniture* (London: Longman, Orme, Brown, Green, and Longmans, 1839), p. 1048.
5. This and other price books were compiled for the use of members of the cabinet- and chairmaking trades. For a standard version of the Philadelphia pillar and claw dining table end, see Robert C. Smith, "The Furniture of Anthony G. Quervelle, Part II: The Pedestal Tables," *Antiques* 104, no. 1 (July 1973): 92, fig. 7.
6. The canted corners are described in *The Philadelphia Cabinet and Chair Makers' Union Book of Prices* (1828), p. 23. The two-part pedestal is a modified version of the table supports pictured as line drawings in plate 9, figs. 1 and 2, in the price book. An eagle-headed claw foot is pictured in plate 8, fig. 6.
7. The carving is comparable to related fruit clusters on a Philadelphia-made desk and bookcase, side chair, sideboard, and dining table. The desk, bookcase, and sideboard are illustrated in Robert C. Smith, "The Furniture of Anthony G. Quervelle, Part IV: Some Case Pieces," *Antiques* 105, no. 1 (January 1974): 183, fig. 4; 186, plate I. The dining table appears in Robert C. Smith, "The Furniture of Anthony G. Quervelle, Part III: The Worktables," *Antiques* 104, no. 2 (August 1973): 264, fig. 7. The carving on the chair is illustrated in Robert C. Smith, "The Furniture of Anthony G. Quervelle, Part V: Sofas, Chairs, and Beds," *Antiques* 105, no. 3 (March 1974): 516, fig. 7; 518, plate I.

CATALOGUE NUMBER 17

1. Various forms of Quervelle's advertisement appeared frequently in several of the city's leading newspapers and periodicals. The earliest notice advertising his "Ware House" at this address appears in the *Philadelphia Directory and Stranger's Guide for 1825* and in issues of the *United States Gazette* for that year. Between 1825 and 1842 he advertised that he was located at 11 Lombard Street and after 1850 at 71 Lombard.
2. For a fuller discussion of Quervelle's career, see Robert C. Smith, "Philadelphia Empire Furniture by Antoine Gabriel Quervelle," *Antiques* 86, no. 3 (September 1964): 304-9, and a series of articles by Smith—"The Furniture of Anthony G. Quervelle, Part I: The Pier Tables," *Antiques* 103, no. 5 (May 1973): 984-94; "The Furniture of Anthony G. Quervelle, Part II: The Pedestal Tables," *Antiques* 104, no. 1 (July 1973): 90-99; "The Furniture of Anthony G. Quervelle, Part III: The Worktables," *Antiques* 104, no. 2 (August 1973): 260-68; "The Furniture of Anthony G. Quervelle, Part IV: Some Case Pieces," *Antiques* 105, no. 1 (January 1974): 180-93; and "The Furniture of Anthony G. Quervelle, Part V: Sofas, Chairs, and Beds," *Antiques* 105, no. 3 (March 1974): 512-21.
3. For more on the French *ébéniste* tradition, see Alexander Pradére, *French Furniture Makers: The Art of the Ébéniste from Louis XIV to the Revolution* (Malibu, Calif.: Getty Museum, 1989). Many eighteenth-century French workshops included specialists; mahogany was traditionally an *ébéniste's* material.
4. See Pierre de la Mésangère, *Meubles et objets de goût. 1796-1830, 678 documents tirés des journaux de modes et de la "collection" de la Mésangère* (Paris, n.d.), plate 158.
5. See Smith, *Collection of Designs for Household Furniture* (London, 1808), plate 106. The overall design of the case relates to a pattern suggested in plate 23.
6. The labeled examples at MWPI and the Philadelphia Museum of Art (PMA) provide the basis for the attribution to Quervelle of three other secretary bookcases. All five examples have related construction, veneer work, carving, and shaped, paneled appliqués. The largest, most ornate version of this group is in the collection of the PMA. A variation, with Gothic-inspired mullions in the top and bottom doors, is in the collection of the Virginia Museum of Fine Arts. For another version, see Smith, "The Furniture of Anthony G. Quervelle, Part IV: Case Pieces," figs. 7 and 8. Another example sold at auction at Freeman's Fine Arts, sale cat. (Philadelphia, April 1977), lot 1046.
7. As quoted in "Report on the Committee on Premiums and Exhibitions of the Fourth Annual Exhibition," *Journal of the Franklin Institute* (1827): 403.
8. For more information concerning the 1829 White House commissions, see Kathleen M. Catalano, "Cabinetmaking in Philadelphia (1820-1840)" (M.A. thesis, University of Delaware, 1972), p. 107.
9. This sketchbook, in the collection of the PMA (accession no. 1995-12-1–13), consists of a full quarto uncut sheet covering fifteen double-sided, half-sheet pages with pen, ink, pencil, and watercolor-wash drawings of numerous furniture forms. These drawings strongly relate to known examples of furniture documented to Quervelle's shop. The sketchbook is attributed to Quervelle on the basis of the resemblance of the drawings to examples of Quervelle's documented furniture and because analytical handwriting comparison with Quervelle's manuscript will (Philadelphia City Hall, Historic Archives, Wills and Inventories) has shown that the notations on the drawings are in Quervelle's hand.
10. The mullion pattern prescribed in this drawing most closely corresponds to the doors of the PMA example.

CATALOGUE NUMBER 18

1. See George Smith, *Collections of Designs for Household Furniture* (London, 1808); Thomas Sheraton, *The Cabinetmaker and Upholsterer's Drawing Book* (London, 1793); and Rudolph Ackermann, *The Repository of Arts, Literature, Commerce, Manufactures, Fashions and Politics* (London: R. Ackermann, 1809-28).
2. The form, when fitted with a mirror on the underside of the top or on a tilting interior hinged frame, is also referred to in several Philadelphia cabinetmakers' daybooks of the period as a toilet or dressing table. The terms seem to have been randomly assigned and interchangeable.
3. Robert C. Smith, "Furniture of Anthony G. Quervelle, Part III: The Worktables," *Antiques* 104, no. 2 (August 1973): 260-68, discusses the known worktables from Quervelle's workshop in detail.
4. This sketchbook is in the collection of the Philadelphia Museum of Art (accession no. 1995-12-1–13). See cat. no. 12, n. 9, for a further description.

CATALOGUE NUMBER 19

1. The furnishings have been attributed to Upjohn largely because he, as a youth in England, had apprenticed to a cabinetmaker for five years. After emigrating to the United States in 1828, he parlayed the lessons of his training, which included a keen sense of proportion and knowledge of current styles, into a long career. Helen Comstock, *American Furniture: Seventeenth, Eighteenth, and Nineteenth Century Styles* (New York: Viking, 1962), nos. 604, 617, 630-32; Katherine S. Howe and David B. Warren, *The Gothic Revival Style in America, 1830-1870* (Houston, Tex.: Museum of Fine Arts, Houston, 1976); Carla Davidson, *The American Heritage History of Antiques* (New York: American Heritage Pub. Co., 1977), no. 330; and John Scherer, *New York Furniture at the New York State Museum* (Alexandria, Va.: Highland House, 1984) all discuss the suite as an Upjohn design.
2. See Charles Lockwood, *Bricks and Brownstone: The New York Row House, 1783-1929: An Architectural and Social History* (New York: Abbeville Press, 1972), p. 205; see also Carol E. Gordon, MWPI, to Katherine Howe, Sept. 19, 1975, MWPI research files.
3. The library suite was donated to MWPI in 1960 by Mrs. Erving C. Pruyn. The gift included five walnut bookcases, a mahogany mantel mirror with matching pedimented cornice, and a walnut library table. Three bookcases are now in the collection of the New York State Museum, Albany. Two of these are presently on loan to Lindenwald, formerly the country house of President Martin Van Buren in Kinderhook, N.Y., for whom Upjohn designed an addition and renovations in 1850. At that time Upjohn designed bookcases (location unknown) for Van Buren's library.
4. National Register Nomination Form, Landmarks Commission, New York, N.Y.
5. The lots were 33⅓ feet rather than the usual 25 feet. Among the Upjohn Papers, Avery Fine Arts and Architectural Library, Columbia University, is a signed, second-floor plan of a bow-front house; the dimensions do not match those of the Kelly house.
6. William Kelly Prentice, *Eight Generations: The Ancestry, Education, and Life of William Packer Prentice* (Princeton, N.J.: n.p., 1947). Prentice was the Kellys' son-in-law.
7. These photographs are at the Museum of the City of New York.
8. The Alexander Roux parlor furniture from the Kelly house is in the collection of the New York State Museum and is one of the largest extant suites bearing Roux's label.
9. Robert Kelly to Richard Upjohn, Feb. 14, 1846, Richard and Richard Michell Upjohn Papers, Rare Books and Manuscripts Collection, New York Public Library. Three letters dated 1847 from Parsons describe his work on a library table, but the first suggests that he had just received the contract, the second that he was hoping to finish the table soon, and the third that he was shipping it from New York City. Little is known about Parsons.
10. Aside from the memorial included in Prentice's book, there are several others to Kelly that stress his intellect and education. These include Edgar S. Van

Winkle, *A Tribute to . . . Robert Kelly June 4, 1856* (New York: Bryant & Co., Printers, 1856), and Alexander S. Leonard, *An Oration before the Associate Alumni of Columbia College, Occasioned by the Death of Robert Kelly, LL.D., Late President of the Association. November 24, 1856* (New York: Sheldon, Blakeman & Co., 1857).
11. The two bookcases have marked differences. One has two slant-fronts, each of which opens to a desk with pigeonholes and six small drawers. The delicate ogee arches above the pigeonholes and the locks in the drawers bespeak expert design and execution. The doors of the lower section of this bookcase have solid wood panels; behind the door at each end are three drawers, and behind the center door, three shelves. The lower section of the MWPI bookcase pictured here has adjustable shelves behind doors with glass panels.
12. The profile of the pediment is a shallower version of porch and window canopies found at several Upjohn houses, such as the entry at the demolished Lyman residence (1844), Brookline, Mass. The foliate pendants relate the mirror to Upjohn's Gothic revival woodwork elsewhere in the Kelly house.
13. This is confirmed by Prentice, *Eight Generations*, p. 193: "The library was of black walnut, and was connected with the parlor by large folding doors, black walnut on one side, and white on the other."

Catalogue Number 20

1. Hobe is first listed in New York directories in 1839-40 as a cabinetmaker. His first business address, 140 Grand, does not appear until 1842-43. Between 1845 and 1847 Hobe relocated his shop to 443 Broadway. By 1853 his shop was at 484 Broadway, where it remained until ca. 1865. In the early 1850s Charles F. Hobe worked with his son Charles J. Hobe; the last listing for Charles F. Hobe and "C. F. Hobe & Son, Tables" is 1864-65. Charles J. Hobe, "cabinetmaker manufacturer of Hobe's patent premium extension tables," continued to be listed through 1868-69.
2. T. Morehead, *New-York Mercantile Register for 1848-49, Containing the Cards of the Principal Business Establishments, Including Hotels and Public Institutions in New-York City* (New York: John P. Prall), p. 93.
3. *New-York Mercantile Register*, p. 93.
4. A descendant of the Kelly family, Mrs. Erving C. Pruyn, gave the library suite and the pedestal table to MWPI. Family tradition held that Upjohn designed all of the pieces.

Catalogue Number 21

1. See Katherine S. Howe and David B. Warren, *The Gothic Revival Style in America, 1830-1870* (Houston, Tex.: Museum of Fine Arts, Houston, 1976).
2. Lyndhurst was built in 1838 for William Paulding. Thirty years later, Davis designed additions for the second owner of the home, George Merritt.
3. For additional information, see Howe and Warren, *Gothic Revival Style in America*.
4. Gothic turrets were added to the house in 1863 and later removed. The rococo revival parlor was left unchanged until 1995.
5. For photographs of Century House, see Russell A. Grills, *Cazenovia: The Story of an Upland Community* (Cazenovia, N.Y.: Cazenovia Preservation Foundation, 1986), pp. 48, 59. I would like to thank Russell A. Grills for his assistance with the historic information on Century House. Many of the home's furnishings were dispersed at a public house sale. The house was sold to a private buyer in 1995.

Catalogue Number 22

1. Andrew Jackson Downing, *The Architecture of Country Houses* (New York: D. Appleton, 1850), p. 432.
2. Thomas Webster, *Encyclopaedia of Domestic Economy* (New York: Harper & Brother, 1845), p. 248.
3. Numerous examples of eighteenth-century French armchairs of this type are included in Bill G. B. Pallot, *The Art of the Chair in Eighteenth-Century France* (Paris: ACR, 1989). The examples pictured on pp. 91, 119, 126, and 161 bear particularly close resemblances to the MWPI chair. The MWPI chair, however, has proportions different from the Parisian prototypes. French armchairs in the rococo style are invariably horizontal in composition, while the MWPI chair has a vertical thrust.
4. Two volumes of these furniture designs, including the one mentioned for a chair, survive in the Bibliothèque National in Paris, France, under the title *L'ameublement*.
5. See Peter Thornton, *Authentic Decor: The Domestic Interior, 1620-1920* (New York: Viking, 1984), p. 271.
6. An upholstered side chair bearing the label of Charles A. Baudouine, in the collection of the Virginia Museum of Fine Arts in Richmond (accession no. 81.86), has carving similar to that which appears on the MWPI example.
7. For a fuller description of flowers and their meanings during the Victorian era, see Mary Ann Bacon, *Flowers and Their Kindred Thoughts* (London: Longman & Co., 1848).

Catalogue Number 23

1. Charles F. Montgomery noted that "most known examples appear to have been made in New York where the form is first listed in the price book of 1810." See his *American Furniture: The Federal Period* (New York: Viking Press, 1966), p. 352.
2. Thomas Sheraton, *The Cabinet Dictionary* (1803; reprint, New York: Praeger Publishers, 1970), pp. 305-6, plate 74.
3. Andrew Jackson Downing, *The Architecture of Country Houses*, as reprinted in John C. Freeman, comp., *Furniture for the Victorian Home* (Watkins Glen, N.Y.: American Life Foundation, 1968), p. 59.
4. Invoice, James Miller to J. Watson Williams, Nov. 4, 1846, MWPI Archives.
5. For additional information on the formation of the MWPI decorative arts collection, see the introductory essay to this catalogue.
6. The address noted on the Williams invoice is 441 Broadway. In 1851-52 Miller is listed in New York City directories at 508 Broome Street as an upholsterer and from 1852-53 through 1854-55 at 108 Thompson Street also as an upholsterer. In the 1853-54 directory Miller's listing cites "upholsterer" and "daguerreotypes."
7. Robert Conner, *The Cabinet Maker's Assistant* (Buffalo, N.Y.: Faxon & Read, 1842); see pp. 19 and 29 for similar table designs. Printed Book and Periodical Collection, Winterthur Museum, Garden and Library, Winterthur, Del.
8. Conner, *Cabinet Maker's Assistant*, plate 19.

Catalogue Number 24

1. Belter filed his application for passport travel to the United States (no. 817) on Aug. 29, 1833, at Osnabruck, Germany. It records that he apparently originally intended to go to Baltimore, but Belter changed his mind and went to New York instead. The original passport application is in the State Records, Bremen, Germany. Photocopy, MWPI research files, courtesy of the author.
2. *The New-York City Directory* (New York: John Doggett Jr., 1844), p. 34.
3. Design patent 19,405 (Feb. 23, 1858), U.S. Patent Office, Washington, D.C. Belter's three other patents were for machinery to saw chair backs (no. 5,208), for the construction of bedsteads (no. 15,552), and for the construction of bureau drawers (no. 26,881).
4. The MWPI research file for this group of furniture contains a document in which the former owner indicates that the sofa was made for a member of the "Shaffer" family of Pottsville, Pa., about 1847 and that it remained in the family until about 1953. The original purchaser may have been John or Killian Shaeffer, both of whom were residents of Pottsville in the 1840s. Even though the document mentions only the sofa, the accompanying chairs were almost certainly made en suite.
5. A sofa, armchair, and the table from the set, along with Belter's itemized bill for them, are pictured and discussed in Michael K. Brown, "A Decade of Collecting at Bayou Bend," *Antiques* 128, no. 3 (September 1985): 516, 517. According to David B. Warren, senior curator and director of the Bayou Bend Collection at the Museum of Fine Arts, Houston, Col. Benjamin Smith Jordan of Milledgeville, Ga., purchased this furniture from Belter on Sept. 5, 1855, on behalf of his sister-in-law, Mrs. Greenhill Jordan.
6. *The Compact Edition of the Oxford English Dictionary* (1971), s.v. "arabesque."

Catalogue Number 25

1. Blackie and Son, *The Cabinet Maker's Assistant* (London, 1853), pp. 50, 51.
2. Andrew Jackson Downing, *The Architecture of Country Houses* (New York: D. Appleton, 1850), p. 456. An étagère is pictured in the context of an elaborate New York City parlor in *Gleason's Pictorial Drawing-room Companion*, Nov. 11, 1854.
3. For comparable French console tables, see Pierre Kjellberg, *Le Meuble Français* (Paris: Les Editions de l'Amateur, 1991), pp. 187-90, and Bill G. B. Pallot, *The Art of the Chair in Eighteenth-Century France* (Paris: ACR, 1989), pp. 152, 154, 155. An informative design for a mid-nineteenth-century French console table in this style, drawn and published by the Parisian cabinetmaker Célestin Allard about 1855, can be seen in Denise Ledoux-Lebard, *Les ébénistes du XIXe siècle, 1795-1889: Leurs œuvres et leurs marques* (Paris: Les éditions de l'Amateur, 1989), p. 28.
4. The laminated components include the carved and pierced skirts under the shelves of both sections.
5. Blackie and Son, *The Cabinet Maker's Assistant*, p. 26.
6. B. Silliman Jr. and C. R. Goodrich, eds., *The World of Science, Art, and Industry* (New York: G. P. Putnam, 1854), p. 19.
7. Other unsigned étagères that appear to be closely related to this example are in the Minneapolis Institute of Arts, Minneapolis, Minn., and the Daughters of the American Revolution Museum, Washington, D.C. A third is illustrated in a Richard and Eileen Dubrow advertisement in *Antiques* 121, no. 5 (May 1982): 1086; and a fourth is in Pettigrew Auction Co., *Important Two Day Estates Auction in Colorado Springs*, sale cat. (Colorado Springs, Colo., Apr. 26-27, 1997), lot 166.

Catalogue Number 26

1. Baudouine's family was of Huguenot descent. Charles Baudouine was born in New York City on May 31, 1808, the son of Abraham Baudouine (d. 1844), also born in New York City. I would like to thank Cynthia Schaffner, who researched Baudouine's career while she was a graduate intern in the Department of American Decorative Arts at the Metropolitan Museum of Art in 1994, and Catherine Hoover Voorsanger, associate curator at the Metropolitan, for making this information available.
2. *Stranger's Guide in the City of New-York, 1852* (New York: Andrews & Co., 1852), p. 58.
3. Catherine Hoover Voorsanger, "From the Bowery to Broadway: The Herter Brothers and the New York Furniture Trade" in Katherine S. Howe, Alice Cooney Frelinghuysen, Catherine Hoover Voorsanger et al., *Herter Brothers: Furniture and Interiors for a Gilded Age* (New York: Harry N. Abrams in association with the Museum of Fine Arts, Houston, 1994), p. 61.
4. Earnest Hagen, "Personal Experiences of an Old New York Cabinet Maker," 1908, Downs Manuscript Collection (col. 32), Winterthur Museum, Garden and Library, Winterthur, Del. The body of this manuscript was reprinted in Elizabeth A. Ingerman, "Personal Experiences of an Old New York Cabinetmaker," *Antiques* 84, no. 5 (November 1963): 576-80. Hagen recalls working for Baudouine from about 1854 to 1856. According to city directories, however, 1854 is the last year Baudouine is listed as a cabinetmaker. In addition, the R. G. Dun report for May 5, 1855, notes: "Removed to 475 Bdway where he has an office—is clos[ing] up the bus." R. G. Dun & Co. Collection, Baker Library, Harvard University Graduate School of Business Administration, Boston, Mass.
5. Hagen, "Personal Experiences." Baudouine married Ann P. Postley of New York City on June 3, 1833. See Henry Hall, ed., *America's Successful Men of Affairs, An Encyclopedia of Contemporaneous Biography* (New York: The New York Tribune, 1895), 1: 65.
6. Hagen, "Personal Experiences."
7. Hagen, "Personal Experiences."
8. *Stranger's Guide*, p. 59. Baudouine's label states that he kept "constantly on hand the largest assortment of Elegant furniture to be Found in the United States." See paper label on laminated chair in the collection of the Virginia Museum of Fine Arts, Richmond, Va. (accession no. 81.86).
9. New York Vol. 191, p. 1421 (Jan. 11, 1853), R. G. Dun & Co. Collection.
10. Anthony Kimbel "worked in New York as the principal designer for Charles Baudouine" prior to 1854. See David L. Barquist, *American Tables and Looking Glasses in the Mabel Brady Garvan and Other Collections at Yale University* (New Haven, Conn.: Yale University Art Gallery, 1992), p. 111. From 1854 to 1862 Kimbel was a partner in Bembé and Kimbel. In 1862 he formed a partnership with Joseph Cabus. The firm Kimbel and Cabus lasted until 1882. See cat. no. 46 and Doreen Bolger Burke et al., *In Pursuit of Beauty: Americans and the Aesthetic Movement* (New York: Metropolitan Museum of Art, 1986), p. 446.
11. In Hagen's reference to furniture with "perforated backs," he may have identified those Baudouine products that constituted an "infringement" on John Henry Belter's patent for rococo-style furniture. Hagen, "Personal Experiences." For John Henry Belter furniture, see cat. no. 24.
12. James Watson Williams to Helen Elizabeth Munson, July 11, 1846, MWPI Archives. A painted and stenciled rococo-style writing table with a paper Baudouine label is in the collection of the Museum of Fine Arts, Boston (accession no. 1979.612).

Catalogue Number 27

1. Invoice in MWPI Archives.
2. One section of the table has a set of wooden screws on the underside; the other section has threaded holes to receive the screws.
3. A similar settee and table are in the collection of the Museum of Fine Arts, Boston (accession nos. 1978.379 and 1981.299, respectively). Tables identical with the MWPI example can be found in the collections of the Museum of Fine Arts, Houston, Tex., and the St. Louis Art Museum, St. Louis, Mo.

Catalogue Number 28

1. For further information on Galusha, see Anna T. D'Ambrosio with Stacy Pomeroy Draper, *Artistry in Rosewood: Furniture by Elijah Galusha* (Utica, N.Y.: Munson-Williams-Proctor Institute, 1995).

Although it is not clear that Galusha trained in Shaftsbury, his age and the presence in the community of established cabinetmakers such as Daniel and Asa Loomis make it probable that Galusha had some training before he moved to Troy. According to Galusha's obituary, he apprenticed with H. M. Smith in Troy (*Troy Daily Times*, July 27, 1871). Smith's cabinetmaking career is not documented.
2. Related services included repairing a "lath bottom of bedstead," hanging pictures, repairing and polishing furniture, gilding objects, and installing floor matting. See invoices in the collection of the Rensselaer County Historical Society (hereafter cited as RCHS), Troy, N.Y. In 1856-57 Henry Galusha, Elijah's son who later opened a grocery store, worked with Elijah.
3. Rosewood was the primary wood used for parlor furniture. Woods used for other furniture forms included cherry, mahogany, maple, and walnut.
4. The RCHS collection includes a signed example of a Galusha frame. Galusha also sold more elaborate gilt items and minor household furnishings such as towel stands, window shades, and footstools that may have been made by other firms.
5. For a discussion of French furniture design sources, especially *Le Garde-Meuble*, see Kenneth L. Ames, "Designed in France: Notes on the Transmission of French Style to America," *Winterthur Portfolio* 12 (1977): 103-14.
6. Surviving furniture and bills of sale demonstrate that Galusha's work was held in high regard. He provided work for the Richard Hart and John Paine Nazro families of Troy, N.Y., and for the Col. Robert Milligan family of nearby Saratoga Springs, who could afford furniture made by prominent New York City cabinetmakers. Numerous pieces made for the Hart family are now in the collection of RCHS. Bills of sale indicate that the Hart family also patronized the New York City firms of Alexander Roux and Léon Marcotte. The Milligan's 1856 parlor is preserved in its entirety at the Brooklyn Museum of Art.
7. An outstanding body of well-documented Galusha furniture from this period survives at MWPI, RCHS, Brooklyn (N.Y.) Museum of Art, the New York State Museum in Albany, and in private collections.
8. New York Vol. 538, p. 80 (1857), R. G. Dun & Co. Collection, Baker Library, Harvard University Graduate School of Business Administration, Boston, Mass.
9. In 1870 the R. G. Dun & Co. credit report observes that Galusha "has only done a small business this year and has a large stock on hand. . . . He is too slow and old fashioned and has owl smart, active competitors." New York Vol. 539, p. 242, R. G. Dun & Co. Collection. The wareroom remained open under Hosea Leach. In 1872 J. Crawford Green and Marcus Waterman took over the firm, and it continued in operation through the turn of the century.

Catalogue Number 29

1. John A. Kouwenhoven, *The Arts in Modern American Civilization* (1948; reprint, New York: W. W. Norton, 1967), pp. 13-74.
2. The phrase is from the title used by Katherine C. Grier, *Culture and Comfort: People, Parlors, and Upholstery, 1850-1930* (Rochester, N.Y.: Strong Museum, 1988).
3. Joseph T. Butler, *American Antiques, 1800-1900* (New York: Odyssey Press, 1965), discusses centripetal chairs under the heading of "Innovative Furniture" and comments only on their springs. The most extensive discussion of centripetal spring chairs, David A. Hanks, *Innovative Furniture in America from 1800 to the Present* (New York: Horizon, 1981), pp. 126-29, argues that the chairs are significant for their use of springs and cast iron but does not comment on their more conventional features. In *Culture and Comfort* Grier has noted the elements that made these chairs examples of technological advancement but also called attention to those that signified refinement. These include the intricate cast-iron ornament and the original, red, stamped plush upholstery in a lush floral pattern, which survives on an example owned by the Strong Museum, Rochester, N.Y. The Metropolitan Museum of Art, ever the advocate of the cultivated tradition, did not include centripetal spring chairs in its landmark 1970 exhibition "19th-Century America."
4. Trade catalogue of Chase Bros. & Co. (Boston, ca. 1855), Hagley Museum and Library, Wilmington, Del. The illustration on p. 36 of the catalogue identifies the MWPI chair as a piano stool and also shows the fringe that may have originally ringed its seat.
5. Hanks, *Innovative Furniture*, p. 126.
6. The Art Journal, *The Industry of All Nations* (London: George Virtue, 1851), p. 152.
7. Siegfried Giedion, *Mechanization Takes Command* (1948; reprint, New York: W. W. Norton, 1969), p. 401. On rocking chairs, see Ellen Denker and Bert Denker, *The Rocking Chair Book* (New York: Mayflower Books, 1979); on American attitudes toward posture, see Kenneth L. Ames, *Death in the Dining Room and Other Tales of Victorian Culture* (Philadelphia: Temple University Press, 1992), pp. 185-232.
8. "In hindsight we can recognize it as the prototype for the pedestal office chair—a form duplicated by the millions in the twentieth century." R. Craig Miller in Neil Harris et al., *The Denver Art Museum: The First Hundred Years* (Denver: Denver Art Museum, 1996), p. 236.
9. Hanks, *Innovative Furniture*, p. 126.
10. Illustrated in Giedion, *Mechanization Takes Command*, p. 404. Like the chair in fig. 101 of Hanks, *Innovative Furniture*, these have wooden, rather than cast-iron, bases.

Catalogue Number 30

1. In the New York City directory of 1838-39 the firm is listed as "Hutchings, E. W. & Co." In the 1842-43 directory it changes to "Hutchings, E. W. & W. & Co." The second W. is dropped from the listing in the following year. By 1851 the firm name is "E. W. Hutchings & Co." although the "& Co." was not always used. In 1866 the firm name became "E. W. Hutchings & Son." Edward Jr. (1840 or 1841-95) joined the firm as early as 1860 (when his business address is the same as his father's) but was not officially made a partner until 1866. See New York Vol. 190, p. 400 (July 12, 1866), R. G. Dun & Co. Collection, Baker Library, Harvard University Graduate School of Business Administration, Boston, Mass. I have relied on the chronology of Hutchings' business that Medill Higgins Harvey compiled for the Department of American Decorative Arts of the Metropolitan Museum of Art in 1994. Catherine Hoover Voorsanger, associate curator, kindly provided access to this material.

Invoice from E. W. Hutchings to James W. Williams, November 1851, MWPI Archives. Williams purchased a dining room étagère for $93. This object is not in the MWPI collection. The invoice is signed by R. C. Hutchings, possibly Edward's son Robert (b. 1836 or 1837). Robert is listed as a lawyer in the 1860 U.S. Census.

2. Bureau of the Census, *Seventh Census of the U.S., Products of Industry*, 1850, City of New York, New York, 8th Ward and N.Y. State Census, 1855, City of New York, 1st District, 8th Ward.

3. While Hutchings' business prospered, he, like many of his colleagues, did not eagerly adopt steam-powered machinery. The 1870 federal census notes that his shop used hand-powered tools.

4. Reviewers of Hutchings' display criticized the sideboard: "We find more to commend in the conception of the design than in its execution. The treatment of the figures in particular is undecided and incorrect, and betrays a want of practical skill in the art of wood sculpture." See B. Silliman Jr. and C. R. Goodrich, *The World of Science, Art and Industry Illustrated: From Examples in the New-York Exhibition, 1853-54* (New York: G. P. Putnam, 1854), p. 189.

5. Hutchings also had business dealings with James W. Vanpelt, a New York City wood merchant. Conceivably Vanpelt supplied wood to Hutchings' cabinet shops. The exact nature of the business association is unclear, but in 1882 cabinetmaker Peter Brunner stated, "Hutchings was in the lumber business in the beginning." See an 1882 article from *Furniture Gazette* quoted in Eileen Dubrow and Richard Dubrow, *American Furniture of the 19th Century, 1840-1880* (Atglen, Pa.: Schiffer Publishing, 1983), p. 24. This statement is corroborated by the fact that from 1847 to 1851 Vanpelt and Hutchings list identical business addresses, and the R. G. Dun & Co. credit-rating report records the dissolution of a business association between Hutchings and Vanpelt in 1851: "J. W. Van Pelt leaving the bus." New York Vol. 190, p. 398 (Aug. 28, 1851), R. G. Dun & Co. Collection. The 1851 Doggett Street Directory includes the listing "Vanpelt" under "E. W. Hutchings & Co."

6. Illinois Vol. 28, p. 14 (Dec. 1, 1856) and New York Vol. 190, p. 398 (Mar. 15 and Dec. 23, 1856), R. G. Dun & Co. Collection. From 1838 through 1857 New York City directories give the same business address for William and for Edward Hutchings. William Hutchings' Chicago business is listed in 1857 at 151 Randolph Street. The 1856 Chicago R. G. Dun & Co. report notes that the goods sold by William Hutchings were "too fine" for the Chicago market. To date, the only extant furniture sold by the Chicago shop of William Hutchings is at Villa Louis of the State Historical Society of Wisconsin, Prairie du Chien. It is documented by two bills of sale for goods William Hutchings sold to Col. Hercules Dousman in 1856 and 1857. After closing his furniture business, William entered the liquor business. Curiously, however, in 1860 Edward Hutchings is listed in the classified section of the Chicago directory under the heading "furniture dealers."

7. The August 1851 R. G. Dun & Co. report that notes Vanpelt's departure from the firm also states, "They had . . . a store in N. O. where 'V. P.' managed." The Dun report of Dec. 1, 1856, on William Hutchings states that Edward's New York business "met some severe losses . . . in Mobile where he established a branch"; New York Vol. 190, p. 398 and Vol. 28, p. 14, R. G. Dun & Co. Collection.

8. Charles Prescott, ed., *The Hotel Guests' Guide to the City of New York* (New York: George W. Averell, 1872), p. 92.

9. Affluent investor and stockbroker LeGrand Lockwood (1820-72) engaged Hutchings to furnish at least two bedrooms in his home, Elm Park, in Norwalk, Conn. (built ca. 1867-69). Herter Brothers executed most of the interior decoration and furnishings for Elm Park. Hutchings may have received this commission because Gustave Herter "formed business connections" with Hutchings in the late 1840s. See *The National Cyclopedia of American Biography* 6 (New York: James T. White, 1896), p. 297, s.v. "Herter, Gustave." There were many interconnections among prominent New York City furniture-making firms. Cabinetmaker and interior decorator Auguste Pottier (1823-96), early in his career, was also affiliated with Hutchings. Pottier, who entered into partnership with William Stymus in 1859, worked as a journeyman sculptor for Hutchings from 1850 to 1853. See Katherine S. Howe, Alice Cooney Frelinghuysen, Catherine Hoover Voorsanger et al., *Herter Brothers: Furniture and Interiors for a Gilded Age* (New York: Harry N. Abrams in association with the Museum of Fine Arts, Houston, 1994), p. 62.

10. New York Vol. 190, p. 400a/23 (May 6, 1885), R. G. Dun & Co. Collection.

11. Plate 25 in *Cabinet Makers Album of Furniture*, an Americanization of a French publication, illustrates a "Lady's Escritoire Louis X. V." with attributes similar to those of the Hutchings desk. See *Cabinet Maker's Album of Furniture Comprising a Collection of Designs for the Newest and Most Elegant Styles of Furniture* (Philadelphia: Henry Carey Baird, 1868). Printed Book and Periodical Collection, Winterthur Museum, Garden and Library, Winterthur, Del.

12. No author. Printed Book and Periodical Collection, Winterthur Museum, Garden and Library.

Catalogue Number 31

1. The business history of the Meeks firm is drawn from a detailed chronology compiled by the author for the Department of American Decorative Arts, the Metropolitan Museum of Art. This work has been expanded into Jodi A. Pollack, "Three Generations of Meeks Craftsmen, 1797-1869: A History of Their Business and Furniture" (M.A. thesis, Program in the History of Decorative Arts, Parsons School of Design and Cooper-Hewitt, National Design Museum, Smithsonian Institution, 1998). Previous literature on the firm includes John N. Pearce, Lorraine W. Pearce, and Robert C. Smith, "The Meeks Family of Cabinetmakers," *Antiques* 85, no. 4 (April 1964): 414-20; John Pearce and Lorraine W. Pearce, "More on the Meeks Cabinetmakers," *Antiques* 90, no. 1 (July 1966): 69-73; Ed Polk Douglas, "Rococo Roses, Part III: Blessed Are the Meeks(s)," *The New York-Pennsylvania Collector* 4 (August 1979): 1, 10-13; and Ed Polk Douglas, "Rococo Roses, Part IV: Faith and Furniture," *The New York-Pennsylvania Collector* 4 (September 1979): 12-15.

2. Bureau of the Census, *Seventh Census of the U. S., Products of Industry*, 1850, City of New York, N.Y., 3d Ward, p. 363. This census indicates that the firm employed 125 male workers at a total average monthly cost of $3,500 and six female workers at an average monthly cost of $100, had invested $150,000 in the business, and produced 2,000 pieces of furniture annually valued at $200,000.

3. New York Vol. 191, p. 404, R. G. Dun & Co. Collection, Baker Library, Harvard University Graduate School of Business Administration, Boston, Mass.

4. The dissolution of the J. & J. W. Meeks firm is discussed in the R. G. Dun & Co. report of Feb. 14, 1859: "Diss[olve]d. the 12th Inst. The outst[an]d[in]g. affairs of the late firm will be settled at thr. late place of bus[iness], Nos. 333 & 335 Fourth st. Cor. Broadway, either ptnr. being authorized to sign in liquidatn. 'Joseph W. Meeks' retires & 'John Meeks' will cont. the Cabinet Furniture bus. at the same place as heretofore on his own a/c." New York Vol. 191, p. 404, R. G. Dun & Co. Collection.

5. Joseph Meeks died July 21, 1868. The final directory listings for John Meeks Jr.'s furniture firm appear in *Trow's New York City Directory for the Year Ending May 1, 1869* (New York: John F. Trow, 1868), and in *Wilson's Business Directory of New York City [1869]* (New York: John F. Trow, 1869). Because the last report filed for the firm by R. G. Dun & Co. is dated Nov. 7, 1868, the firm appears to have dissolved between that date and Apr. 30, 1869.

6. "Chit-Chat of New-York," *The New Mirror*, Mar. 9, 1844, p. 367. I am grateful to Jeni L. Sandberg for bringing this reference to my attention.

7. I wish to thank Richard Dubrow and Eileen Dubrow for informing me of a second example of this form, also bearing the stenciled label of J. & J. W. Meeks, in a private collection.

8. The MWPI games table is identified by a black stenciled label, with the firm's address from 1836 to 1855, on the interior of the drawer.

Catalogue Number 32

1. Andrew Jackson Downing, *The Architecture of Country Houses*, as reprinted in John C. Freeman, comp., *Furniture for the Victorian Home* (Watkins Glen, N.Y.: American Life Foundation, 1968), pp. 84-85.

2. The MWPI chair has modern upholstery. Nineteenth-century publications illustrating similar chairs show examples with deeper seat rails and an upholstery treatment that includes fringe above the carving on the seat rail.

3. While there is a growing body of research on Galusha's career, we still do not know whether he retailed the works of other cabinetmakers. He may have purchased elaborate frames and fashionable rococo looking glasses from New York City makers and had them shipped to Troy via the Hudson River.

4. The Shaftsbury Historical Society records its chair as "donated by Marjorie Prentice Rose, daughter of Mary Galusha Spence Rose, Troy, N.Y." The donor, a Galusha descendant, identified Galusha as the maker of the chair.

5. Two other examples of this design that appear to be from the same cabinet shop are in the collection of the Bennington Museum, Bennington, Vt.

6. Printed Book and Periodical Collections, Winterthur Museum, Garden and Library, Winterthur, Del.

7. See John Scherer, *New York Furniture at the New York State Museum* (Alexandria, Va.: Highland House Publishers, 1984), p. 95, for an example of this motif in Galusha's work.

Catalogue Number 33

1. A labeled side chair in the collection of the Virginia Museum of Fine Arts, Richmond, provides the basis for the attribution of this and numerous other pieces of seating furniture to Baudouine. A related sofa is in the collection of the Art Institute of Chicago. See Eileen Dubrow and Richard Dubrow, *American Furniture of the 19th Century, 1840-1880* (Atglen, Pa.: Schiffer Publishing, 1983), p. 117. Two of the three sections of the tripartite back of the sofa parallel the Virginia chair. The third section is more ornately embellished; the crest features a grotesque face formed from vegetation. The Virginia chair and Chicago sofa directly parallel a suite at Glenmont, Edison National Historical Site, West Orange, N.J. The faces on the crests of the two sofas in the Glenmont suite are more ornate and have horns sprouting from their heads and vegetation emerging from their mouths. An analogous suite, formerly in the collection of Lockwood-Mathews Mansion Museum in Norwalk, Conn., was sold at auction; see Neal Auction Co., "Autumn Estates Auction," sale cat. (New Orleans, La., Oct. 4, 1997), lot 358.

2. See William Anderson, *Green Man: The Archetype of Our Oneness with the Earth* (San Francisco: HarperCollins, 1990).

3. Printed Book and Periodical Collection, Winterthur Museum, Garden and Library, Winterthur, Del. A chair that is an exact likeness of the line drawing in these publications is in the collection of MWPI (accession no. 59.85). The carved decoration on the legs of this chair includes a male face with an open mouth with vegetation spilling out. The same chair design was published in Guilmard's *Le Garde-Meuble Ancien et Moderne, Journal D'Ameublement*, Paris, Mar. 15, 1851.

Catalogue Number 34

1. For more information about Shaker history and theology, see Stephen J. Stein, *The Shaker Experience in America* (New Haven, Conn.: Yale University Press, 1992), and Priscilla J. Brewer, *Shaker Communities, Shaker Lives* (Hanover, N.H.: University Press of New England, 1986).

2. A Shaker family could have as few as twelve or as many as 130 members, and a Shaker community or village might have as few as two families or as many as eight.

3. The village at New Lebanon, N.Y., had eight families—the Church, Center, Second, North, East, South, Upper Canaan, and Lower Canaan families. Over the years chair shops were located within several of these families. In 1861, when a post office was established in the village, the community's name was changed to Mount Lebanon to differentiate it from the town of New Lebanon. New Lebanon is used here for consistency.

4. See Edward Deming Andrews, *The Community Industries of the Shakers* (Albany: The University of the State of New York, 1933), for a description of the production of Shaker chairs for sale to the "outside world."

5. Gilbert Avery lived and made chairs at the Upper Canaan Family, Benjamin Lyon at the Center Family, and John Bishop at the Second Family.

6. For further discussion and illustrations of New Lebanon Shaker chairs from different periods, see Charles R. Muller and Timothy D. Rieman, *The Shaker Chair* (Winchester, Ohio: The Canal Press, 1984).

7. The earliest references to the use of cloth as a seating material for Shaker chairs suggest that the Shakers used listing, a narrow strip of selvage from woven cloth hemmed on its raw edge, to make a tape that was then woven for the seat. Later, the Shakers wove material, variously called tape braid, webbing, and lace, especially for chair seats. When New Lebanon Shakers began to make chairs for commercial purposes, factory-woven worsted tape was purchased for the chairs.

8. Design patent 8771, U.S. Patent Office, Washington, D.C. The patent was granted on Mar. 2, 1852, to George O. Donnell for "a new and improved mode of preventing the wear and tear of carpets and the marring of floors caused by the corners of the back posts of chairs as they take their natural motion of rocking backward and forward."

9. Although the chair does not retain its original finish and its seat has been replaced with a replica of Shaker webbing, the chair closely matches a number of other New Lebanon chairs that survive in public and private collections.

Catalogue Number 35

1. A similar cabinet, also of unknown manufacture, is owned by the Henry Ford Museum in Dearborn, Mich. The placement and design of key elements of each cabinet are identical, although the two differ in many details. Measurements, tracings, or construction features of the Ford Museum and MWPI cabinets have not been compared to determine if the cabinets were produced in the same shop.

2. Much of Marcotte's known furniture is more fully grounded in historical antecedents than this flamboyantly inventive cabinet. Roux's best-known work is in earlier styles. While Herter Brothers' furniture displays similar design motifs, nothing illustrated in Katherine S. Howe, Alice Cooney Frelinghuysen, Catherine Hoover Voorsanger et al., *Herter Brothers: Furniture and Interiors for a Gilded Age* (New York: Harry N. Abrams in association with the Museum of Fine Arts, Houston, 1994) suggests authorship of the MWPI cabinet. The firm of Pottier & Stymus remains a possibility. The partnership may have provided some of the furnishings for the A. T. Stewart House in New York (1869), many of which are in a style close to that of the MWPI cabinet. For discussion and images, see Jay E. Cantor, "A Monument of Trade: A. T. Stewart and the Rise of the Millionaire's Mansion in New York," *Winterthur Portfolio* 10 (1975): 165-97.

3. The most extensive treatment of furniture in this manner, Howe et al., *Herter Brothers*, describes its characteristics and origins in some detail (esp. pp. 22-77). Looking primarily at Herter furniture, however, provides little basis for distinguishing the work of competing firms in New York or elsewhere.

4. The style is conventionally described as "Renaissance revival," a too-simple term that masks its complexity. It could more accurately be termed "mannerist revival." Nineteenth-century Boston-based Anglophile designer and writer Charles Wyllys Elliott had his own names for this furniture. In "Household Art," he called it the "German-French-Roman-Greek style" and, less approvingly, the "German-French-bastard style" (*The Art Journal* 1 [1875]: 299). Neither of these terms is likely to catch on today, although Elliott's identification of the German aspect of this furniture is significant. As Howe et al. point out in *Herter Brothers*, the style was largely French in inspiration but was often created and, presumably, influenced by German designers and artisans.

5. For a discussion of the courtly paradigm, see Kenneth L. Ames, *Death in the Dining Room and Other Tales of Victorian Culture* (Philadelphia: Temple University Press, 1992), esp. pp. 87-88, 93-95.

6. See, for example, the famous passage comparing the relative appropriateness of upscale and mid-level sideboards for households in republican America in Benjamin Silliman Jr. and C. R. Goodrich, eds., *The World of Science, Art, and Industry Illustrated: From Examples in the New-York Exhibition, 1853-54* (New York: G. P. Putnam, 1854), p. 185.

7. Twentieth-century discussions of furniture of this era comment on its historicizing and eclectic aspects but often fail to acknowledge its creative dimension. Implicit here, it seems to me, is an assumption that cabinetmakers are less imaginative (lesser artists?) than painters and architects, an assumption not borne out by close study of American and European objects. Like painting and architecture of the same era, American furniture often reveals considerable design innovation, even if the design vocabulary is the same as that used in Europe. American objects sometimes replicate European models but more often do not.

8. Many of the intricate or unusual features of the MWPI cabinet are not immediately apparent. Among them are doors on the sides of the upper section that provide access to small recesses behind the concave niches.

9. The form of the cabinet is also historically referential, traceable through French cabinets-on-stand of the seventeenth century to likely prototypes in the style of Henri II. For examples, see Pierre Kjellberg, *Le meuble Français et Européen du moyen âge a nos jours* (Paris: Les Editions de l'Amateur, 1991), pp. 29-31.

10. See, for instance, Allan David Bloom's best-selling *The Closing of the American Mind* (New York: Simon & Schuster, 1987).

Catalogue Number 36

1. Dianne D. Hauserman, "Alexander Roux and His 'Plain and Artistic Furniture,'" *Antiques* 93, no. 2 (February 1968): 210-17.

2. Alexander Roux is first listed in New York City directories in 1837, but some of his labels read, "Established in 1836."

3. A circa 1866 Roux paper label heralds him as a "FRENCH CABINET MAKER AND IMPORTER OF FANCY BUHL AND MOSAIC FURNITURE." See Catherine Hoover Voorsanger, "From the Bowery to Broadway: The Herter Brothers and the New York Furniture Trade," in Katherine S. Howe, Alice Cooney Frelinghuysen, Catherine Hoover Voorsanger et al., *Herter Brothers: Furniture and Interiors for a Golden Age* (New York: Harry N. Abrams in association with the Museum of Fine Arts, Houston, 1994), p. 67, fig. 46.

4. New York Vol. 190, p. 397 (Aug. 12, 1851), R. G. Dun & Co. Collection, Baker Library, Harvard University Graduate School of Business Administration, Boston, Mass. In 1848 the stenciled label used by the business reads, "A. & F. Roux." See Hauserman, "Alexander Roux," p. 211.

5. I am grateful to Catherine Hoover Voorsanger for sharing an undated copy of this advertisement and the Ledoux-Lebard citation from the scholarship files of the Department of American Decorative Arts, Metropolitan Museum of Art, and for her assistance with this entry. Beginning in 1856 Frédéric Roux is listed at the Paris address on the Alexander Roux paper label. See Denise Ledoux-Lebard, *Le mobilier français du XIXe siècle, 1795-1889: Dictionnaire des*

ébénistes et des menuisiers (Paris: Les éditions de l'Amateur, 1989), pp. 565-66.
6. *Wilson's Business Directory of New York City*, 1858, 1859. New York Vol. 190, p. 397 (Dec. 14, 1858, and Jan. 10, 1860), R. G. Dun & Co. Collection lists the firm as "Roux and Co." It appears that the firm of Roux & Cabus existed from December 1858 through about January 1860. Joseph Cabus was a partner with Anthony Kimbel from 1862 to 1882.
7. New York Vol. 190, p. 400H (May 23, 1865), R. G. Dun & Co. Collection. In light of this secondary connection the stylistic similarities of work by Roux and by Pottier & Stymus are of interest. The partnership with Chatain dissolved by Dec. 16, 1865. Chatain later established his own furniture business.
8. New York Vol. 190, p. 301E (Nov. 13, 1877), R. G. Dun & Co. Collection, states, "Their factory has been totally destroyed by the recent fire." On May 20, 1878, the Dun reports record that Roux's business had been "burnt out twice within six months."
9. New York Vol. 190, p. 301E (May 8, 1880), R. G. Dun & Co. Collection.
10. Andrew Jackson Downing, *The Architecture of Country Houses*, as reprinted in John C. Freeman, comp., *Furniture for the Victorian Home* (Watkins Glen, N.Y.: American Life Foundation, 1968), pp. 42, 62.
11. For a more general discussion of French drawing room cabinets, see cat. no. 35.
12. For a discussion of the conservation work executed on the MWPI cabinet, see Wendy M. Watson et al., *Altered States: Conservation, Analysis, and the Interpretation of Works of Art* (South Hadley, Mass.: Mount Holyoke College Art Museum, 1994), pp. 154-57.
13. Several mounts on a cabinet attributed to Roux in the collection of the Toledo Museum of Art are marked "RC." It is speculated that this is an abbreviation for "Roux et Cie" (Roux and Company). Patricia J. Whitesides, Registrar, Toledo Museum of Art, to author, July 31, 1997.
14. N.Y. State Census, 1855, City of New York, 1st District, 8th Ward. In 1860 the census cites eighty employees, and the company's annual production is listed as $100,000. Bureau of the Census, *Eighth Census of the U.S., Products of Industry*, City of New York, N.Y., 8th Ward.
15. The same impressed mark has been found on other examples of Roux's work, such as a carved sideboard made about 1853 in the collection of the Newark Museum, Newark, N.J. Several different paper labels and two stenciled marks are documented to the Roux firm. For labels and marks see Howe et al., *Herter Brothers*, p. 67; Hauserman, "Alexander Roux," figs. 1a, 6a, and 17a; Eileen Dubrow and Richard Dubrow, *American Furniture of the 19th Century, 1840-1880* (Atglen, Pa.: Schiffer Publishing, 1983), p.167; and John L. Scherer, *New York Furniture at the New York State Museum* (Alexandria, Va.: Highland House Publishing, 1984), fig. 95a. For additional examples of Roux drawing room cabinets see *19th-Century America: Furniture and Other Decorative Arts* (New York: Metropolitan Museum of Art, 1970), cat. no. 164; Christopher P. Monkhouse and Thomas S. Michie, *American Furniture in Pendleton House* (Providence, R.I.: Rhode Island School of Design, Museum of Art, 1986), entry 54; and Gerald W. R. Ward, *American Case Furniture in the Mabel Brady Garvan and Other Collections at Yale University* (New Haven, Conn.: Yale University Art Gallery, 1988), no. 224. Also see the collections of the Walker Art Gallery, Bowdoin College, Brunswick, Me; the Strong Museum, Rochester, N.Y.; the Museum of the City of New York; and the Toledo Museum of Art, Toledo, Ohio. The cabinets in the RISD and Toledo collections are nearly identical with MWPI's. The cabinet at the Metropolitan Museum of Art is similar but larger and has an additional column and door in the center section. A cabinet nearly identical with the Metropolitan's, formerly in the collection of the Virginia Museum of Fine Arts, sold at the North East Auctions, *New Hampshire Auction*, sale cat. (Hampton, N.H., Nov. 1-2, 1997), lot 143.

Catalogue Number 37

1. Reports by Ed Polk Douglas and Mimi Findlay (MWPI research file) list and describe several of the cabinets in this group.
2. A cabinet formerly in the collection of the Lockwood-Mathews Mansion Museum in Norwalk, Conn., sold at Neal Auction Co., *Autumn Estates Auction*, sale cat. (New Orleans, La., Oct. 4-5, 1997), lot 355, may well be from the same shop or factory, but it, too, is undocumented. See also Christie's, *Important American Furniture, Folk Art and Decorative Arts*, sale cat. (New York, Oct. 8, 1998), lot 90. See also Christie's, *Important American Furniture, Folk Art and Decorative Arts*, sale cat. (New York, Oct. 8, 1998), lot 90.
3. An accurate, if graceless, stylistic label may be "Upscale New York Franco-German 1860s."
4. Although the marquetry, metal mounts, and porcelain plaques that adorn this body of furniture have antecedents in French courtly work of the eighteenth century, horizontal-format cabinets are largely a later nineteenth-century invention, only loosely patterned on commodes with doors from the eighteenth and early nineteenth centuries. For eighteenth-century antecedents, see Pierre Kjellberg, *Le meuble Français et Européen du moyen âge a nos jours* (Paris: Les Editions de l'Amateur, 1991), pp. 330, 368. An early example of the form that would become popular in the 1860s was exhibited at the London Crystal Palace in 1851 by the Parisian cabinetmaker Ringuet-LePrince, whose partner and brother-in-law, Léon Marcotte, was a leading cabinetmaker in New York when the MWPI cabinet was manufactured. See Art Journal, *The Industry of All Nations* (London: George Virtue, 1851), p. 197. Marcotte may have introduced this form to New York.
5. The tripartite mirror arrangement is more typical of cabinets and sideboards produced in the 1850s. For examples, see Art Journal, *Industry of All Nations*, pp. 70, 186, 222, 302.

Catalogue Number 38

1. For further information on Herter Brothers, see Katherine S. Howe, Alice Cooney Frelinghuysen, Catherine Hoover Voorsanger et al., *Herter Brothers: Furniture and Interiors for a Gilded Age* (New York: Harry N. Abrams in association with the Museum of Fine Arts, Houston, 1994).
2. *Bildhauer* appears in the papers that Herter signed on June 29, 1850, at the Württemberg consulate in New York; these documents renounce his Württemberg citizenship and proclaim his intention to become a United States citizen. The description of Herter's abilities is from an R. G. Dun & Co. report (New York Vol. 191, p. 451 [Sept. 12, 1854]), R. G. Dun & Co. Collection, Baker Library, Harvard University Graduate School of Business Administration, Boston, Mass.
3. "Began here about May '51," in the first report on Bulkley and Herter by R. G. Dun & Co. in 1854, can be interpreted as suggesting that Gustave Herter's association with Erastus Bulkley started as early as 1851, although the exact meaning of the sentence is ambiguous. New York Vol. 191, p. 451 (Sept. 12, 1854), R. G. Dun & Co. Collection. Bulkley & Herter is first listed in the New York City directories in 1853. Christian is mentioned in association with Gustave's monumental, sculpted organ case made between 1860 and 1863 for the Boston Music Hall. See Catherine Hoover Voorsanger, "Gustave Herter, Cabinetmaker and Decorator," *Antiques* 147, no. 5 (May 1995): 740-51, especially n. 20.
4. The dates used here for the Lockwood mansion—called Elm Park—differ slightly from those in Howe et al., *Herter Brothers*. Construction of the house began in 1867 while the Lockwood family was on an extended stay in Europe. Although the main public rooms were not entirely complete, the house was occupied in 1869. Lockwood lost his fortune in the gold market crash of September 1869 and mortgaged the house to pay his debts. He was unlikely to have ordered additional goods and services after this date.
5. The use of metal in Herter marquetry is relatively uncommon. This particular marquetry band does not appear on the other Herter music cabinet of this form (see n. 8). It does appear—with brass instead of pewter—on four cabinets that are identical in form to a Herter cabinet original to Thurlow Lodge, a home decorated by Herter Brothers in 1872 and 1873 for one-time California governor Milton Slocum Latham. One of these four cabinets is in the Los Angeles County Museum (see Howe et al., *Herter Brothers*, cat. no. 17). The brass version of this pattern also appears on several oval tables of a type associated with Thurlow Lodge. Three of the four cabinets share with the MWPI music cabinet the second marquetry pattern that surrounds the central door on each piece. Among the distinguishing characteristics of this marquetry band are the small loops that connect each palmette in the marquetry to the rosewood background. Another version of this band—black wood against a bird's-eye maple ground—was used in the Lockwood card room, decorated by Herter Brothers between 1867 and 1869.
6. The interior is divided into four vertical sections above a single horizontal one. The contrast of exterior and interior woods is a consistent feature in Herter Brothers furniture and was also a common feature of parlor cabinets by other New York makers in the third quarter of the nineteenth century.
7. Monique Riccardi-Cubitt, *The Art of the Cabinet* (London: Thames and Hudson, 1992). See passages indexed under "cabinet-on-stand."
8. This statement appears to be true also of other New York firms contemporary with Herter Brothers. One other Herter example of this form, on the New York art market in 1998, is known. Although it has identical marquetry on the door and a variation of the surrounding border (the loops attached to the palmettes are contained within the framework of the border), this music cabinet conveys quite a different visual effect. Maple spindles (in place of rosewood) contrast with the rosewood carcass, the marquetry border around the door is repeated under the cornice (in lieu of the marquetry band with pewter), the engaged columns are not stop-fluted, and the flutes are gilded from top to bottom. For a black-and-white illustration, see Sotheby's, *19th Century Furniture, Decorations, and Works of Art*, sale cat. 6634 (New York, Sept. 16, 1992), lot 189. Another music cabinet-on-stand attributed to Herter Brothers,

inscribed "De Forest" on top of the base and decorated with a figure painted in grisaille on each of two doors, is about the same date as the MWPI cabinet but is horizontal in orientation and markedly more delicate in proportions. See Neal Alford Co., Auction, sale cat. (New Orleans, La., Oct. 7, 1989), lot 633, in which the piece was not recognized as being by Herter Brothers. Other variations of the cabinet-on-stand form by Herter Brothers are illustrated in Butterfield & Butterfield, *English, American and Continental Furniture and Decorative Arts in Los Angeles*, sale cat. (Los Angeles, Calif., Nov. 6, 1990), lot 437; and in Howe et al., *Herter Brothers*, cat. no. 41.

Catalogue Number 39

1. Barry R. Harwood, *The Furniture of George Hunzinger: Invention and Innovation in Nineteenth-Century America* (Brooklyn, N.Y.: Brooklyn Museum of Art, 1997). All biographical information about Hunzinger and his firm is taken from this source.
2. On Oct. 17, 1877, a fire devastated Hunzinger's rented factory at 141-143 7th Avenue.
3. The last patent—for an armchair with collapsible writing tables on either side—was granted to Hunzinger's heirs in 1899, the year after his death.
4. Harwood, *Furniture of George Hunzinger*, plates 3, 5. The two illustrated versions of this chair, identical in form to the MWPI example, retain their original upholstery and demonstrate the range of choices available to the consumer. The chair in plate 3 is stained dark brown, while the one in plate 5 is ebonized with gilded incised decoration. Although the elaborate, tufted upholstery scheme is the same in each case, and both chairs incorporate the same machine-woven, floral tapestry panel on the back, the ebonized version is tufted in silk, while the less expensive stained version is tufted in cotton rep.
5. Harwood, *Furniture of George Hunzinger*, fig. 13. The store sign on the front of Hunzinger's factory showroom on West 16th Street, illustrated on the letterhead of his stationery, stated that he was a manufacturer of "Fancy Chairs and Ornamental Furniture."
6. The original patent drawing shows a somewhat simpler chair. Hunzinger applied the technical innovation in this patent to a variety of designs–at least twenty-five distinct models are known to incorporate it. In addition to the diagonal brace, all of these variations include paired vertical supports that extend from the bottom front seat rail to the front cross stretcher. The diversity and originality of these variations underline Hunzinger's seemingly tireless creativity and enthusiasm for reworking design ideas. A chronology for these variations is, however, difficult to reconstruct. Hunzinger could have used this diagonal brace at any point in his career, but if he followed the letter of the law, all chairs impressed with the 1869 patent stamp would have been made between 1869 and the expiration of the patent in 1886.
7. Page Talbott, "Portability," in *Innovative Furniture in America from 1800 to the Present*, ed. David A. Hanks. (New York: Horizon Press, 1981), pp. 125-30. Several manufacturers, including Pierre J. Hardy in New York, made folding chairs that refer to campaign stools with similar designs on their backs.

Catalogue Number 40

1. Casting directly from a cast-iron model resulted in the loss of fine details, and the end product was up to 3 percent smaller than the original because the iron shrank after cooling.
2. The Coalbrookdale Company in England registered the "Fern and Blackberry Settee" in 1858 with the Designs Office in London. See Georg Himmelheber, *Cast-iron Furniture and All Other Forms of Iron Furniture* (London: Philip Wilson Publishers, Ltd., 1996), p. 32. Himmelheber has noted that copies of this pattern were available from companies in Glasgow, Stockholm, the United States, and perhaps Melbourne and has stated that the pattern was also available as an armchair.
3. *19th-Century America: Furniture and Other Decorative Arts* (New York: Metropolitan Museum of Art, 1970), cat. no. 119.
4. Esther Mipaas, "Cast-Iron Furnishings: Sitting Pretty in the Garden," *American Art & Antiques* 2, no. 3 (May-June 1979): 41.
5. See Sotheby's, *Sotheby's Summers Place Auction*, sale cat. 7073 (New York, Sept. 23, 1997), lots 254-55, 266, for illustrations of fern and blackberry-patterned settees showing an iron slat seat, a wooden slat seat, and a pierced cast-iron seat of latticework and scrolls, respectively.
6. Ellen Marie Snyder, "Victory over Nature: The Elevation and Domestication of Victorian Cast-Iron Seating Furniture" (M.A. thesis, Winterthur Program in Early American Culture, 1984), p. 38.
7. In her master's thesis, Snyder analyzed five settees and discussed the Victorian desire to express control over nature through seating furniture. During the nineteenth century, cast-iron furniture changed forms—pieces tended to become more controlled and confined and less naturalistic. Snyder described the fern settee as a step in the evolution between the rustic settees and curtain settees (rectilinear in composition). See Snyder, "Victory over Nature," p. 38.
8. Snyder, "Victory over Nature," p. 33. The fern settee is illustrated in a Phoenix Iron Works advertisement in the 1877 Utica city directory. The fern settee also appears in several trade catalogues of A. B. and W. T. Westervelt and Samuel S. Bent and Son of New York and E. T. Barnum Wire and Tool Works of Detroit, Mich.; see *19th-Century America: Furniture and Other Decorative Arts*, cat. no. 218, and Mipaas, "Cast-iron Furnishings," p. 38. The fern settee with wooden slat seat is illustrated in an 1870s catalogue and a 1924 catalogue of J. W. Fiske of New York; see Printed Book and Periodical Collection, Winterthur Museum, Garden and Library, Winterthur, Del. The Coalbrookdale Company of Shropshire, Eng., illustrated the fern settee in its catalogue of 1875. See Sotheby's, *Summers Place Auction*, illustration for lot 254, and *The Coalbrookdale Illustrated Spring Catalogue*, April 1888, Printed Book and Periodical Collection, Winterthur Museum, Garden and Library.
9. John J. Walsh, *Vignettes of Old Utica* (Utica: Utica Public Library, 1982), p. 274. Palmer is listed as a master builder and foundry owner from 1843 through 1859, after which he is listed as foundry owner.
10. One of the company's principal products was the well-known Phoenix furnace. Chauncey and son Cyrus Palmer also expanded their business to include the distribution of the Utica Sewing Machine as well as their own highly advertised Palmer Patent Clothes Dryer. See Utica city directories, 1866 and 1906.
11. Obituary for Cyrus F. Palmer, *The Utica Observer*, Sept. 19, 1906.

In the early 1880s, according to the Utica Mercantile and Manufacturing Association, Chauncey is listed under the category of "Iron Industries" as an employer of ten workers. See *Utica Mercantile and Manufacturing Association* (Utica: Curtiss & Childs, Printers, 1881), p. 44. By 1892 his son Cyrus, then presiding owner, employed twenty-five "of the most skilled mechanics in the city." See J. A. Miller, *A Descriptive Review of the D., L. & W. R. R. Co.'s Route* (Syracuse: Hall & McChesney, 1892), p. 39. There is no listing for Phoenix Iron Works in the Utica city directories after 1906.

Catalogue Number 41

1. A similar pedestal, without the chains and putti, is in the collection of the Metropolitan Museum of Art. An identical sewing table sold at the Neal Auction Company, sale cat. (New Orleans, La., Oct. 5, 1996), lot 326.
2. [Kilian Brothers], *Album of Photographs* (n.p., n.d.), Maercklein Collection, col. 305, Joseph Downs Collection of Manuscript and Paper Ephemera; Winterthur Museum, Garden and Library, Winterthur, Del. This album features photographs of the firm's furniture, including one on the first page of a folding chair below a sign that reads "Kilian's Patent Folding Chair, pat'd, April 5th, 1870." This is the only place in the album where the firm's name appears. The MWPI pieces vary slightly from the examples featured in the album. The Kilian "catalogue" of ca. 1870, among the papers of upholsterer H. Maercklein of Hartford, Conn., illustrates every aspect of the company's business. For information on Maercklein, see Andrew Passeri and Robert Trent, "The Wheelwright and Maercklein Inventories and the History of the Upholstery Trade in America, 1750-1900," *Old-Time New England* 72 (1987): 312-54. The firm name, "Kilian Brothers," is also cited in the original text of Earnest Hagen's "Reminiscence of a New York City Cabinetmaker" (Joseph Downs Collection, col. 32, Winterthur Museum, Garden and Library), but Hagen does not elaborate on the firm or its products.
3. Francis A. Walker, ed., *United States Centennial Commission. International Exhibition, 1876. Reports and Awards*, vol. 4, *Groups III-VII* (Washington, D.C.: Government Printing Office, 1880), p. 739. The company's display at the exhibition included easels, a parlor table, music stand, table, and card receiver. *International Exhibition, 1876: Official Catalogue* (Philadelphia: John R. Nagle and Company, 1876), p. 114.
4. Frederick Kilian is first listed in a New York City directory of 1851-52 as a chairmaker. Theodore is listed as a cabinetmaker by 1856-57, and the first listing for William appears in an 1860-61 directory.
5. New York Vol. 192, p. 526 (Feb. 15, 1869[?]), R. G. Dun & Co. Collection, Baker Library, Harvard University Graduate School of Business Administration, Boston, Mass. Bureau of the Census, *Ninth Census of the United States, Products of Industry*, City of New York, N.Y., 19th District, 20th Ward.
6. Kilian Brothers, *Price List* (New York: Kilian Brothers, 1872), Printed Book and Periodical Collection, Winterthur Museum, Garden and Library.
7. See V. Quetin, *Le Magasin de Meubles*, no. 10, Printed Book and Periodical Collection, Winterthur Museum, Garden and Library. See especially plates 62 and 39 for parallel examples. This periodical is not dated but is believed to be from the early 1870s. The forms depicted in *Le Magasin de Meubles* may be derived from an earlier nineteenth-century French furniture model called an *athénienne*, a classically

decorated tripod form used as a washstand, plant stand, or a perfume burner. See Daniel Alcouffe, Anne Dion-Tenenbaum, and Amaury Lefébure, *Furniture Collections in the Louvre, Vol. I* (Dijon, France: Éditions Faton, 1993), 1: 305.

Catalogue Number 42

1. Other examples in this group include pieces in three public collections–the Dallas Museum of Art, the Metropolitan Museum of Art, and the Newark Museum. For information on them see Charles L. Venable, *American Furniture in the Bybee Collection* (Austin, Tex.: University of Texas Press, 1989), pp. 158-61; Ulysses G. Dietz, "Edwin Van Antwerp's Jelliff Furniture," *Antiques* 137, no. 4 (April 1990): 907; and Marshall B. Davidson and Elizabeth Stillinger, *The American Wing at the Metropolitan Museum of Art* (New York: Alfred A. Knopf, 1985), p. 91.

2. The MWPI chair and related objects are regularly ascribed to Jelliff by collectors, dealers, and auction houses, as well as curators. In "Edwin Van Antwerp's Jelliff Furniture," Ulysses Dietz, curator of decorative arts at the Newark Museum, illustrates the museum's armchair (which apparently differs only from the MWPI example in its use of a carved shell boss on the crest rail) and explains that it was part of the Van Antwerp furniture made by Jelliff in 1858 and documented by a bill of sale. While some precursors of the Renaissance revival style were made in the late 1850s, full-blown examples of this style of seating furniture were not made in this country until the late 1860s. The popularity of such pieces reached its peak in the early 1870s, and the style faded from fashion after 1875. The set at the Metropolitan Museum, for example, was ordered by Jedediah Wilcox of Meriden, Conn., in 1870. The popularity of the style in the 1870s prompted several manufacturers to produce "Grande Duchess" suites. In addition to Schrenkeisen, the New York City firms of Jordan & Moriarty and J. W. Hamburger made suites of similar design. A period advertisement showing a Jordan & Moriarty suite is in the Landauer Collection at the New-York Historical Society. For an illustration of Hamburger's offerings, see his trade catalogue, *Parlor Furniture* (New York: J. W. Hamburger, ca. 1870), Winterthur Museum, Garden and Library, Winterthur, Del. These references and additional research on Schrenkeisen were provided from copies in the MWPI research files.

3. M. & H. Schrenkeisen, *Trade Price List for M. & H. Schrenkeisen* (New York: M. & H. Schrenkeisen, 1873), pp. 2-4, 14-15, Printed Book and Periodical Collection, Winterthur Museum, Garden and Library.

4. The original upholstery was a satin-weave fabric with a cotton warp and mohair weft. The original weave structure have been recreated in the chair's reproduction upholstery. The tufting pattern is original.

5. M. & H. Schrenkeisen, *Parlor Furniture* (New York: M. & H. Schrenkeisen, 1869), preface. Printed Book and Periodical Collection, Winterthur Museum, Garden and Library. John M. Schrenkeisen is listed in New York City directories from 1858-59 until 1860-61.

6. There is a New York City listing for Martin F. Schrenkeisen as "furniture" or "upholsterer" until 1921.

7. New York Vol. 413, p. 215 (May 18, 1874), R. G. Dun & Co. Collection, Baker Library, Harvard University Graduate School of Business Administration, Boston, Mass.

8. New York Vol. 412, p. 200 (Dec. 9, 1871) and New York Vol. 413, p. 298 (May 27,1885), R. G. Dun & Co. Collection.

9. For images of these premises see *Parlor Furniture* (1869), cover; and M. & H. Schrenkeisen, *Parlor Furniture* (New York: M. & H. Schrenkeisen, after 1874), rear endpage. These catalogues are at the Cooper-Hewitt, National Museum of Design, Smithsonian Institution, New York, N. Y. The quotation is from New York Vol. 413, p. 215 (Jan. 24, 1874), R. G. Dun & Co. Collection. M. & H. Schrenkeisen, *Illustrated Catalogue of M. & H. Schrenkeisen* (New York: M. & H. Schrenkeisen, 1879), pictures the medal the firm was awarded for a patent rocker. This catalogue is in the Printed Book and Periodical Collection, Winterthur Museum, Garden and Library.

10. While important efforts have been made in the study of this confusing industry, much work remains to be done. See Katherine S. Howe, Alice Cooney Frelinghuysen, Catherine Hoover Voorsanger et al., *Herter Brothers: Furniture and Interiors for a Gilded Age* (New York: Harry N. Abrams in association with the Museum of Fine Arts, Houston, 1994), pp. 56-77.

11. Schrenkeisen, *Parlor Furniture* (1869), pp. 104-9, shows mainly late rococo revival furnishings. M. & H. Schrenkeisen, *Trade Price List of M. & H. Schrenkeisen* (New York: M. & H. Schrenkeisen, 1871), lists numerous suites in the Renaissance revival style. This catalogue is in the Printed Book and Periodical Collection, Winterthur Museum, Garden and Library. Also in Winterthur's collection are M. & H. Schrenkeisen, *Supplement to Illustrated Catalogue* (New York: M. & H. Schrenkeisen, 1872), and M. & H. Schrenkeisen, *Trade Price List of M. & H. Schrenkeisen* (New York: M. & H. Schrenkeisen, [1873]), which are dominated by furniture in the Renaissance revival style. The same is true of Schrenkeisen, *Parlor Furniture* (after 1874).

12. Platform rockers with aesthetic-style upholstery are depicted in the company's 1879 catalogue. See Schrenkeisen, *Illustrated Catalogue of M. & H. Schrenkeisen* (1879), p. 61.

Catalogue Number 43

1. Original upholstery from several chairs of the suite (see note 5) was salvaged and preserved on two chairs, MWPI's and one now in the Brooklyn Museum of Art, Brooklyn, New York.

2. Conservation analysis by Katherine C. Grier of a mate to MWPI's chair revealed these colors; Andrew W. Mellon Foundation Curatorial-Conservation Survey, Brooklyn Museum of Art, 1994. Information courtesy Barry Harwood, associate curator, Brooklyn Museum of Art.

3. This information was provided to the author by Barry Harwood and Katherine Grier. McDonough, Wilsey & Co., *Catalogue* (Chicago, 1878), State Historical Society of Wisconsin, Madison. Grier has noted that although figured silks of this type were predominantly imported, by 1880 they were being made in Philadelphia.

4. M. & H. Schrenkeisen, *Illustrated Catalogue of M. & H. Schrenkeisen* (New York: M. & H. Schrenkeisen, 1879), pp. 61, 87, Printed Book and Periodical Collection, Winterthur Museum, Garden and Library, Winterthur, Del. The commentary on furniture coverings notes that the fabrics were "manufactured in endless variety; in fact, there is no limit to patterns and colorings" and that many of the fabrics "are our own patterns and imported especially for us" (p. 87).

5. According to the auction catalogue, there were ten pieces in the set—two settees and eight chairs. The chairs are described as "carved oak chair upholstered in velvet and tapestry." See Butterfield & Butterfield, *Sherwood Hall: The Estate of the Late Mary E. Hopkins (Mrs. Timothy Hopkins)*, sale cat. (San Francisco, Calif., Oct. 5, 1942), lots 297-306. The author wishes to thank Jon King for supplying a copy of this catalogue listing.

6. This Menlo Park, Calif., residence (originally named Thurlow Lodge) was built for Milton Slocum Latham. The interior decor was supplied by Herter Brothers. In 1883 Mrs. Mark Hopkins purchased the home, fully furnished, for her adopted son Timothy. Subsequently, Timothy Hopkins inherited part of the Mark Hopkins estate in San Francisco, another Herter Brothers commission. See Katherine S. Howe, Alice Cooney Frelinghuysen, Catherine Hoover Voorsanger et al., *Herter Brothers: Furniture and Interiors for a Gilded Age* (New York: Harry N. Abrams in association with the Museum of Fine Arts, Houston, 1994), pp. 158, 180-81. The suite could originally be from either of these structures. The author thanks Alex Brammer for his comments concerning the provenance of the chair.

7. Wood analysis by Bruce Hoadley, March 1997, for MWPI. Hoadley noted that western Pacific cedar was not often used on the East Coast until the last quarter of the twentieth century.

8. The inventory tag from Universal Studios remains nailed to the bottom seat rail of the chair. The chair in MWPI's collection was attributed to Daniel Pabst (1826-1910) in Butterfield & Butterfield, *Sherwood Hall*. Stylistic examination combined with provenance and wood analysis indicate that Pabst did not make the chair.

Catalogue Number 44

1. The now-faded stamp appears to read, "Kimbel and Cabus/Cabinet Makers/and/Decorators/7 & 9 E. 20th St. N. Y." This photograph album is one of two that descended in the Kimbel family; the second documents later nineteenth-century, or perhaps early twentieth-century, furniture by A. Kimbel & Sons. Both albums were given to the library of the Cooper-Hewitt, National Design Museum, Smithsonian Institution, New York, N.Y.

2. Joseph Cabus's father, Charles, first appears in New York City directories in 1838 and is listed as a cabinetmaker. Joseph Cabus was first listed as a cabinetmaker in 1850. Between 1857 and 1862, before he joined Kimbel, Cabus worked for Alexander Roux as a foreman and was a partner in the Roux firm for a little more than one year between 1858 and 1860.

3. The firm dissolved because, ostensibly, the principals wanted to form separate companies with their sons. The business history of Kimbel & Cabus is drawn from an unpublished chronology compiled in 1995 by Medill Higgins Harvey for the Department of American Decorative Arts at the Metropolitan Museum of Art. Information about Kimbel's early history is from Heidrun Zinnkann, *Mainzer Möbelschreiner der ersten Hälfte des 19. Jarhunderts*, Schriften des Historischen Museums Frankfurt am Main, XVII (Frankfurt: Dr. Waldemar Kramer Verlag, 1985), which also cites Kimbel's association with Charles Baudouine.

4. The most well-known example is the rosewood cabinet now in the Brooklyn Museum of Art (accession

no. 45.96), Brooklyn, N.Y., that was made for the George Bliss family of New York. A related example is in the High Museum of Art (accession no. 1985.317), Atlanta, Ga. Two versions of the form, one of which is ebonized, are in private collections in California.
5. Two examples of the firm's highest-quality cabinetwork are a diminutive mahogany bonheur-du-jour (private collection) and the oak and mahogany woodwork executed for Company K in the Seventh Regiment Armory, New York City, to the designs of Sidney V. Stratton of the architectural firm McKim, Mead & White.
6. Christopher Dresser, *Studies in Design* (London: Cassell, Petter & Calpin, [1876]), plate VI, described the motifs as "grotesque 'powderings,' suitable for the wall ornaments of a smoking-room." Dresser scholar Stuart Durant has explained that *Studies* was a "demy-folio" book published in a series of twenty parts beginning in November 1874 and completed in the fall of 1876. Thus, the published compendium must date from 1876, but since individual plates would have been available earlier, I have used 1874-76. Durant also mentioned that certain grotesque designs were probably by J. Moyr Smith, although he did not identify specific plates. See Durant, *Christopher Dresser* (London: Academy Editions, 1993), pp. 27-28.
7. For example, the Museum of Fine Arts, Houston, owns a walnut desk with inset Minton tiles decorated in black on a turquoise ground. An ebonized fall-front desk in the Brooklyn Museum of Art bears two porcelain tiles (thought to be French), a geometric plaque of different colored woods, and gilded incising. The Victoria & Albert Museum, London, owns an ebonized desk with painted and gilded panels.

Catalogue Number 45

1. Design patent 8163, *Design for Chairs*, U.S. Patent Office, Washington, D.C.; Barry R. Harwood, "Two Early Thonet Imitators in the United States: The Henry I. Seymour Chair Manufactory and the American Chair-Seat Company," *Studies in the Decorative Arts* 2, no. 1 (Fall 1994): 92-113. All information about the Henry I. Seymour Chair Manufactory and its principals is taken from this article.
2. Charles R. Muller and Timothy D. Rieman, *The Shaker Chair* (Winchester, Ohio: Canal Press, 1984), Appendix A, p. 4. One of the characteristics that differentiates Seymour rockers from Shaker rockers is the use of continuous bent members for the runners in the former and carved runners in the latter.
3. The Seymours lived in the family house at 162 4th Street, Troy, owned after 1852 by their widowed mother until her death in 1875. The family was a large and prosperous one and had moved to Troy from Hartford, Conn., in the late eighteenth century. From 1852 Henry Seymour is listed in the city directory as a chair manufacturer along with George Seymour.
4. The Taylor, Seymour Company was listed in the city directory at Erie and Auburn Streets in West Troy. Robert M. Taylor resided at 34 Rochester St., Troy.
5. Beginning in 1865 George Seymour is no longer listed as a chair manufacturer but rather as a stoneware manufacturer; presumably he left his active role in the furniture business to join the pottery, an older family enterprise. In 1877 George Seymour is identified as an "insurance agent" with offices at 153 River Street, Troy.
6. In addition to the two patents he secured with Harwood, Wood secured patent no. 42,150 on Mar. 29, 1864, for an innovative slatted chair seat design.
7. Harwood's name is also absent from the directories between 1866 and 1869. Perhaps the pair went elsewhere to try their hand in the furniture business. After 1873 Harwood was listed in the Troy directory, but his profession was not specified. From 1886 through 1895 New York City directories list Harwood as an attorney in lower Manhattan. There is no evidence that Harwood continued his interest in chair design after his move to New York City.
8. John L. Scherer, *New York Furniture at the New York State Museum* (Alexandria: Highland House Publishers, 1984), pp. 108-10. The New York State Museum in Albany has three labeled examples of Seymour furniture—a child's conventional Shaker-style rocking chair, a walnut side chair patented Sept. 28, 1862, and a hickory and ash side chair patented May 31, 1870, patterned after Thonet model number 4. A version of the latter is also in the collection of the Metropolitan Museum of Art. An unmarked chair of the same design as the MWPI example, with original red and white tape on the seat and back, is in the Brooklyn Museum of Art.
9. Harwood, "Two Early Thonet Imitators," p. 98 and n. 21. The firm's interest in Shaker design did not begin with this rocker. Previously, on Sept. 9, 1870, Harwood and Wood patented a more conventional rocking chair without bent members that is more closely related to Shaker rockers. They also assigned the production of this chair to the Seymour Company.
10. The tape back on the MWPI chair is original to the object; the tape seat is a reproduction.
11. Muller and Rieman, *The Shaker Chair*, Appendix A, p. 4.
12. Harwood, "Two Early Thonet Imitators," p. 92. Although Thonet Brothers did not open a retail store in the United States until 1873, beginning in the 1860s their wares were available from agents in this country.

Catalogue Number 46

1. The surviving fabric has been replicated on the exterior of the drawer.
2. See cat. no. 28 in Katherine S. Howe, Alice Cooney Frelinghuysen, Catherine Hoover Voorsanger et al., *Herter Brothers: Furniture and Interiors for a Gilded Age* (New York: Harry N. Abrams in association with the Museum of Fine Arts, Houston, 1994).
3. Two rooms from this residence are installed at the Museum of the City of New York. I am grateful to Deborah Dependahl Waters for allowing me to examine and photograph this furniture. A dressing table believed to be from this home is now in the collection of the High Museum of Art, Atlanta, Ga., and the smoking parlor is installed at the Brooklyn Museum of Art, Brooklyn, N.Y. For additional information on the dressing table at the High Museum, see David Hanks, "George A. Schastey & Co.," *Art and Antiques* 6, no. 5 (September-October 1983): 54-57.
4. George A. Schastey to John D. Rockefeller Sr., Jan. 21 and Oct. 29, 1884. Copies of these letters are in the research files of the Museum of the City of New York and were generously made available to me by Deborah Dependahl Waters. Schastey is also listed in the Springfield, Mass., directory from 1891 to 1902. See Caroline Mortimer, "The George Walter Vincent Smith Art Museum, Springfield, MA, I: The Building and Its Decoration," *The International Journal of Museum Management and Curatorship* 6 (1987): 353-72, and "George Walter Vincent Smith: The Man and His Museum" (M.A. thesis, Program in the History of Decorative Arts, Parsons School of Design and Cooper-Hewitt, National Design Museum, Smithsonian Institution, 1984).
5. New York Vol. 438, p. 582 (Oct. 13, 1873), R. G. Dun & Co. Collection, Baker Library, Harvard University Graduate School of Business Administration, Boston, Mass. This report also notes that Schastey worked for "Her[?]te & C." Perhaps this should read either "Herter" or "Herts." For a full discussion of the attribution of the interior work at 4 West 54th Street, see Catherine Hoover Voorsanger, "From the Bowery to Broadway: The Herter Brothers and the New York Furniture Trade," in Howe et al., *Herter Brothers*, p. 75 and n. 89 on p. 246.
6. See George A. Schastey Company, *Occasional Pieces of Choice and Useful Furniture* (Springfield, Mass.: George A. Schastey Company, n.d.), Archives Center, National Museum of American History, Smithsonian Institution, Washington, D.C.

Catalogue Essay 47

1. The Matthews & Willard Co., *Price List of Art Brass Goods* (Waterbury, Conn.: The Matthews & Willard Co., 1886), Printed Books and Periodical Collection, Winterthur Museum, Garden and Library, Winterthur, Del.
2. The Meriden Britannia Co., *The Meriden Britannia Silver-plate Treasury* (Meriden, Conn.: Meriden Britannia, 1886-87), collection of the Meriden Historical Society, Meriden, Conn.
3. This illustration was discovered by Hyman Myers. I would like to thank Ulysses Dietz of the Newark Museum for alerting me to it.
4. In 1854 Nathaniel L. Bradley (b. 1829) and Walter Hubbard (b. 1828) founded the business. Bradley and Hubbard Mfg. Co. was organized in 1875 and operated until 1940, when it was purchased by the Charles Parker Co. C. Bancroft Gillespie, *A Century of Meriden, "The Silver City"* (Meriden, Conn.: Journal Publishing Co., 1906), p. 65. I wish to acknowledge Allen Weathers, curator of the Meriden Historical Society, for his assistance.
5. *Souvenir of the Centennial Exhibition: or, Connecticut's Representation at Philadelphia, 1876* (Hartford, Conn.: Geo. D. Curtis, 1877), p.106.
6. For an in-depth discussion of the aesthetic movement, see Doreen Bolger Burke, Jonathan Freedman, Alice Cooney Frelinghuysen et al., *In Pursuit of Beauty: Americans and the Aesthetic Movement* (New York: Rizzoli and the Metropolitan Museum of Art, 1986).
7. Similar stands are in the Brooklyn Museum of Art, Brooklyn, N.Y.; the Newark Museum, Newark, N.J.; and the Wadsworth Atheneum, Hartford, Conn. Although the tiles on the Newark example were made by Minton and Company, Stoke-on-Trent, Staffordshire, England, they were probably retailed by Meriden Flint Glass Company. See Burke et al., *In Pursuit of Beauty*, p. 281.

Catalogue Number 48

The author gratefully acknowledges the assistance of William C. Clendaniel, Eileen Dubrow, Richard Dubrow, Jonathan Fairbanks, Timothy Neuman, William T. Nicholas, and Gerald W. R. Ward in the preparation of this essay.
1. Edward S. Cooke Jr., "The Boston Furniture Industry in 1880," *Old-Time New England* 80 (1980): 84, 95.
2. Cooke, "Boston Furniture Industry," p. 96. Cooke

has included Kilborn Whitman & Company in his list of "Furniture Firms Categorized by Product" but refers to it as "Kilborn, Whitman & Company." Cooke cited Kilborn Whitman & Co. as a maker of first-class furniture when the company was actually a "specialty firm."

3. Documentation in the MWPI research file demonstrates either the sale or use of Whitman merchandise in Massachusetts, Maine, New York, and Texas.

4. For illustrations of Whitman merchandise, see Eileen Dubrow and Richard Dubrow, *Furniture Made in America, 1875-1905* (Exton, Pa.: Schiffer Publishing, 1982), pp. 56-58, 65, 66, 79. Items on p. 245 are incorrectly labeled Kilborn Whitman & Company.

5. See *Boston Almanac and Business Directory* (Boston: various publishers, 1876-96), and Massachusetts Vol. 83, p. 176, R. G. Dun & Co. Collection, Baker Library, Harvard University Graduate School of Business Administration, Boston, Mass., for the various sites of the firm between 1876 and 1896.

6. Palmer was a former sales representative of Palmer Embury & Company, New York, N.Y., active 1870 to 1876. See New York Vol. 434, p. 100-A-50; and Vol. 436, pp. 230 and 300, R. G. Dun & Co. Collection. For Beal & Hooper, see Massachusetts Vol. 69, pp. 83A, 527, 599O, 599P, R. G. Dun & Co. Collection. For Palmer & Whitman, see Massachusetts Vol. 83, pp. 176-77, R. G. Dun & Co. Collection, and *Boston Almanac and Business Directory*, 1871-76. Palmer & Whitman's origins were modest, but the firm had warerooms initially at 13 Charlestown Street (and later at 34 Canal Street) and a factory in Chelsea, Mass., and specialized in parlor furniture, desks, and bookcases. See Massachusetts Vol. 83, pp. 176-77, R. G. Dun & Co. Collection, and *Boston Almanac and Business Directory*, 1876, p. 1279.

7. Charles A. Jones had been the accountant for Palmer & Whitman. See Massachusetts Vol. 83, pp. 176-77, R. G. Dun & Co. Collection, and *Boston Almanac and Business Directory*, 1876, p. 1279.

8. Printed Book and Periodical Collection, Winterthur Museum, Garden and Library, Winterthur, Del. Items in the Renaissance revival style from Kilborn Whitman & Company appear in plates 4 and 8.

9. At the bottom of his full-page advertisement (unnumbered) in Kimball's *Book of Designs*, Whitman urged potential clients to "Send for Catalogue."

10. *Kilborn Whitman & Co., Parlor Furniture Manufacturers, 34 Canal Street, Boston, Mass., U. S. A.* (Boston: by the author, n.d. [ca. 1880]). A copy of this catalogue survives in a private collection; reconfigured selections from it appear in Dubrow and Dubrow, *Furniture Made in America*, pp. 57, 58, 66. The MWPI chair form is no. 5 at the bottom of p. 58. While the catalogue has no printed date, authors Dubrow and Dubrow speculate that it was published May 1, 1880 (p. 314).

11. For information on the decoration of panels on more expensive contemporary furniture, see Katherine S. Howe, Alice Cooney Frelinghuysen, Catherine Hoover Voorsanger et al., *Herter Brothers: Furniture and Interiors for a Gilded Age* (New York: Harry N. Abrams in association with the Museum of Fine Arts, Houston, 1994), p. 222.

12. "The gilded surface is revealed under ultraviolet light as a complex and detailed surface treatment. . . . The surface appears to be oil gilt [with] a separate resin varnish coating . . . used over the gilding to highlight selected areas." See Williamstown Art Conservation Center "Examination Record" (1997), MWPI research files, for a more detailed analysis of the finish. For comments on the design and use of such small chairs in American interiors of the 1870s and 1880s, see Howe et al., *Herter Brothers*, pp. 144-45, 170-71, 175-78, 193-94, 202-3. A comprehensive study of gilded furniture in the United States has yet to appear. By the 1880s this costly mode of decoration was less expensive and thus more prevalent in middle-class homes. Whitman offered gilded pieces from the beginning of his business: the chair from his manufactory shown in plate 4 of Kimball's *Book of Designs* was available at extra cost in a gilded finish.

13. For related British design, see Edward T. Joy, *Pictorial Dictionary of British 19th Century Furniture Design* (Woodbridge, Eng.: Antique Collectors' Club, 1977), pp. 200-203, 225-27, 245-46, 576-79, 582-83, and Jeremy Cooper, *Victorian and Edwardian Decor, From the Gothic Revival to Art Nouveau* (New York: Abbeville Press, 1987), pp. 115-52. For similar objects shown at the international exhibitions, see *The Art Journal*, new ser. 2 (1876), 4 (1878), and 5 (1879), and Walter Smith, *The Masterpieces of the Centennial International Exhibition, 2, Industrial Art* (Philadelphia: Gebbie & Barrie, 1875 [1876]).

14. See Doreen Bolger Burke, Jonathan Freedman, Alice Cooney Frelinghuysen et al., *In Pursuit of Beauty: Americans and the Aesthetic Movement* (New York: Rizzoli and the Metropolitan Museum of Art, 1986), pp. 110-75, 438-40, 446-47, and Howe et al., *Herter Brothers*, pp. 36-77.

15. Charles L. Eastlake, *Hints on Household Taste in Furniture, Upholstery, and Other Details* (London: Longmans, Green, 1868; Boston: James R. Osgood, 1872), plate IV ("Window in Dining-room, Cothele, Devon [*sic*]"), p. 35.

16. Eastlake, *Hints*, pp. 162-63, and Clarence Cook, *The House Beautiful: Essays on Tables, Stools and Candlesticks* (New York: Scribner, Armstrong and Co., 1878), p. 76.

Catalogue Number 49

1. The Ruppert chairs are pictured in *Artistic Houses: Being a Series of Interior Views of a Number of the Most Beautiful and Celebrated Homes in the United States, with a Description of the Art Treasures Contained Therein* (New York: D. Appleton, 1883-84) 2: part 1, near p. 103. The rosewood chair is discussed in Katherine S. Howe, Alice Cooney Frelinghuysen, Catherine Hoover Voorsanger et al., *Herter Brothers: Furniture and Interiors for a Gilded Age* (New York: Harry N. Abrams in association with the Museum of Fine Arts, Houston, 1994), cat. no. 40; an identical chair from the same suite and with the impressed number "454" is in the collection of the Philadelphia Museum of Art (accession no. 1975-043-001). Since *Herter Brothers* was published, an upholstered chair from the same suite, with the pencil inscription "Mrs. C. Vanderbilt," has come to light (Margot Johnson to author, 1996). A pair of ebonized chairs with a garland motif on each crest is said to have come from the Ohio residence of President James A. Garfield. An ebonized variation of the form (which differs in the treatment of its crest rail) may have been part of Jay Gould's ebonized Anglo-Japanese bedroom suite. The suite is in the Metropolitan Museum of Art; the chair is at Lyndhurst, formerly Gould's country home in Tarrytown, N.Y. A pair of gilded chairs in the collections of the Metropolitan and the Museum of Fine Arts, Houston, respectively, are the only other gilded versions of the form currently known. Each bears the impressed number "5595" and retains nearly all of its original gilding. Each crest rail is decorated with a "necklace" of flowers carved in bas-relief, and the stiles are studded with "strung coins," an ancient motif Herter Brothers favored during this period. The Houston chair has the name "Mills" inscribed in pencil on the top of the proper right seat rail, which links it to Darius Ogden Mills' New York domicile decorated in 1880.

2. For further information about Herter Brothers see MWPI cat. no. 38 and Howe et al., *Herter Brothers*. Most gilded furniture Herter Brothers manufactured seems to have been designed for urban residences in the years around 1880. See Howe et al., *Herter Brothers*, cat. nos. 4, 25, 29, 37, 42, and p. 52 for illustrations of gilded pieces. During the 1860s and early 1870s the firm imported gilded reception chairs from France for use in interiors such as the music room in Thurlow Lodge, Menlo Park, Calif., decorated about 1872-73; see Howe et al., *Herter Brothers*, p. 161, for a photograph illustrating this practice.

3. The use of mother-of-pearl in Herter Brothers furniture dates to the years around 1880. See Howe et al., *Herter Brothers*, pp. 116-17, cat. no. 41, for discussion of a rosewood cabinet inlaid with mother-of-pearl garlands and ribbons.

4. *Artistic Houses* 2: part 1, p. 88. Christian Herter announced his retirement from the firm in 1879 but occupied himself with the William H. Vanderbilt commission with the understanding that it would be his last project (Howe et al., *Herter Brothers*, p. 231). Although Herter's associates, including Bigelow, have not received much attention to date, with the circumstances of Christian Herter's "retirement" and the number of commissions Herter Brothers embarked upon around 1880, it is probable that other members of the firm were directly involved in overseeing some of these projects.

5. *Artistic Houses* 2: part 1, p. 88.

6. The gilded surface and original upholstery were lacking when MWPI acquired the chair in 1982. A conservation report from 1986 in the MWPI research files mentions yellow and gold threads found on the chair. The conservation report concludes that the whole chair, except the inlaid face of the crest rail, was originally water-gilded; traces of original gilding are on the underside of the seat rails, on the underside of the crest rail, and on the piercing of the hand-hold. There is also indication of a thin gesso ground with a sienna/burnt sienna bole and a yellow ochre wash on the edges of the seat frame. The chair bears an impressed number—891—on the underside of the seat rail. There are two inscriptions written in blue crayon on the frame of the seat—"891 Gilt" and "Store"; the latter is crossed out in pencil. The initials "DE H" on a brass tag affixed to the chair are neither those of Robert or Mary Stuart, nor of Mrs. Stuart's executors, who were slated to receive some of her household furnishings after her death; the tag may refer to a subsequent owner of the chair. (See "Many Public Bequests/Mrs. Robert L. Stuart's Will Filed for Probate," *New York Times*, Jan. 6, 1892, p. 8.)

7. For an illustration of one of the two surviving gilded chairs from the Vanderbilt commission, see Howe et al., *Herter Brothers*, cat. no. 37, and, for further comparison, cat. nos. 21 and 25. The distinctive turned leg with flared conical foot bears a relationship to ancient furniture, such as Egyptian stools and chairs that appear in Greek and Roman reliefs and wall paintings. For representative examples see Helena Hayward, ed., *World Furniture* (London: Hamlyn Publishing Group, 1981), p. 12, ill. 10, and Maxwell Anderson, "Pompeian Frescoes in the Metropolitan Museum of Art," *The Metropolitan*

Museum of Art Bulletin 45, no. 3 (Winter 1987-88): 28-29. I am grateful to Mimi Findlay for providing me with additional illustrations of this distinctive feature.

CATALOGUE NUMBER 50

1. For a Tiffany advertisement promoting its plated wares of the 1860s, see Charles Carpenter and Mary Grace Carpenter, *Tiffany Silver* (New York: Dodd, Mead & Company, 1978), p. 213. In this advertisement Tiffany's address is 550 and 552 Broadway in New York, the firm's location from 1854 to 1870.

2. Thomas Shaw apprenticed with Elkington, Mason & Co. in Birmingham, England, before emigrating in the mid-1860s to Providence, R.I., where he worked for the Gorham Company. According to the Newark city directories, Shaw was a "manufacturing silversmith" working at the address listed for "Tiffany & Co. Silversmiths." He served as superintendent of the Tiffany plant until his retirement in 1898. C. C. Adams also worked for the Gorham Company before joining Shaw about 1874. Carpenter, *Tiffany Silver*, p. 214.

3. Gorham Manufacturing Company is the only other American silver maker known to have made furniture. For an illustration of a silver dressing table and stool in the Martelé style, see Charles L. Venable, *Silver in America, 1840-1940: A Century of Splendor* (Dallas and New York: Harry N. Abrams for the Dallas Museum of Art, 1995), p. 257.

4. For an illustration of a portion of the display, which included a dinner set comprising sixty-seven pieces, a smoking set, terrapin dishes, a water set, and a lunch set, see "The Tiffany Exhibit at the World's Fair," *The Jeweler's Review* 22 (Oct. 16, 1893): 60. Receiving fifty-six medals for its display, Tiffany won awards in every division in which it participated. On Oct. 3, 1893, the firm was honored with a medal for its "plated ware," most likely as a result of its "beautiful silver table." See "Tiffany Exhibit," p. 44.

5. Quoted in "Tiffany Exhibit," p. 44.

6. Frank Shaw died of tuberculosis at the age of twenty-four, a tragic loss of a talented designer and silversmith. Carpenter, *Tiffany Silver*, pp. 214-15.

7. Cited in Tiffany & Co., *Catalogue of Tiffany & Co.'s Exhibit* (New York: Tiffany & Co., 1893), p. 84.

8. Quoted in "Tiffany Exhibit," p. 44.

9. For an illustration of the tea and coffee service, see "The Silverware Department," *The Jeweler's Weekly* 8 (May 30, 1889): 44, 45. The overall floral design on the salver from this set is rendered in a manner similar to the MWPI table top—a plethora of flowers intertwined with ferns; both have ornate floral borders.

At the Chicago fair Tiffany displayed a sterling silver tea and coffee service, once again elaborately chased with American flora; perhaps it was intended to complement the MWPI table. For an illustration of this set, see "Tiffany Exhibit," p. 48.

10. A listing with the heading, "Catalogue of Books," Tiffany Archives, Parsippany, N.J., includes 908 books, catalogues, portfolios, and periodicals assembled by the company from the 1870s until 1908. *Native Flowers and Ferns of the United States* by Meeham is listed on page 29, item nos. 148-51. The portfolios of photographs of the ferns are listed on p. 54, item nos. 547 and 548.

11. For an illustration, see "Tiffany Exhibit," p. 52. For more information about the toilet table, see Major Ben. C. Truman, *History of the World's Fair, Being a Complete and Authentic Description of the Columbian Exposition from Its Inception* (Philadelphia: Mammoth Publishing Co., 1893), p. 217.

CATALOGUE NUMBER 51

1. A "spring seat" uses metal springs, fastened into the chair frame in a state of tension, to make the seat resilient. The springs are covered with stuffing materials and under-upholstery before the show fabric is added. The use of springs in chairs in the United States began in the 1820s but was not common until the 1850s. Until the twentieth century the typical upholstery spring was formed into a coil; these have been supplanted in inexpensive and midpriced furniture by band or sinuous springs, which are less flexible and often have shorter useful lives but are easier to install.

2. Until the last twenty-five years, such chairs were little appreciated or preserved. Modernist design historian Siegfreid Giedion bemoaned the era of their creation as a "Reign of the Upholsterer" and decried designs like this one as "blubbery" and "boneless." Siegfreid Giedeon, *Mechanization Takes Command: A Contribution to Anonymous History* (New York: Oxford University Press, 1948), pp. 364, 366.

3. For a general discussion of French- and Turkish-style upholstery in America, including this early history, see Katherine C. Grier, *Culture and Comfort: People, Parlors, and Upholstery, 1850-1930* (Rochester, N.Y.: Strong Museum, 1988), pp. 163-99.

4. Denise Ledoux-Lebard, *Muebles et ensembles époque second empire* (Paris: Editions Charles Massin, 1966), p. 33 ("*chaise capitonnée á dossier renversé*").

5. *Le Magasin de Meubles No. 17. Album de Sièges de Fantaisie* (ca. 1860): plates 55, 83, 84.

6. William C. Richards, *A Day at the New York Crystal Palace, and How to Make the Most of It* (New York: G. P. Putnam, 1853), p. 44.

7. An armless chair of this style is one of the pieces of a large suite in the Turkish style, upholstered with a very large floral print, that was part of the furnishings of the circa 1885 New York City reception rooms of Mrs. George Frederic Jones (mother of the novelist Edith Wharton). See Peter Thornton, *Authentic Decor: The Domestic Interior, 1620-1920* (London: Weidenfield and Nicholson, 1984), p. 343, plate 459.

8. The forms of furniture in the Turkish manner that did achieve popularity with American consumers were the "Turkish rocker" and the backless couch, which was often upholstered with cotton fabric woven in imitation of Oriental rugs. For a fuller discussion of the impact of French and "Turkish" upholstery styles in America, see Grier, *Culture and Comfort*, pp. 163-99.

9. Grier, *Culture and Comfort*, pp. 24, 32-35.

10. For an X-frame chair with a mauve satin cover with needlework strip, see Albert Keim, *Le décoration et le mobilier à l'époque romantique et sous le second empire* (Paris: Éditions Nillson [1929]), plate 3, no. 10. See also Grier, *Culture and Comfort*, pp. 110, 269, plates 9, 20, 37.

CATALOGUE NUMBER 52

1. William Hosley, *The Japan Idea: Art and Life in Victorian America* (Hartford, Conn.: Wadsworth Atheneum, 1990) is the most recent study of Japanese taste in America in the last half of the nineteenth century. Imitation bamboo is discussed on pp. 141-42. By 1869 Léon Marcotte, a leading French-born furniture maker working in New York, was making imitation bamboo furniture. Marcotte's upholstered imitation bamboo chair is illustrated and discussed in Nina Gray, "Léon Marcotte: Cabinetmaker and Interior Decorator," in *American Furniture 1994*, ed. Luke Beckerdite (Milwaukee, Wis.: Chipstone Foundation, 1994): 66-67 and fig. 32 on 68. Other New York City furniture firms, such as Herter Brothers, also embraced Japanese taste by using ebonized and marquetry surfaces.

2. Another New York City firm, Kilian Brothers, illustrated faux bamboo in its 1876 catalogue. The plate is reprinted in Marshall B. Davidson, *The American Heritage History of American Antiques from the Civil War to World War I* (New York: American Heritage Publishing Company, 1969), p. 172, no. 223.

3. Clarence Cook, *The House Beautiful: Essays on Beds and Tables, Stools and Candlesticks* (New York: Scribner, Armstrong and Co., 1878), pp. 74-75.

4. Highly figured bird's-eye maple panels provide visual contrast for the turned-maple imitation bamboo elements. These elements are consistent on most of the imitation bamboo examples now in museum collections. The Wadsworth Atheneum in Hartford, Conn., owns an imitation bamboo maple desk (Hosley, *The Japan Idea*, p. 143). A dressing bureau, less elaborate than the MWPI example, is in the Metropolitan Museum of Art and is illustrated in Marshall B. Davidson and Elizabeth Stillinger, *The American Wing at The Metropolitan Museum of Art* (New York: Alfred A. Knopf for the Metropolitan Museum of Art, 1985), p. 192, fig. 300.

CATALOGUE NUMBER 53

1. Robert J. Horner was first listed as a clerk in New York City directories in 1883. According to his obituary in the *New York Times*, Feb. 27, 1922, p. 13, as a boy Horner worked at Mills and Gibb, a New York lace retailer, "remaining with them for many years and working himself up to a responsible position." Horner may have been a clerk at Mills and Gibb when he was listed in the 1883 directory. By 1892 R. J. Horner & Co.'s address had been listed in different years as 61, 63, and 65 West 23rd Street. According to the 1886 *New York Times* advertisement cited in the text, the firm actually occupied all three addresses on West 23rd Street from its inception; the full address is given on surviving furniture labels, including the one on the MWPI desk.

2. Christian Herter died in 1883, but new partners took over the management of Herter Brothers. Alexander Roux (d. 1886) retired in 1881 and left the business under his son's management. Out of the dissolution of Kimbel & Cabus in 1880 came A. Kimbel and Sons.

3. Robert P. Lyon, comp., *The Official Reference Book of the Furniture Trade Giving the Names, Addresses and Credit Rating of the Furniture, Carpet, Upholstery, Undertaking, Wall Paper, Picture Frame, Looking Glass, Bedding and Cabinet Wood Trades, January, 1889* (n.p. [probably New York]: Robert P. Lyon, 1889), pp. 19-20.

4. At the time of the move to West 36th Street (1912), R. J. Horner was the company's president and R. J. Horner Jr. was vice president. For several years R. J. Horner & Co. and George C. Flint and Co. were listed in directories at 20 West 36th Street along with Flint and Horner. The exact working relationships among the firms remain unclear. Horner's obituary stated that he had retired "three years ago" (ca. 1919) from the furniture business.

5. The desk does not have the usual pull supports

in the apron; a sliding brass bar mechanism on the interior supports the fall-front when open.

6. William C. Ketchum Jr. with the Museum of American Folk Art, *American Cabinetmakers: Marked American Furniture, 1640-1940* (New York: Crown Publishers, 1995), pp. 172-73, illustrates a desk with details adapted from a French Empire prototype. An American colonial revival desk, ca. 1895, is in the Strong Museum, Rochester, N.Y.; Nicolas Ricketts, Strong Museum, to D. Scott Bell, MWPI, June 20, 1996, MWPI research files. An advertisement for R. J. Horner & Co. in *The Philadelphia Carpet Trade* (May 1, 1887): 382, notes, "Everything, from the colonial-primitive to the renaissance can be found here." Photocopy in the scholarship file, Department of American Decorative Arts, Metropolitan Museum of Art.

Catalogue Number 54

1. For a discussion of the successful development of Shaker communities in the antebellum period, see Priscilla J. Brewer, *Shaker Communities, Shaker Lives* (Hanover, N.H.: University Press of New England, 1986). For a general discussion of the growth of Shaker industry and agriculture, see Edward Deming Andrews, *The Community Industries of the Shakers* (Albany: University of the State of New York, 1932).

2. For a detailed history of the development of the New Lebanon chair factory, see Charles R. Muller and Timothy D. Rieman, *The Shaker Chair* (Winchester, Ohio: The Canal Press, 1984).

3. Henry Blinn's diary, Canterbury, N.H., 1872, as quoted in Muller and Rieman, *The Shaker Chair*, p. 169.

4. See, for example, "Illustrated Catalogue and Price List of Shakers' Chairs Manufactured by the Society of Shakers" (R. M. Wagan & Co., ca. 1876), reproduced in Robert F. W. Meader, *Illustrated Guide to Shaker Furniture* (New York: Dover Publications, Inc., 1972), p. 126ff.

5. Receipt, Boston & Albany Railroad, Apr. 5, 1895, Edward Deming Andrews Memorial Shaker Collection (no. SA 934), Winterthur Museum, Garden and Library, Winterthur, Del. Also described in E. Richard McKinstry, comp., *The Edward Deming Andrews Memorial Shaker Collection* (New York: Garland Publishing, Inc., 1987), manuscript no. 1147.

6. *The Manifesto* (July 1895). The publication was printed at the Canterbury, N.H., Shaker Village under various titles between January 1871 and December 1899.

Catalogue Number 55

1. See Anna Tobin D'Ambrosio and Leslie Greene Bowman, *"The Distinction of Being Different": Joseph P. McHugh and the American Arts and Crafts Movement* (Utica, N.Y.: Munson-Williams-Proctor Institute Museum of Art, 1993).

2. "The Mission Furniture: Its Design and Execution," *The Upholstery Dealer and Decorative Furnisher* 1 (October 1901): 52.

Index